BEAT THE STORY DRUM

AUTHORS

ELAINE MEI AOKI
VIRGINIA A. ARNOLD
JAMES FLOOD
JAMES V. HOFFMAN
DIANE LAPP
MIRIAM MARTINEZ

ANNEMARIE SULLIVAN
 PALINCSAR
MICHAEL PRIESTLEY
NANCY ROSER
CARL B. SMITH

WILLIAM H. TEALE
JOSEFINA VILLAMIL
 TINAJERO
ARNOLD W. WEBB
PEGGY E. WILLIAMS
KAREN D. WOOD

MACMILLAN/McGRAW-HILL SCHOOL PUBLISHING COMPANY

NEW YORK   CHICAGO   COLUMBUS

AUTHORS, CONSULTANTS, AND REVIEWERS

WRITE IDEA! Authors

Elaine Mei Aoki, James Flood, James V. Hoffman, Diane Lapp, Ana Huerta Macias, Miriam Martinez, Ann McCallum, Michael Priestley, Nancy Roser, Carl B. Smith, William Strong, William H. Teale, Charles Temple, Josefina Villamil Tinajero, Arnold W. Webb, Peggy E. Williams

The approach to writing in Macmillan/McGraw-Hill Reading/Language Arts is based on the strategies and approaches to composition and conventions of language in Macmillan/McGraw-Hill's writing-centered language arts program, WRITE IDEA!

Multicultural and Educational Consultants

Alma Flor Ada, Yvonne Beamer, Joyce Buckner, Helen Gillotte, Cheryl Hudson, Narcita Medina, Lorraine Monroe, James R. Murphy, Sylvia Peña, Joseph B. Rubin, Ramon Santiago, Cliff Trafzer, Hai Tran, Esther Lee Yao

Literature Consultants

Ashley Bryan, Joan I. Glazer, Paul Janeczko, Margaret H. Lippert

International Consultants

Edward B. Adams, Barbara Johnson, Raymond L. Marshall

Music and Audio Consultants

John Farrell, Marilyn C. Davidson, Vincent Lawrence, Sarah Pirtle, Susan R. Snyder, Rick and Deborah Witkowski

Teacher Reviewers

Terry Baker, Jane Bauer, James Bedi, Nora Bickel, Vernell Bowen, Donald Cason, Jean Chaney, Carolyn Clark, Alan Cox, Kathryn DesCarpentrie, Carol L. Ellis, Roberta Gale, Brenda Huffman, Erma Inscore, Sharon Kidwell, Elizabeth Love, Isabel Marcus, Elaine McCraney, Michelle Moraros, Earlene Parr, Dr. Richard Potts, Jeanette Pulliam, Michael Rubin, Henrietta Sakamaki, Kathleen Cultron Sanders, Belinda Snow, Dr. Jayne Steubing, Margaret Mary Sulentic, Barbara Tate, Seretta Vincent, Willard Waite, Barbara Wilson, Veronica York

ACKNOWLEDGMENTS

The publisher gratefully acknowledges permission to reprint the following copyrighted material:

"Arctic Memories" is from ARCTIC MEMORIES by Normee Ekoomiak. Copyright © 1988 by Normee Ekoomiak. Reprinted by permission of Henry Holt and Company, Inc. Used by permission also of The Rights Agency, Montreal, Quebec.

"Big Friend, Little Friend" is from BIG FRIEND, LITTLE FRIEND: A BOOK ABOUT SYMBIOSIS by Susan Sussman and Robert James. Copyright © 1989 by Susan Sussman and Robert James. Reprinted by permission of Houghton Mifflin Company.

"Bird and Boy" by Leslie Norris appeared in STORIES AND RHYMES, a BBC Publication in 1980. It is reprinted by permission of the author.

"Creation of a California Tribe: Grandfather's Maidu Indian Tales" is from CREATION OF A CALIFORNIA TRIBE: GRANDFATHER'S MAIDU INDIAN TALES by Lee Ann Smith-Trafzer & Clifford E. Trafzer. Copyright © 1988 by Lee Ann Smith-Trafzer and Clifford E. Trafzer. Published by Sierra Oaks Publishing Co. Reprinted by permission.

"Dear Bronx Zoo" is from DEAR BRONX ZOO by Joyce Altman & Sue Goldberg. Text copyright © 1990 by Joyce Altman and Sue Goldberg. Reprinted with permission of Macmillan Publishing Company.

"Do Not Disturb: The Mysteries of Animal Hibernation and Sleep" is from DO NOT DISTURB: THE MYSTERIES OF ANIMAL HIBERNATION AND SLEEP by Margery Facklam with illustrations by Pamela Johnson. Copyright © 1989 by Margery Facklam. Illustrations copyright © 1989 by Pamela Johnson. By permission of Little, Brown and Company in association with Sierra Club Books.

"Dreams" from THE DREAM KEEPER AND OTHER POEMS by Langston Hughes. Copyright © 1932 by Alfred A. Knopf, Inc. and renewed 1960 by Langston Hughes. Reprinted by permission of the publisher.

Cover permission for EL CHINO by Allen Say. Copyright © 1990 by Allen Say. Reprinted by permission of Houghton Mifflin Company.

"Érase Una Vez"/"Once Upon a Time" by Juan Goytisolo from EXPRESION ORAL INFANTIL compiled, selected, and arranged by Noe Solchaga Zamudio and Luisa Aurora Solchaga Peña. Copyright © by Editorial Avante, S. A. and used with their permission.

Cover permission for the Trophy Edition of THE FACTS AND FICTIONS OF MINNA PRATT by Patricia MacLachlan. Used by permission of Harper Collins Publishers.

"Felita" is from FELITA by Nicholasa Mohr. Copyright © 1979 by Nicholasa Mohr. Used by permission of Dial Books for Young Readers, a division of Penguin Books USA Inc.

Cover permission for FLOSSIE AND THE FOX by Patricia C. McKissack, pictures by Rachel Isadora. Copyright © 1986 by Rachel Isadora for pictures. Used by permission of Dial Books for Young Readers, a division of Penguin Books USA Inc.

"Going Green: A Kid's Handbook to Saving the Planet" is from GOING GREEN: A KID'S HANDBOOK TO SAVING THE PLANET by John Elkington, Julia Hailes, Douglas Hill, and Joel Makower. Illustrated by Tony Ross. Text copyright © 1990 by John Elkington, Julia Hailes, Douglas Hill and Viking Penguin, a division of Penguin Books USA Inc. Illustrations copyright © 1990 by Tony Ross. Used by permission of Viking Penguin, a division of Penguin Books USA Inc. By permission also of Victor Gollancz Ltd. By permission also of McLelland & Stewart for the Canadian edition which is titled THE YOUNG GREEN CONSUMER GUIDE.

"Good Books, Good Times" by Lee Bennett Hopkins. Copyright © 1985 by Lee Bennett Hopkins. Reprinted by permission of Curtis Brown, Ltd.

"Grandmother's Brook" from POEMS by Rachel Field. Copyright 1934 by Macmillan Publishing Company, renewed 1962 by Arthur S. Pederson. Reprinted with permission of Macmillan Publishing Company.

(continued on page 575)

1995 Printing

Wish A Wish

Let's Find Out!

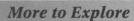

SIDE BY SIDE

250

Teammates

A biographical story
by Peter Golenbock, illustrated by Paul Bacon
**Notable Children's Trade Book in the Field
of Social Studies, 1990**

The first African American to play on a major league baseball team, Jackie Robinson finds great difficulties in his new role. He also finds a friend and supporter in teammate Pee Wee Reese.

THE CHOICE IS OURS

11

Remember When...

Twice Upon A Time

454

The Three Little Pigs and the Fox

An Appalachian folk tale
*by William H. Hooks,
illustrated by S. D. Schindler*
ALA Notable Book, 1990

This time-honored tale has a new twist, as a young piglet tries to outwit the wily fox to save herself and her two brothers.

474

Mufaro's Beautiful Daughters

An African folk tale
written and illustrated by John Steptoe
**Boston Globe–Horn Book Award, 1987;
Coretta Scott King Award, 1988;
Caldecott Honor Book, 1988**

Two beautiful sisters—one spiteful and cruel, the other kind and helpful—follow the same path to the city, but with very different results.

424

Yeh-Shen: A Cinderella Story from China

A fairy tale
retold by Ai-Ling Louie, illustrated by Ed Young
School Library Journal Best Book of the Year, 1982; Boston Globe–Horn Book Honor Award, 1983

Caldecott Award–winning illustrator

In this variant tale from China, a young girl overcomes the cruelty of a stepmother with the help of a magic fish.

CONTENTS

WISH A WISH · WISH A

WISH A WISH

When you wish upon a star
Makes no difference who
you are. . . .

NED WASHINGTON

Author's Note

One of our family treasures is a rare picture of my grandparents dated 1906, five years before they were married. They were teenagers at the time and had just won a cakewalk. As winners, they'd been awarded an elaborately decorated cake.

First introduced in America by slaves, the cakewalk is a dance rooted in Afro-American culture. It was performed by couples who strutted and pranced around a large square, keeping time with fiddle and banjo music. As the dancers paraded by, doing flamboyant kicks and complicated swirls and turns, the elders judged them on appearance, grace, precision, and originality of moves. The winning couple took home a cake.

It's never been difficult for me to imagine my grandparents strutting around a square with their backs arched, their toes pointed, and their heads held high. . . . They were full of life's joy, especially Mama. Papa used to say he believed Mama had captured the Wind. I believed it too.

Patricia C. McKissack

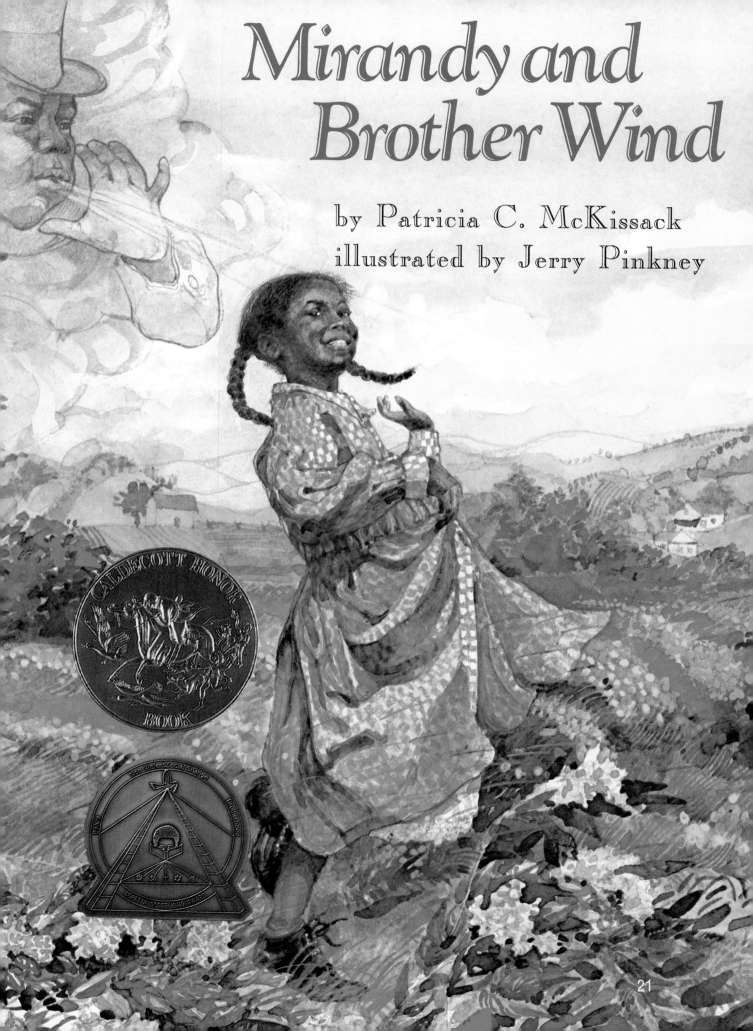

Mirandy and Brother Wind

by Patricia C. McKissack
illustrated by Jerry Pinkney

Swish! Swish!

It was spring, and Brother Wind was back. He come high steppin' through Ridgetop, dressed in his finest and trailing that long, silvery wind cape behind him.

Swoosh! Swoosh! Swoosh!

"Sure wish Brother Wind could be my partner at the junior cakewalk tomorrow night," say Mirandy, her face pressed against the cool cabin window. "Then I'd be sure to win."

Ma Dear smiled. "There's an old saying that whoever catch the Wind can make him do their bidding."

"I'm goin' to," say Mirandy. And she danced around the room, dipping, swinging, turning, wheeling. "This is my first cakewalk. And I'm gon' dance with the Wind!"

When the sky turned morning pink, Mirandy set out to capture Brother Wind. Grandmama Beasley was out back feeding her chickens when Mirandy come up asking all excited, "Do you know how to catch Brother Wind? I want to make him be my partner at the cakewalk tonight."

Grandmama Beasley studied on the notion. "Can't nobody put shackles on Brother Wind, chile. He be special. He be free."

Mirandy asked all her neighbors the same question, but nobody seemed to have an answer.

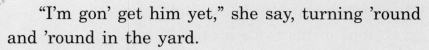

"I'm gon' get him yet," she say, turning 'round and 'round in the yard.

"Get who?"

She didn't even have to look around to know it was that clumsy boy Ezel. Mirandy didn't answer but walked toward the road. Ezel came too, walking backward to face her. He was sure to trip any minute. And he did.

"Why you been asking everybody how to catch the Wind?"

"Ma Dear tol' me whoever catch the Wind can make him do their bidding. I want him to be my partner at the cakewalk tonight."

"But I thought I . . ." After a moment Ezel flashed his good-natured smile. His eyes sparkled like sun glints on branch water. He say, "What do you think Orlinda would say if I asked her to be my partner?"

"Orlinda! Skinny Orlinda! Ask her and find out," say Mirandy, and she strutted away.

At the corner store Mr. Jessup told Mirandy that a great-aunt of his from Ipsala, Mississippi, said to put black pepper in Brother Wind's footprints. That would make him sneeze. "While he's busy sneezing, slip up behind and throw a quilt over him."

Mirandy rushed home and got the black-pepper mill and one of Ma Dear's quilts. Wasn't long 'fore Brother Wind came strolling through the meadow, his wind cape hovering gentle-like over the grasses.

Sneaking up behind him, Mirandy commenced to grinding pepper. Then she threw the quilt. But—*whoosh!* Brother Wind was gone.

Mirandy was still sneezing when she told Ezel what happened.

"I could have tol' you the Wind don't leave footprints," he say as he milked the family cow. He was sure to spill some. And he did.

Mirandy sneezed again.

"Did you ask Orlinda 'bout being your partner?" she say, changing the subject.

"Sure did, and she said—"

"I don't care what she said," Mirandy interrupted, and rushed away.

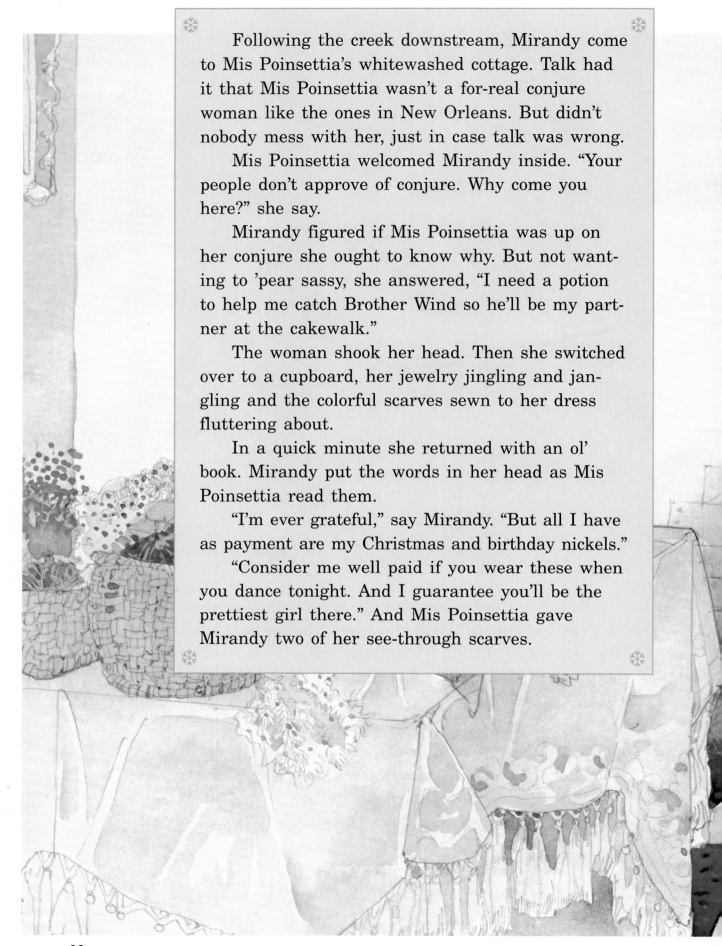

Following the creek downstream, Mirandy come to Mis Poinsettia's whitewashed cottage. Talk had it that Mis Poinsettia wasn't a for-real conjure woman like the ones in New Orleans. But didn't nobody mess with her, just in case talk was wrong.

Mis Poinsettia welcomed Mirandy inside. "Your people don't approve of conjure. Why come you here?" she say.

Mirandy figured if Mis Poinsettia was up on her conjure she ought to know why. But not wanting to 'pear sassy, she answered, "I need a potion to help me catch Brother Wind so he'll be my partner at the cakewalk."

The woman shook her head. Then she switched over to a cupboard, her jewelry jingling and jangling and the colorful scarves sewn to her dress fluttering about.

In a quick minute she returned with an ol' book. Mirandy put the words in her head as Mis Poinsettia read them.

"I'm ever grateful," say Mirandy. "But all I have as payment are my Christmas and birthday nickels."

"Consider me well paid if you wear these when you dance tonight. And I guarantee you'll be the prettiest girl there." And Mis Poinsettia gave Mirandy two of her see-through scarves.

Mirandy hurried home. Like the conjure spell said, she found a crock bottle . . . washed it in water from the rain barrel . . . and poured in a measure of cider. Then she made her way to the big willow down by the branch and set the bottle on the tree's north side. Nothing left to do but wait.

'Fore long Brother Wind come out the woods. Mirandy had never seen a body stand so tall or hold his head so high. The conjure was working. He smelled the cider. With a big *whoosh* he jumped into the bottle.

"I got you!" Mirandy pushed in the cork and danced 'round and 'round. But when she looked, Brother Wind was on the other side of the branch, bent over laughing. Then, flicking the tail of the wind cape, he vanished. *Swoosh!*

33

"How did he get in and out of that bottle so
fast?" she asked Ezel at the woodpile. He'd pulled
the wrong log, and the whole pile had come crash-
ing down on him. Mirandy was helping him restack
it. "What am I gon' do?"

Ezel laughed. "Looks like you gon' need
a partner."

Mirandy got purely upset. "You laughing, but
just wait! I'll catch him yet!" she shouted, and left
in a huff.

The cakewalk was only a few hours away, and Mirandy was moping on the front porch swing when Brother Wind swooped over the hedges, kicking up dust. He leaped over the lilacs, around the snowball tree, and into the barn.

While he was inside shaking the rafters and scaring Ma Dear's hens, Mirandy slipped up quietlike and slammed the door. No way for him to get out, 'cause Pa had stuffed all the cracks.

"I got you!" she say, clapping her hands. "Now you've got to do whatever I ask."

At dusk the neighbors from the Ridge started gathering at the schoolhouse, everybody dressed in their Sunday best. The fiddlers stood in one corner, and Grandmama Beasley and the other elder folk sat in the judges' seats. Elder Thomas brought in two big triple-decker cakes—one for the junior cakewalk winners and the other for the grown-up winners. Somebody drew a big square in the middle of the floor, and the cakewalk jubilee began.

First thing, Orlinda come siding up to Mirandy, asking, "Who gon' be yo' partner?"

Mirandy tried not to act excited. "He's real special." Then she added, "I wish you and Ezel luck. Y'all gon' need it."

"Me and Ezel? Girl, don't be silly. He asked, but I wouldn't dance with that ol' clumsy boy for nothing," she say, fanning herself. "Why, he can't even now walk and breathe at the same time. I didn't want him tripping over my feet in front of the whole county." And the girls laughed.

Mirandy put her hands on her hips and moved right in close to Orlinda. "You just hush making fun of Ezel, you hear?" she say quiet-like. "He's my friend, and it just so happens *we're* gon' win that cake!" And she tossed her head in the air and hurried away.

Outside Mirandy wondered why she'd said such a tomfool thing. She'd caught Brother Wind. Ezel couldn't be her partner. But an idea came.

"Brother Wind," she called. "You still in there?" The barn door rattled and almost shook off its hinges. "I'm ready with my wish." She whispered it, then hurried to find Ezel.

Weeks passed, and still Ridge folk talked 'bout how Mirandy and Ezel had won the junior cakewalk. That night they'd pranced 'round and 'round, cutting corners with style and grace. *Swish! Swish!* And when the music had changed to a fast gait, they'd arched their backs, kicked up their heels, and reeled from side to side. *Swoosh! Swoosh!*

Folk still talked about how Mirandy was a picture of pretty, dressed in yellow with two colorful scarves tied 'round each wrist. And everybody agreed Ezel had never stood taller or held his head higher.

When Grandmama Beasley had seen Mirandy and Ezel turning and spinning, moving like shadows in the flickering candlelight, she'd thrown back her head, laughed, and said, "Them chullin' is dancing with the Wind!"

Meet Patricia C. McKissack and Jerry Pinkney

"What if . . ." Patricia McKissack used to ask herself after she read a story. "What if something different had happened, instead of what did?"

As a child, McKissack made up new endings to the stories she loved. She also began to write. Once a week she wrote to a pen pal in Hawaii, describing her family, her life, and her feelings. She is still writing about her family and their stories.

For McKissack, joy is having others read and like her stories. "Writing is important," she says, "but it is just as important to have my writing read by someone else."

Another of her stories that you might enjoy is *Flossie & the Fox*. It is based on a folk tale, told to McKissack by her grandfather when she was a child, about a wily fox who meets his match when he encounters a bold little girl.

❋

Jerry Pinkney uses real people as models for his illustrations. In fact, the artist himself appears as Brother Wind in *Mirandy and Brother Wind*. And Jerry Pinkney's wife, Gloria, was the model for Mis Poinsettia.

To help him illustrate stories, Pinkney often asks his models to dress as the characters and to act out the events.

Pinkney's watercolors for *Mirandy and Brother Wind* seem to fill the pages. He explains his large illustrations by saying, "There's a lot of movement in this story. I wanted the reader to feel that the page goes on and on, that the tale just keeps going."

Teachers in Jerry Pinkney's elementary school used to ask him to draw in front of the class. The artist recalls, "There was a kind of reward and satisfaction I got from someone saying that I'd done something well and people being pleased by what I'd done and curious about it." He still thinks that reaching people is the most important part of his work.

Another book that is beautifully illustrated by Jerry Pinkney is *Home Place*, a story about a family that makes an interesting discovery while out for a hike.

45

Her Dreams

In her dreams

there are sometimes trees

on which hang ornaments

as tall as she

she lifts her arms

to touch them

if she can stretch

high enough to

claim them

they will become

the jewelled moments

of her life.

Eloise Greenfield

Mr. Amos Ferguson's folk painting of a young girl in the Bahamas was the inspiration for the poem by Eloise Greenfield.

Meet Marc Harshman

To Marc Harshman, writing a story is like solving a jigsaw puzzle. At first, he isn't sure what pieces he has or how they will fit together.

Harshman put together several puzzle pieces to write *A Little Excitement*. He remembered his car catching on fire and thought of the smoke and flames. That started him thinking about fires in houses. In rural West Virginia, where he lives, houses often catch fire because of the wood-burning stoves people use to heat their homes.

Marc Harshman had two pieces of a story—a fire and wood-burning stoves. When he added his memories of growing up on a farm, he completed the puzzle and created *A Little Excitement*.

Meet Ted Rand

Ted Rand lives in a rural area in Washington State. In his drawings for *A Little Excitement,* he captures the feeling of day-to-day life in the country, as well as the drama of a house in flames on a dark, snowy night.

Rand encourages children to draw and to enjoy the fun of it. He says, "Drawing is a second language to me and I hope it becomes that to you."

A LITTLE EXCITEMENT

by Marc Harshman
illustrated by Ted Rand

Winter on Pleasant Ridge had gone on long enough. Sure, I loved sledding and snowmen, snowballs and snowforts. But they can be boring, especially when you live so far in the country that your only companions are a pair of older sisters. Half the time they didn't even want to play, and the other half when they did, they were always too bossy. Mom said maybe I was too fussy. Anyway, I was tired of winter and tired of being bossed.

And what else was there? Not much. Get up. Go out in the dark and carry hay while Dad milked. Eat. Go to school. Go home and carry hay again. Eat. Study. And put up with Annie and Sarah. Not much fun I can tell you.

Annie and Sarah would tease me about the girl that the bus driver made me sit beside. When we played games, it was always them against me, and if I cheated—just to make it fair—they complained!

Mom tried. She'd offer to play checkers and sometimes we did. But you can't tell your friends when they ask what you did last night: "Oh, played checkers with Mom." I liked working with Dad but winter wasn't the fun time for that. Winter work was all mud and buckets and cow manure. And at night after chores, Dad could only slump in his chair, too tired to do much with any of us. I wondered if he would ever get his old summer strength back.

Some days it seemed all I could wish for was that something exciting might happen. One Sunday when we visited Grandma after church, I listened to her tell about her winters as a girl. She would ride to town on a sleigh behind two black mares. There were blizzards that topped the roof of the old porch. And sometimes her school would be closed for weeks at a time. It all sounded pretty good, and lots more exciting than my winter. But when I told her this, she said, "Be careful what you wish for, Willie, you might just get it."

Well, I didn't quite understand that. I didn't see why you'd have to be careful. I thought the best thing in the world that could happen to this winter would be a little excitement.

Mom heard the strange, loud roar first. She woke up Dad and he ran down the stairs, switched on the light, and saw the glow from the overheated stove. Dad's weariness had caught up with him. When he loaded up the stove with as much wood as it could hold that cold night, he forgot to shut out the air. So, instead of burning slowly, the fire swelled white hot and ignited the tar built up inside the chimney. He hollered everyone awake, but it was Sarah who yelled at me, pulled off the covers, and stumbled beside me down the stairs. Was this what I'd wished for?

I was cold and the snow lay deep on the hill. In our pajamas we stood shivering, and in the dark at the top of the roof, out of the red brick chimney, roared a red-thick fire. Dad ran back in and closed the stove and hoped enough air would be stopped to slow the burning.

As the blaze crackled and spit above us, Dad and Annie set up the ladder and I ran for buckets. The heat from the burning tar could crack the chimney and set the house on fire inside and we couldn't do anything about that. But outside we could at least make sure the roof didn't catch fire. We broke ice on the spring and hauled up—carefully, carefully—that black water to keep the roof safe from sparks and cinders. And while that dark, moonless night was lit by the fiery torch atop our helpless house, there were no jokes but lots of "hurry-up" and silence.

Side by side with Annie I worked, quietly and hard and quickly, to keep the buckets coming to Dad. Later I saw his hands bloody from fighting to keep a hold on that slippery roof. *Roar* and *whoosh* were the sounds the fire made, and I was more scared than excited.

While we worked with the water, Mom and Sarah braved the house to pack what we'd need if the worst happened, if the whole house burned. Everyone seemed brave that night. I kept thinking how Annie's hands must be frozen like mine but she never said a word.

Eventually the Piney Volunteer Fire Department gathered: Jimmy up from Adeline, and Harry from Dutch Fork, Bob from Clouston, and Dan Creary from Sleepy Creek Hollow. They all came in pickups since the pump truck was froze up solid over at Dixon's. Neighbors from across the valley and down the ridge would arrive, too, before it was over. But, of course, the first one there was Dad himself—he joked later that no one had ever been quicker than that to a fire, and if they had, he'd eat his Sunday pants.

The night was beautiful, all white and black
beyond the fire. Somewhere in that black a deer
must have lifted her nose from grass pawed clear of
snow, looked over our way, and wondered—too smart
and too quick to be scared. I felt better when I heard
Jimmy and Bob, Harry and Dan shouting and laughing, even when it seemed they shouldn't. But finally
we watched the orange flames fall back until one
hour after it had started, Bob Jackson shone his
flashlight down the flue and announced: "She's all
gone, folks! Get on in the house and get to bed."
And, of course, we didn't.

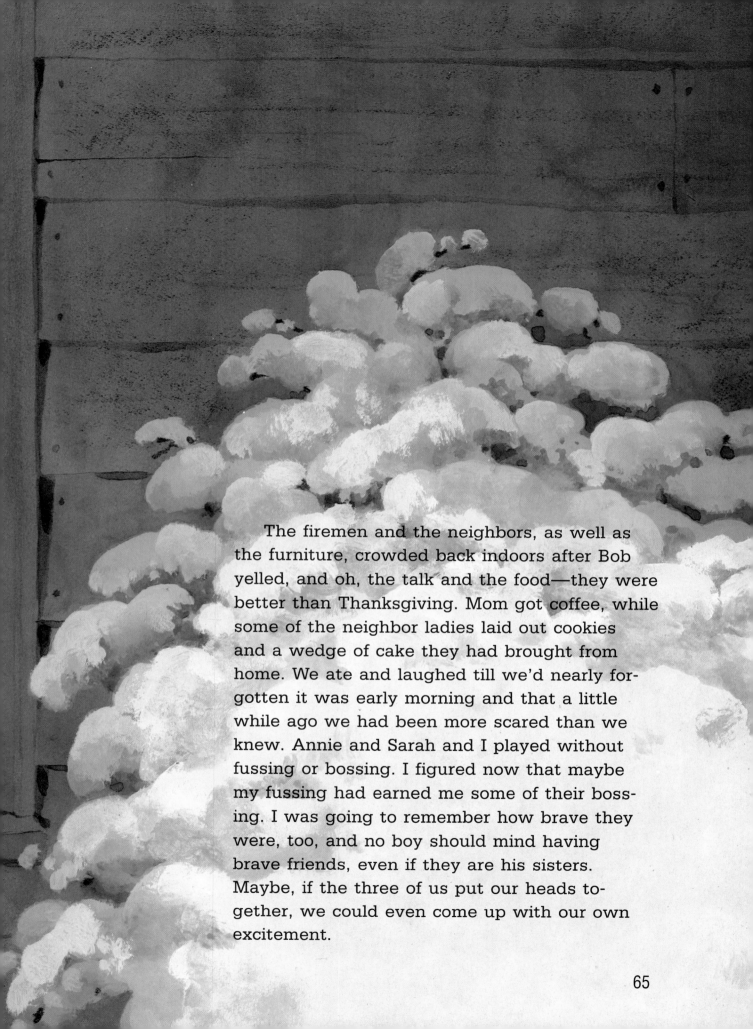

The firemen and the neighbors, as well as the furniture, crowded back indoors after Bob yelled, and oh, the talk and the food—they were better than Thanksgiving. Mom got coffee, while some of the neighbor ladies laid out cookies and a wedge of cake they had brought from home. We ate and laughed till we'd nearly forgotten it was early morning and that a little while ago we had been more scared than we knew. Annie and Sarah and I played without fussing or bossing. I figured now that maybe my fussing had earned me some of their bossing. I was going to remember how brave they were, too, and no boy should mind having brave friends, even if they are his sisters. Maybe, if the three of us put our heads together, we could even come up with our own excitement.

65

Sunrise came absolutely quiet to our hilltop farm.
A new powder of snow had fallen sometime after we
got back to sleep. The black ash and soot from the
blaze had already disappeared under it. It felt good to
see that everything was safe. I hoped when I saw
Grandma that she wouldn't mention what she had
said on Sunday. Besides, she wouldn't have to worry
about reminding me. I'm not likely to forget.

Be

Who

You

Want

To

Be

Zeely

by Virginia Hamilton
illustrated by
Symeon Shimin
Aladdin, 1986

"But you *are* different," Geeder said. "You are the most different person I've ever talked to."

"Am I?" Zeely said, her voice kind. "And you want to be different, too?"

A Man Named Thoreau

by Robert Burleigh
illustrated by
Lloyd Bloom
Atheneum, 1985

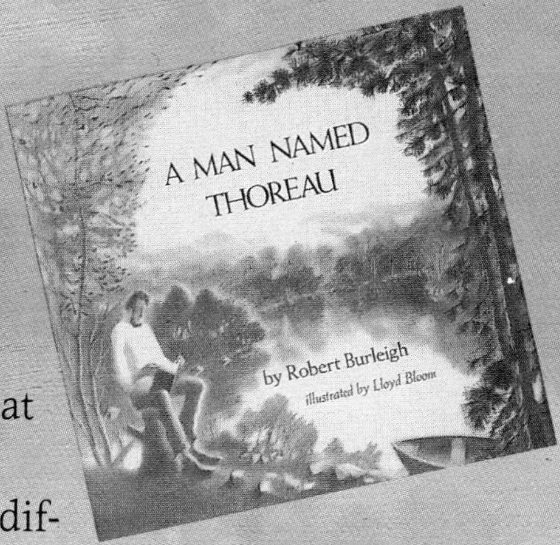

Above all, Thoreau wanted to live his own kind of life. He believed that a person might live differently from his neighbor because he heard a "different drummer."

69

THE Lost Lake

by Allen Say

I went to live with Dad last summer.

Every day he worked in his room from morning to night, sometimes on weekends, too. Dad wasn't much of a talker, but when he was busy he didn't talk at all.

I didn't know anybody in the city, so I stayed home most of the time. It was too hot to play outside anyway. In one month I finished all the books I'd brought and grew tired of watching TV.

One morning I started cutting pictures out of old magazines, just to be doing something. They were pictures of mountains and rivers and lakes, and some showed people fishing and canoeing. Looking at them made me feel cool, so I pinned them up in my room.

Dad didn't notice them for two days. When he did, he looked at them one by one.

"Nice pictures," he said.

"Are you angry with me, Dad?" I asked, because he saved old magazines for his work.

"It's all right, Luke," he said. "I'm having this place painted soon anyway."

He thought I was talking about the marks I'd made on the wall.

That Saturday Dad woke me up early in the morning and told me we were going camping! I was wide awake in a second. He gave me a pair of brand-new hiking boots to try out. They were perfect.

In the hallway I saw a big backpack and a knapsack all packed and ready to go.

"What's in them, Dad?" I asked.

"Later," he said. "We have a long drive ahead of us."

In the car I didn't ask any more questions because Dad was so grumpy in the morning.

"Want a sip?" he said, handing me his mug. He'd never let me drink coffee before. It had lots of sugar in it.

"Where are we going?" I finally asked.

"We're off to the Lost Lake, my lad."

"How can you lose a lake?"

"No one's found it, that's how." Dad was smiling! "Grandpa and I used to go there a long time ago. It was our special place, so don't tell any of your friends."

"I'll never tell," I promised. "How long are we going to stay there?"

"Five days, maybe a week."

"We're going to sleep outside for a whole week?"

"That's the idea."

"Oh, boy!"

We got to the mountains in the afternoon.

"It's a bit of a hike to the lake, son," Dad said.

"I don't mind," I told him. "Are there any fish in the lake?"

"Hope so. We'll have to catch our dinner, you know."

"You didn't bring any food?"

"Of course not. We're going to live like true outdoorsmen."

"Oh..."

Dad saw my face and started to laugh. He must have been joking. I didn't think we were going very far anyway, because Dad's pack was so heavy I couldn't even lift it.

Well, Dad was like a mountain goat. He went straight up the trail, whistling all the while. But I was gasping in no time. My knapsack got very heavy and I started to fall behind.

Dad stopped for me often, but he wouldn't let me take off my pack. If I did I'd be too tired to go on, he said.

It was almost suppertime when we got to the lake.

The place reminded me of the park near Dad's apartment. He wasn't whistling or humming anymore.

"Welcome to the *Found* Lake," he muttered from the side of his mouth.

"What's wrong, Dad?"

"Do you want to camp with all these people around us?"

"I don't mind."

"Well, I do!"

"Are we going home?"

"Of course not!"

He didn't even take off his pack. He just turned and started to walk away.

Soon the lake was far out of sight.

Then it started to rain. Dad gave me a poncho and it kept me dry, but I wondered where we were going to sleep that night. I wondered what we were going to do for dinner. I wasn't sure about camping anymore.

I was glad when Dad finally stopped and set up the tent. The rain and wind beat against it, but we were warm and cozy inside. And Dad had brought food. For dinner we had salami and dried apricots.

"I'm sorry about the lake, Dad," I said.

He shook his head. "You know something, Luke? There aren't any secret places left in the world anymore."

"What if we go very far up in the mountains? Maybe we can find our own lake."

"There are lots of lakes up here, but that one was special."

"But we've got a whole week, Dad."

"Well, why not? Maybe we'll find a lake that's not on the map."

"Sure, we will!"

We started early in the morning. When the fog cleared we saw other hikers ahead of us. Sure enough, Dad became very glum.

"We're going cross-country, partner," he said.

"Won't we get lost?"

"A wise man never leaves home without his compass."

So we went off the trail. The hills went on and on. The mountains went on and on. It was kind of lonesome. It seemed as if Dad and I were the only people left in the world.

And then we hiked into a big forest.

At noontime we stopped by a creek and ate lunch and drank ice-cold water straight from the stream. I threw rocks in the water, and fish, like shadows, darted in the pools.

"Isn't this a good place to camp, Dad?"

"I thought we were looking for our lake."

"Yes, right..." I mumbled.

The forest went on and on.

"I don't mean to scare you, son," Dad said. "But we're in bear country. We don't want to surprise them, so we have to make a lot of noise. If they hear us, they'll just go away."

What a time to tell me! I started to shout as loudly as I could. Even Dad wouldn't be able to beat off bears. I thought about those people having fun back at the lake. I thought about the creek, too, with all those fish in it. That would have been a fine place to camp. The Lost Lake hadn't been so bad either.

It was dark when we got out of the forest. We built a fire and that made me feel better. Wild animals wouldn't come near a fire. Dad cooked beef stroganoff and it was delicious.

Later it was bedtime. The sleeping bag felt wonderful. Dad and I started to count the shooting stars, then I worried that maybe we weren't going to find our lake.

"What are you thinking about, Luke?" Dad asked.

"I didn't know you could cook like that," I said.

Dad laughed. "That was only freeze-dried stuff. When we get home, I'll cook you something really special."

"You know something, Dad? You seem like a different person up here."

"Better or worse?"

"A lot better."

"How so?"

"You talk more."

"I'll have to talk more often, then."

That made me smile. Then I slept.

Dad shook me awake. The sun was just coming up, turning everything all gold and orange and yellow. And there was the lake, right in front of us.

For a long time we watched the light change on the water, getting brighter and brighter. Dad didn't say a word the whole time. But then, I didn't have anything to say either.

After breakfast we climbed a mountain and saw our lake below us. There wasn't a sign of people anywhere. It really seemed as if Dad and I were all alone in the world.

I liked it just fine.

MEET
ALLEN SAY
ALLEN SAY

For Allen Say, who writes and illustrates many of his own stories, pictures always come first. When he makes up a story, he begins by drawing pictures without having words or even ideas to go with them. *The Lost Lake* grew out of pictures Say drew of a camping trip. He unexpectedly remembered hiking to a mountain lake many years before and finding the area completely ruined by litter.

Say has been an artist almost all of his life. He originally dreamed of being a cartoonist. At thirteen he already had a job drawing backgrounds for a famous cartoonist in Japan. Say eventually came to the United States. He never lost his interest in art and later began to write and illustrate stories.

Other books by this writer and illustrator that you might enjoy are *El Chino,* a book about Bill Wong, the first Chinese bullfighter, and *Tree of Cranes*, a book Say dedicated to the man he learned from and first worked for, the Japanese cartoonist Noro Shinpei.

87

FIRST AID

What about first aid?
It's a good idea to bring a simple first-aid kit, even on a short hike.

What do I wear?
If you are hiking where hungry insects hunt, cover your arms and legs. Be kind to your feet, too! Wear sturdy, comfortable shoes.

LET'S HIT THE TRAIL

How can you experience the best nature has to offer? Why, take a hike in the great outdoors! Just follow this trail to help you get ready.

Should
I bring food?
Definitely! Always carry water or juice. To keep up your energy, pack a trail snack—dried fruit and cereal mixed with nuts.

For an all-day hike, pack sandwiches and fruit. All that walking will make you thirsty and hungry.

Now you're ready to hit the trail. Ask friends and an adult to go. (It's a good idea to hike in a group.) Keep your eyes and ears open, step carefully, and enjoy the scenery!

Uh, oh!
Which way to go?
Carry a compass and a map and you'll always know where you're going.

Hint: To keep yourself on course, put your map on the ground and the compass on top of the map. Line up the north arrows on the map and the compass. Knowing where you are in relation to north will help you know which way to go.

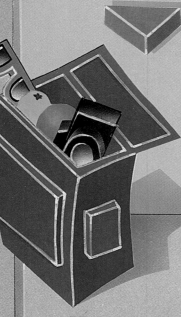

How can I carry
my hiking gear?
You can use a small backpack or hip pack.

Bird and Boy

So you want to fly. Why?
 You haven't any feathers.
Do you think it's good fun
 Being out in all weathers?
Said Bird to Boy.

You haven't any wings,
 You can't build a nest.
Why aren't you satisfied.
 With the things you do best?
Said Bird to Boy.

What would it be like?
 A sky full of boys,
Their arms flapping, their big feet—
 And the noise!
Said Bird to Boy.

Have you ever tried perching
 In some old tree
When it's snowing? It's not funny,
 Believe me!
Said Bird to Boy.

Be comfortable, do your own thing,
 Your skateboard, your bike,
Your football, all the other
 Things you like.
 Why try to fly?
 Stay out of the sky,
Said Bird to Boy.

Yes, you're right, I can't just
 Flap my arms and fly.
But I dream about it often,
 Winging through the sky,
Above the houses, the streets.
 I'd like to try.
Said Boy to Bird.

Leslie Norris

illustrated by **Burton Silverman**

Sarah, Plain and Tall

AND

by Patricia MacLachlan

Anna and Caleb's mother died the day after Caleb was born. Papa and Anna miss Mama, and Caleb longs for a mother to love and care for him. When Papa decides to advertise for a wife, Sarah Elisabeth Wheaton answers the advertisement from Maine. After trading a few letters with Papa, Anna, and Caleb, Sarah decides to visit them in their prairie home for a month. She writes that they will recognize her at the train station because she is "plain and tall." Sarah brings Seal, her cat, and gifts from the ocean she loves so much. Papa, Caleb, and Anna wonder if Sarah will be content to stay and make her new home with them, so far from the sea.

The dandelions in the fields had gone by, their heads soft as feathers. The summer roses were opening.

Our neighbors, Matthew and Maggie, came to help Papa plow up a new field for corn. Sarah stood with us on the porch, watching their wagon wind up the road, two horses pulling it and one tied in back. I remembered the last time we had stood here alone, Caleb and I, waiting for Sarah.

Sarah's hair was in thick braids that circled her head, wild daisies tucked here and there. Papa had picked them for her.

Old Bess and Jack ran along the inside of the fence, whickering at the new horses.

"Papa needs five horses for the big gang plow," Caleb told Sarah. "Prairie grass is hard."

Matthew and Maggie came with their two children and a sackful of chickens. Maggie emptied the sack into the yard and three red banty chickens clucked and scattered.

"They are for you," she told Sarah. "For eating."

Sarah loved the chickens. She clucked back to them and fed them grain. They followed her, shuffling and scratching primly in the dirt. I knew they would not be for eating.

The children were young and named Rose and Violet, after flowers. They hooted and laughed and chased the chickens, who flew up to the porch roof, then the dogs, who crept quietly under the porch. Seal had long ago fled to the barn to sleep in cool hay.

Sarah and Maggie helped hitch the horses to the plow, then they set up a big table in the shade of the barn, covering it with a quilt and a kettle of flowers in the middle. They sat on the porch while Caleb and

Matthew and Papa began their morning of plowing.
I mixed biscuit dough just inside the door, watching.

"You are lonely, yes?" asked Maggie in her soft voice.

Sarah's eyes filled with tears. Slowly I stirred the dough.

Maggie reached over and took Sarah's hand.

"I miss the hills of Tennessee sometimes," she said.

Do not miss the hills, Maggie, I thought.

"I miss the sea," said Sarah.

Do not miss the hills. Do not miss the sea.

I stirred and stirred the dough.

"I miss my brother William," said Sarah.

"But he is married. The house is hers now. Not mine any longer. There are three old aunts who all squawk together like crows at dawn. I miss them, too."

"There are always things to miss," said Maggie. "No matter where you are."

I looked out and saw Papa and Matthew and Caleb working. Rose and Violet ran in the fields. I felt something brush my legs and looked down at Nick, wagging his tail.

"I would miss you, Nick," I whispered. "I would." I knelt down and scratched his ears. "I miss Mama."

"I nearly forgot," said Maggie on the porch. "I have something more for you."

I carried the bowl outside and watched Maggie lift a low wooden box out of the wagon.

"Plants," she said to Sarah. "For your garden."

"My garden?" Sarah bent down to touch the plants.

"Zinnias and marigolds and wild feverfew," said Maggie. "You must have a garden. Wherever you are."

Sarah smiled. "I had a garden in Maine with dahlias and columbine. And nasturtiums the color of the sun when it sets. I don't know if nasturtiums would grow here."

"Try," said Maggie. "You must have a garden."

We planted the flowers by the porch, turning over the soil and patting it around them, and watering. Lottie and Nick came to sniff, and the chickens walked in the dirt, leaving prints. In the fields, the horses pulled the plow up and down under the hot summer sun.

Maggie wiped her face, leaving a streak of dirt.

"Soon you can drive your wagon over to my house and I will give you more. I have tansy."

Sarah frowned. "I have never driven a wagon."

"I can teach you," said Maggie. "And so can Anna and Caleb. And Jacob."

Sarah turned to me.

"Can you?" she asked. "Can you drive a wagon?"

I nodded.

"And Caleb?"

"Yes."

"In Maine," said Sarah, "I would walk to town."

"Here it is different," said Maggie. "Here you will drive."

Way off in the sky, clouds gathered. Matthew and Papa and Caleb came in from the fields, their work done. We all ate in the shade.

"We are glad you are here," said Matthew to Sarah. "A new friend. Maggie misses her friends sometimes."

Sarah nodded. "There is always something to miss, no matter where you are," she said, smiling at Maggie.

Rose and Violet fell asleep in the grass, their bellies full of meat and greens and biscuits. And when it was time to go, Papa and Matthew lifted them into the wagon to sleep on blankets.

Sarah walked slowly behind the wagon for a long time, waving, watching it disappear. Caleb and I ran to bring her back, the chickens running wildly behind us.

"What shall we name them?" asked Sarah, laughing as the chickens followed us into the house.

I smiled. I was right. The chickens would not be for eating.

And then Papa came, just before the rain, bringing Sarah the first roses of summer.

The rain came and passed, but strange clouds hung in the northwest, low and black and green. And the air grew still.

In the morning, Sarah dressed in a pair of overalls and went to the barn to have an argument with Papa. She took apples for Old Bess and Jack.

"Women don't wear overalls," said Caleb, running along behind her like one of Sarah's chickens.

"This woman does," said Sarah crisply.

Papa stood by the fence.

"I want to learn how to ride a horse," Sarah told him. "And then I want to learn how to drive the wagon. By myself."

Jack leaned over and nipped at Sarah's overalls. She fed him an apple. Caleb and I stood behind Sarah.

"I can ride a horse, I know," said Sarah. "I rode once when I was twelve. I will ride Jack." Jack was Sarah's favorite.

Papa shook his head. "Not Jack," he said. "Jack is sly."

"I am sly, too," said Sarah stubbornly.

Papa smiled. "Ayuh," he said, nodding. "But not Jack."

"Yes, Jack!" Sarah's voice was very loud.

"I can teach you how to drive a wagon. I have already taught you how to plow."

"And then I can go to town. By myself."

"Say no, Papa," Caleb whispered beside me.

"That's a fair thing, Sarah," said Papa. "We'll practice."

A soft rumble of thunder sounded. Papa looked up at the clouds.

"Today? Can we begin today?" asked Sarah.

"Tomorrow is best," said Papa, looking worried. "I have to fix the house roof. A portion of it is loose. And there's a storm coming."

"We," said Sarah.

"What?" Papa turned.

"*We* will fix the roof," said Sarah. "I've done it before. I know about roofs. I am a good carpenter. Remember, I told you?"

There was thunder again, and Papa went to get the ladder.

"Are you fast?" he asked Sarah.

"I am fast and I am good," said Sarah. And they climbed the ladder to the roof, Sarah with wisps of hair around her face, her mouth full of nails, overalls like Papa's. Overalls that *were* Papa's.

Caleb and I went inside to close the windows. We could hear the steady sound of hammers pounding the roof overhead.

"Why does she want to go to town by herself?" asked Caleb. "To leave us?"

I shook my head, weary with Caleb's questions. Tears gathered at the corners of my eyes. But there was no time to cry, for suddenly Papa called out.

"Caleb! Anna!"

We ran outside and saw a huge cloud, horribly black, moving toward us over the north fields. Papa slid down the roof, helping Sarah after him.

"A squall!" he yelled to us. He held up his arms and Sarah jumped off the porch roof.

"Get the horses inside," he ordered Caleb. "Get the sheep, Anna. And the cows. The barn is safest."

The grasses flattened. There was a hiss of wind, a sudden pungent smell. Our faces looked yellow in the strange light. Caleb and I jumped over the fence and found the animals huddled by the barn. I counted the sheep to make sure they were all there, and herded them into a large stall. A few raindrops came, gentle at first, then stronger and louder, so that Caleb and I covered our ears and stared at each other without speaking. Caleb looked frightened and I tried to smile at him. Sarah

carried a sack into the barn, her hair wet and streaming down her neck. Papa came behind, Lottie and Nick with him, their ears flat against their heads.

"Wait!" cried Sarah. "My chickens!"

"No, Sarah!" Papa called after her. But Sarah had already run from the barn into a sheet of rain. My father followed her. The sheep nosed open their stall door and milled around the barn, bleating. Nick crept under my arm, and a lamb, Mattie with the black face, stood close to me, trembling. There was a soft paw on my lap, then a gray body. Seal. And then, as the thunder pounded and the wind rose and there was the terrible crackling of lightning close by, Sarah and Papa stood in the barn doorway, wet to the skin. Papa carried Sarah's chickens. Sarah came with an armful of summer roses.

Sarah's chickens were not afraid, and they settled like small red bundles in the hay. Papa closed the door at last, shutting out some of the sounds of the storm. The barn was eerie and half lighted, like dusk without a lantern. Papa spread blankets around our shoulders and Sarah unpacked a bag of cheese and bread and jam. At the very bottom of the bag were Sarah's shells.

Caleb got up and went over to the small barn window. "What color is the sea when it storms?" he asked Sarah.

"Blue," said Sarah, brushing her wet hair back with her fingers. "And gray and green."

Caleb nodded and smiled.

"Look," he said to her. "Look what is missing from your drawing."

Sarah went to stand between Caleb and Papa by the window. She looked a long time without speaking. Finally, she touched Papa's shoulder.

"We have squalls in Maine, too," she said. "Just like this. It will be all right, Jacob."

Papa said nothing. But he put his arm around her, and leaned over to rest his chin in her hair. I closed my eyes, suddenly remembering Mama and Papa standing that way, Mama smaller than Sarah, her hair fair against Papa's shoulder. When I opened my eyes again, it was Sarah standing there. Caleb looked at me and smiled and smiled until he could smile no more.

We slept in the hay all night, waking when the wind was wild, sleeping again when it was quiet. And at dawn there was the sudden sound of hail, like stones tossed against the barn. We stared out the window, watching the ice marbles bounce on the ground.

And when it was over we opened the barn door and walked out into the early-morning light. The hail crunched and melted beneath our feet. It was white and gleaming for as far as we looked, like sun on glass. Like the sea.

It was very quiet. The dogs leaned down to eat the hailstones. Seal stepped around them and leaped up on the fence to groom herself. A tree had blown over near the cow pond. And the wild roses were scattered on the ground, as if a wedding had come and gone there. "I'm glad I saved an armful" was all that Sarah said.

Only one field was badly damaged, and Sarah and Papa hitched up the horses and plowed and replanted during the next two days. The roof had held.

"I told you I know about roofs," Sarah told Papa, making him smile.

Papa kept his promise to Sarah. When the work was done, he took her out into the fields, Papa riding Jack who was sly, and Sarah riding Old Bess. Sarah was quick to learn.

"Too quick," Caleb complained to me as we watched from the fence. He thought a moment. "Maybe she'll fall off and have to stay here. Why?" he asked, turning to me. "Why does she have to go away alone?"

"Hush up, Caleb," I said crossly. "Hush up."

"I could get sick and make her stay here," said Caleb.

"No."

"We could tie her up."

"No."

And Caleb began to cry, and I took him inside the barn where we could both cry.

Papa and Sarah came to hitch the horses to the wagon, so Sarah could practice driving. Papa didn't see Caleb's tears, and he sent him with an ax to begin chopping up the tree by the pond for firewood. I stood and watched Sarah, the reins in her hands, Papa next to her in the wagon. I could see Caleb standing by the pond,

one hand shading his eyes, watching, too. I went into the safe darkness of the barn then, Sarah's chickens scuttling along behind me.

"Why?" I asked out loud, echoing Caleb's question.

The chickens watched me, their eyes small and bright.

The next morning Sarah got up early and put on her blue dress. She took apples to the barn. She loaded a bundle of hay on the wagon for Old Bess and Jack. She put on her yellow bonnet.

"Remember Jack," said Papa. "A strong hand."

"Yes, Jacob."

"Best to be home before dark," said Papa. "Driving a wagon is hard if there's no full moon."

"Yes, Jacob."

Sarah kissed us all, even my father, who looked surprised.

"Take care of Seal," she said to Caleb and me. And with a whisper to Old Bess and a stern word to Jack, Sarah climbed up in the wagon and drove away.

"Very good," murmured Papa as he watched. And after a while he turned and went out into the fields.

Caleb and I watched Sarah from the porch. Caleb took my hand, and the dogs lay down beside us. It was sunny, and I remembered another time when a wagon had taken Mama away. It had been a day just like this day. And Mama had never come back.

Seal jumped up to the porch, her feet making a small thump. Caleb leaned down and picked her up and walked inside. I took the broom and slowly swept the porch. Then I watered Sarah's plants. Caleb cleaned out the wood stove and carried the ashes to the barn, spilling them so that I had to sweep the porch again.

"I *am* loud and pesky," Caleb cried suddenly. "You said so! And she has gone to buy a train ticket to go away!"

"No, Caleb. She would tell us."

"The house is too small," said Caleb. "That's what it is."

"The house is not too small," I said.

I looked at Sarah's drawing of the fields pinned up on the wall next to the window.

"What is missing?" I asked Caleb. "You said you knew what was missing."

"Colors," said Caleb wearily. "The colors of the sea."

Outside, clouds moved into the sky and went away again. We took lunch to Papa, cheese and bread and lemonade. Caleb nudged me.

"Ask him. Ask Papa."

"What has Sarah gone to do?" I asked.

"I don't know," said Papa. He squinted at me. Then he sighed and put one hand on Caleb's head, one on mine. "Sarah is Sarah. She does things her way, you know."

ANNA

"I know," said Caleb very softly.

Papa picked up his shovel and put on his hat.

"Ask if she's coming back," whispered Caleb.

"Of course she's coming back," I said. "Seal is here." But I would not ask the question. I was afraid to hear the answer.

We fed the sheep, and I set the table for dinner. Four plates. The sun dropped low over the west fields. Lottie and Nick stood at the door, wagging their tails, asking for supper. Papa came to light the stove. And then it was dusk. Soon it would be dark. Caleb sat on the porch steps, turning his moon snail shell over and over in his hand. Seal brushed back and forth against him.

Suddenly Lottie began to bark, and Nick jumped off the porch and ran down the road.

"Dust!" cried Caleb. He climbed the porch and stood on the roof. "Dust, and a yellow bonnet!"

Slowly the wagon came around the windmill and the barn and the windbreak and into the yard, the dogs jumping happily beside it.

"Hush, dogs," said Sarah. And Nick leaped up into the wagon to sit by Sarah.

Papa took the reins and Sarah climbed down from the wagon.

Caleb burst into tears.

"Seal was very worried!" he cried.

Sarah put her arms around him, and he wailed into her dress. "And the house is too small, we thought! And I am loud and pesky!"

Sarah looked at Papa and me over Caleb's head.

"We thought you might be thinking of leaving us," I told her. "Because you miss the sea."

Sarah smiled.

"No," she said. "I will always miss my old home, but the truth of it is I would miss you more."

Papa smiled at Sarah, then he bent quickly to un-hitch the horses from the wagon. He led them to the barn for water.

Sarah handed me a package.

"For Anna," she said. "And Caleb. For all of us."

The package was small, wrapped in brown paper with a rubber band around it. Very carefully I un-wrapped it, Caleb peering closely. Inside were three colored pencils.

"Blue," said Caleb slowly, "and gray. And green."

Sarah nodded.

Suddenly Caleb grinned.

"Papa," he called. "Papa, come quickly! Sarah has brought the sea!"

We eat our night meal by candlelight, the four of us. Sarah has brought candles from town. And nasturtium seeds for her garden, and a book of songs to teach us. It is late, and Caleb is nearly sleeping by his plate and Sarah is smiling at my father. Soon there will be a wedding. Papa says that when the preacher asks if he will have Sarah for his wife, he will answer, "Ayuh."

Autumn will come, then winter, cold with a wind that blows like the wind off the sea in Maine. There will be nests of curls to look for, and dried flowers all winter long. When there are storms, Papa will stretch a rope from the door to the barn so we will not be lost when we feed the sheep and the cows and Jack and Old Bess. And Sarah's chickens, if they aren't living in the house. There will be Sarah's sea, blue and gray and green, hanging on the wall. And songs, old ones and new. And Seal with yellow eyes. And there will be Sarah, plain and tall.

Meet

PATRICIA MacLACHLAN

Although Patricia MacLachlan did not write as a child, she made up stories in her head. She imagined kings and queens, heroes and villains. When MacLachlan became an adult, kings and queens no longer captured her imagination. Instead, her children and the relatives she had known and heard about as a child became models for her characters.

MacLachlan becomes old friends with the people in her stories before she begins to write. "I . . . have all sorts of conversations with myself and with characters I make up. . . . I talk with characters in the car, over a sink full of dishes, in the garden."

MacLachlan's story ideas may begin with people, but she also thinks a lot about the setting. Because she was born in Wyoming and raised in Minnesota, she says, "the western landscape has always been a powerful force in my life."

In the Newbery Award-winning story *Sarah, Plain and Tall*, character and place cannot be separated. Sarah, a mail-order bride—like one of MacLachlan's distant relatives—leaves her home on the eastern seacoast to begin a new life in the West. To the prairie she brings her love of Maine and her longing for the sea.

Other books by MacLachlan that you might enjoy are *The Facts and Fictions of Minna Pratt* and *Arthur, for the Very First Time*.

DREAMS

Hold fast to dreams
For if dreams die
Life is a broken-winged bird
That cannot fly.

Hold fast to dreams
For when dreams go
Life is a barren field
Frozen with snow.

Langston Hughes

CONTENTS

LET'S FIND OUT!

There is wonder past all wonder
in the ways of living things,
in a worm's intrepid wriggling,
in the song a blackbird sings, . . .

In a fish's joyful splashing
in a snake that makes no sound,
in the smallest salamander
there is wonder to be found.

JACK PRELUTSKY
from "The Ways of Living Things"

118

Dear Bronx Zoo

BY JOYCE ALTMAN
AND
SUE GOLDBERG

Every day, letters arrive at the Bronx Zoo. Most come from children—children who've recently come to the zoo, or who live too far away to visit. When they write, they ask about all aspects of animal and zoo life, everything from "Do bats always hang upside down?" and "Why does the rattlesnake have a rattle?" to "Where do the animals sleep at night when it's cold?"

The letters are answered by the Friends of the Zoo, a group of volunteers who work with the zoo's education department to teach and inform zoo visitors about animals. In answering these letters, as well as the questions posed at the zoo by young zoo visitors, Sue Goldberg and I, both members of the Friends of the Zoo, conceived the idea for Dear Bronx Zoo—a collection of the best and most frequently asked zoo-related questions. The answers explain how animals live in nature and captivity, how the zoo operates and cares for over 4,200 animals on a day-to-day basis, and what role modern-day zoos play in species preservation.

Joyce Altman

121

What is a zoo?

For many people, especially those who live in cities, the only way to ever see wild animals is by visiting a zoo. In the past, most zoos only displayed strange and unusual animals for people to look at, but today they do much more than that. Modern zoos not only exhibit animals, but also teach people about wildlife and the environment, and even help to preserve animals that are losing their homes in nature.

The Bronx Zoo exhibits animals from all parts of the world, sends researchers into the field to study animals in the wild, and working together with other zoos, helps preserve many **endangered species**—those animals that are in danger of dying out, or becoming **extinct.** As animals lose more

and more of their natural ranges, called **habitats,** zoos help provide substitute homes for them.

In the past, zoos tried to display as many different types of animals as possible. Modern zoos, instead, keep fewer kinds of animals, or animal **species,** so that they can care for and **breed** larger numbers of each. By doing so, they give the animals a better chance of survival. ●

When did the Bronx Zoo open? How big is it?

The Bronx Zoo opened in 1899, four years after the New York Zoological Society was formed. Although not the oldest zoo in the United States (the Cincinnati and Philadelphia zoos are older), it is one of the country's largest and most successful urban zoos, with 265 acres of meadows and woodlands.

From the beginning, animal exhibition at the Bronx Zoo was different than at many other zoos of the day. Instead of small pens, the zoo housed many of its animals in open areas similar to their natural habitats. Large North American animals, such as deer, elk, and bison, ranged in large enclosed meadows, and the natural landscapes helped give zoo visitors a truer sense of the animals' nature and ways.

Today's exhibits are designed to resemble natural habitats even more closely. For example, one of the newer exhibits at the Bronx Zoo, the Himalayan Highlands, houses red pandas, rare white-naped cranes, tragopan pheasants, and a highly endangered species of cat called the snow leopard in large mountainous and marshy outdoor areas created especially for them. In the JungleWorld building, Asian mammals, birds, and reptiles of all descriptions live in huge, barless habitats, so real that it's easy to imagine what it's like in the Asian wilderness. ●

Where does the Bronx Zoo get its animals from?

Because zoos today are concerned with protecting animal populations, they generally no longer seek animals captured in the wild for their collections. Also, it is very upsetting for any animal to be taken from its home or family. Many captured animals do not survive. For some rare species, taking individuals from the wild may push the species closer to extinction.

Instead of collecting animals from the wild, pairs or groups of animals live together in zoos and produce babies. Animals that breed in zoos are called **captive bred.** Since not all zoos breed all species of animals, exchanges and loans are often made between zoos. Zookeepers keep records on their animals—such as the age, sex, and condition of each—so that loans (sometimes long term) can be made. These loans and exchanges are important when it comes to efforts to save endangered species. In order for a species that has lost a lot of its population to remain healthy and survive, its remaining members must breed and produce young with nonrelated members of the same species. Most zoos do not have the facilities to keep a large number of animals of each species, so exchanging animals from one zoo with those from another becomes essential.

In a single year, the Bronx Zoo may exchange as many as five hundred animals with over one hundred other institutions. When one of the zoo's animals is sent to another zoo for a temporary or long-term stay for breeding purposes, that animal is on "breeding loan." ●

and other reptiles and amphibians on display. There are many rare and unusual creatures in this building. One is called the Lake Titicaca frog. It can remain submerged in water almost indefinitely, getting oxygen through its skin. When water comes into contact with the frog's loose folds of thin skin, the frog extracts the oxygen it needs from the water.

Another is the Gila monster, a smallish (17- to 24-inch) lizard from the southwestern part of the United States, and one of only two poisonous lizards in the world. (The other is the Mexican beaded lizard.)

The Elephant House is another favorite building. It houses Asian elephants, Indian rhinoceroses, and Malayan tapirs.

Among the outdoor exhibits, the Children's Zoo is also quite popular. Here children can see animals at close range—prairie dogs and herons, raccoons and skunks, foxes and porcupines, ducks and goats, and many more. And they can learn how these animals use their senses, build homes, and defend themselves. ●

What is the most popular building at the zoo?

The Reptile House, the zoo's oldest building, is always filled with visitors who come to see the many species of snakes, turtles, crocodiles, frogs, toads, lizards,

What do animals at the zoo eat, and how often are they fed?

Each animal in the zoo has its own special diet and eating schedule, which vary depending on what type of animal it is. The zoo's nutritionist works with the curators, keepers, and **veterinarians** (zoo doctors) to determine the exact foods necessary for the good health of each species. Sometimes a diet must be invented, such as proper baby food for an orphaned sea lion or for a litter of snow leopard cubs.

Some animals, like birds and tigers, may eat only once a day. Others, like sea lions, are fed twice daily. Snakes may eat only once a week.

Meat, chicken, and fish for the carnivores are usually bought in large quantities, then frozen and stored in a warehouse until needed. Polar bears sometimes enjoy being fed their fish still frozen in a block of ice, so they can play with it as it melts.

Some of the animals at the zoo eat very large quantities of food. Elephants are each fed about seventeen pounds of sweet grain daily, along with as much hay as they want (usually about three ninety-pound bales a day), six apples, six carrots, six loaves of bread, and vitamin and mineral supplements. Every other day they also eat about five pounds of **hydroponic** grass, a special nutritious grass grown at the zoo in water instead of soil.

Rhinos eat about thirty pounds of grain, one to three bales of hay, six potatoes, and six carrots daily. Every third day, they also eat twenty pounds of hydroponic grass, and sometimes they get a special treat of mulberry branches or other **browse** (leaves and twigs).

It's important for elephants and rhinos to be accustomed to eating foods such as apples and potatoes. This is because, should they ever become ill, medication can be hidden inside these types of foods and hand-fed to the animals by their keepers.

Fruits and vegetables are purchased for primates and birds. Throughout the warm months of the year, keepers collect browse from the trees in the zoo. This is frozen and saved for use later in the year. Each zoo building has a spotlessly clean kitchen used for preparing animal meals. The keepers prepare the meals following directions written on a blackboard that detail each animal's diet. ●

Where do the animals sleep at night when it's cold?

Almost all of the zoo's animals are brought indoors to sleep at night whether it is cold or not. Most often, their indoor quarters are connected to their outdoor exhibit area. Taking the animals in at night protects them from bad weather and gives the keepers a chance to observe them closely and make sure they are feeling well. If they are ill, one of the zoo's veterinarians will be called in.

In the winter, some animals—such as lions, zebras, elephants, and giraffes—are not allowed to go outdoors at all. This is because they come from Africa, Asia, or other warm parts of the world, and cannot withstand the cold temperatures. Other animals, those that are native to cooler northern climates, stay outdoors in the winter. These include bison and bears, which have long, thick coats of fur to keep them warm.

In the summer, when the temperature often rises above 90° Fahrenheit in New York, bears help keep themselves cool by remaining fairly inactive and by swimming in the large pools of cool water in their exhibits. Reptiles, many of which come from very hot climates, live year-round in exhibits where the temperature is kept over 90° F.

Animals often live longer in zoos than they would in the wild. This is because they are fed nutritious meals, receive medical care when needed, and are protected from other animals that might harm them. ●

How are the animals and their exhibits cleaned?

Each morning before the zoo opens to the public, zookeepers are hard at work cleaning the exhibits. Most of the time the animals are transferred to a holding area next to their exhibit, so that the keepers can work quickly without disturbing the animals or being in any danger. Cleaning may include hosing down floors and walls, scrubbing artificial rocks and plants, and washing glass windows. After the exhibit is thoroughly cleaned, the animals are returned.

Most animals take care of their own hygiene. Birds such as ducks, flamingos, and penguins bathe in the pools and lakes in their exhibit areas. Condors and bluebirds use their beaks to clean their feathers instead of bathing.

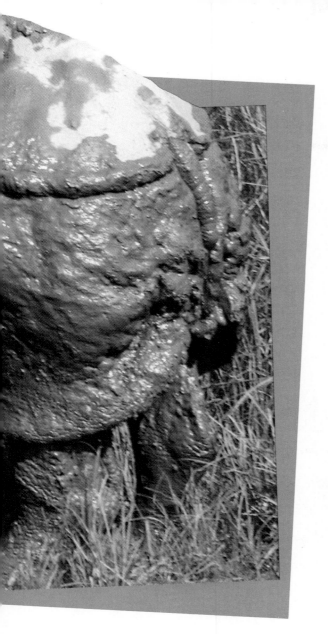

Do the keepers brush the animals' teeth?

It isn't necessary for wild animals to have their teeth brushed. The foods they eat usually keep them in good dental health. But if an animal must be anesthetized (put into a deep sleep) for some medical reason, the veterinarian will usually take care of any necessary dental work at that time. ●

Large cats, like lions, clean their fur with their rough tongues, just as housecats do. Rhinos take mud baths, digging mud holes to lie in to cool themselves and keep their sensitive skin from drying out.

A few animals, however, need to be cleaned by their keepers. For example, elephants are bathed by hand with soap and water, and then given a hose shower, which they love! ●

animals to rest in until they are well enough to return to their exhibits. ●

What does a zoo veterinarian do?

A veterinarian is a doctor who treats animals. The zoo veterinarian's job is not just to take care of animals when they are sick; it is also to make sure the animals are kept healthy, and to plan for any special care needed by baby animals born at the zoo. Helping the Bronx Zoo's veterinarians with these tasks is a staff of pathologists, radiologists, and other medical technicians and interns, as well as a full-time nutritionist. The zoo opened a large new health center in 1985. It has operating rooms with examination tables small enough for rodents and large enough for elephants. There are also fully equipped laboratories, and quarters for the

Does the zoo train any of its animals?

The zoo prefers to keep its wild animals as close to their natural wild state as possible. However, it is sometimes important to train some of the animals so that they can be cared for properly. For that reason, elephants are trained to do "tricks" like lifting a foot or sitting down on command, which is useful if a veterinarian needs to examine them. ●

Can people buy animals from the zoo?

No. Zoo animals are not for sale to the public. All of the animals at the zoo are wild, and it is the zoo's policy that wild animals should not be kept as pets. A wild animal requires special care in terms of food, habitat, and veterinary attention, and does not make a good—or safe—pet. ●

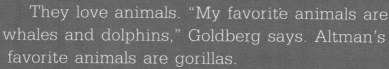

Meet JOYCE ALTMAN AND SUE GOLDBERG

Joyce Altman and Sue Goldberg have learned about animals by helping out at the Bronx Zoo in New York. They answer schoolchildren's letters, and they give classes and talks about the zoo animals. The two authors give demonstrations with snakes and small mammals. Can you imagine holding a boa constrictor or a ferret or a chinchilla? Altman and Goldberg get to hold these and more!

They love animals. "My favorite animals are whales and dolphins," Goldberg says. Altman's favorite animals are gorillas.

When they're not helping out at the zoo, Joyce Altman and Sue Goldberg work at regular jobs: Altman works as an editor, and Goldberg is a computer science teacher.

Joyce Altman

Sue Goldberg

133

DON'T FEED

IF YOU THINK UNUSUAL ANIMALS ARE FOUND ONLY IN ZOOS, TAKE ANOTHER LOOK.

Deborah Reich practices the art of topiary as she shapes plants into the forms of animals. Her condor appeared at the San Diego Zoo as part of an exhibition called "Animals in the Garden." If this condor wants to stay in shape, it'll need to have its wings clipped from time to time!

This creature might look ferocious, but it "wood" never bite you. Felipe Archuleta carved the animal from cottonwood.

Mr. Archuleta was one of the first woodcarvers in New Mexico to create realistic-looking–and life-size–wooden animals. He used chain saws, hammers, and knives to create all

134

THE ANIMALS

kinds of animals from rabbits to elephants. To add details, he used paint and bits of glass, rope, wire, and rubber. Although Mr. Archuleta recently died, his son, Leroy, and other woodcarvers carry on the tradition of crafting wooden animals.

Some buckets and shovels and a few gallons of colored water are all that's needed to sculpt magnificent creatures. In Casper, Wyoming, piles of snow were shaped into this huge white tiger, complete with stripes.

After shaping and carving the snow, the sculptors added details, using colored water. All this tiger needs to keep its shape is freezing-cold weather.

I

How do they know—
the sparrows and larks—
when it's time to return
to the meadows and parks?

How do they know
when fall is still here
it's the "thing" to go south
that time of the year?

Do you think that a bird
is just smart, or, instead,
that he carries a calendar
'round in his head?

II

How do they know—
the hornets and bees—
what direction to take
through the woods and the trees,

How far they should go,
how long they should roam,
and which way to turn
when it's time to go home?

Do you think that a bee
knows north from northwest—
or has he a compass
tucked under his vest?

Aileen Fisher

137

DO NOT DISTURB

THE MYSTERIES OF
ANIMAL HIBERNATION AND SLEEP

BY MARGERY FACKLAM
ILLUSTRATED BY PAMELA JOHNSON

A 300-pound grizzly bear shuffled through a dry autumn meadow in Yellowstone National Park. She stopped to catch a mouse with one swat of her huge paw and then ambled on toward a clear stream. At the water's edge she stood on her hind legs to look around and sniff the air before she plunged into the cold water. In a moment she caught a salmon with a swoop of her paw and gulped it down. She devoured two more fish before she waded out and shook the water from her thick, gray-tipped "grizzled" fur, which glistened in the sun.

Day after day the grizzly loped through the meadows in avid search of insects, berries, and small rodents, stopping once for a real picnic when she found the carcass of an elk. Food seemed to be the only thing on her mind.

But as she grew fatter and the air grew colder, she began to search for something else—her winter den. Like other grizzlies, who are the largest land carnivores (meat-eaters) in the world and are part of the bigger family of brown bears, she looks for a fresh new den each year. When she found a place that suited her, on a steep north-facing slope at the base of a large fir tree, she began to dig. Dirt flew as she scooped out a tunnel with her long claws. It was a tight fit as she tunneled under the tree roots that would make a strong roof for her den, but she needed room enough only to squeeze through to her bedroom. In the spring, after four or five months of a deep sleep called hibernation, she would be much thinner.

The hollowed-out bedroom was just big enough for her to curl up in, head to tail. During her winter sleep, she would give birth to two tiny cubs, but they wouldn't take up much space. The cubs of a 300-pound grizzly bear are so small that they can both sit on a saucer.

For several weeks the grizzly crawled in and out of her den to arrange her bedding. Some bears use moss and grass, but this one liked the soft branches of a fir tree.

Late in November, when the temperature had dropped below freezing, the big grizzly no longer raced with the speed of a horse across the open meadow. Day after day she acted as though she were walking in her sleep. Her head drooped, and she dragged one foot after the other. Then one day, when the wind whipped the snow in swirls around her, the bear crawled into her den. All night it snowed, covering the opening to her tunnel until it disappeared. No one would be able to find it. The grizzly was safe for the winter, cozy and warm beneath the blanket of snow. She would not eat, drink water, urinate, or defecate until spring. Her heart rate would slow down from its usual 40 or 50 beats a minute to 10 or 12. Her temperature would drop a few degrees, and she would breathe slowly, just as a person in a deep sleep would do.

Like their grizzly cousins, the black bears also sleep through winter, but they don't tunnel or dig deep dens. Some scratch out a hollow at the base of a tree. Others like to sleep under a pile of brush and fallen logs, and still others curl up in small caves. They, too, build cozy beds of moss, leaves, pine needles, or bark and branches that will keep them as warm as down sleeping bags.

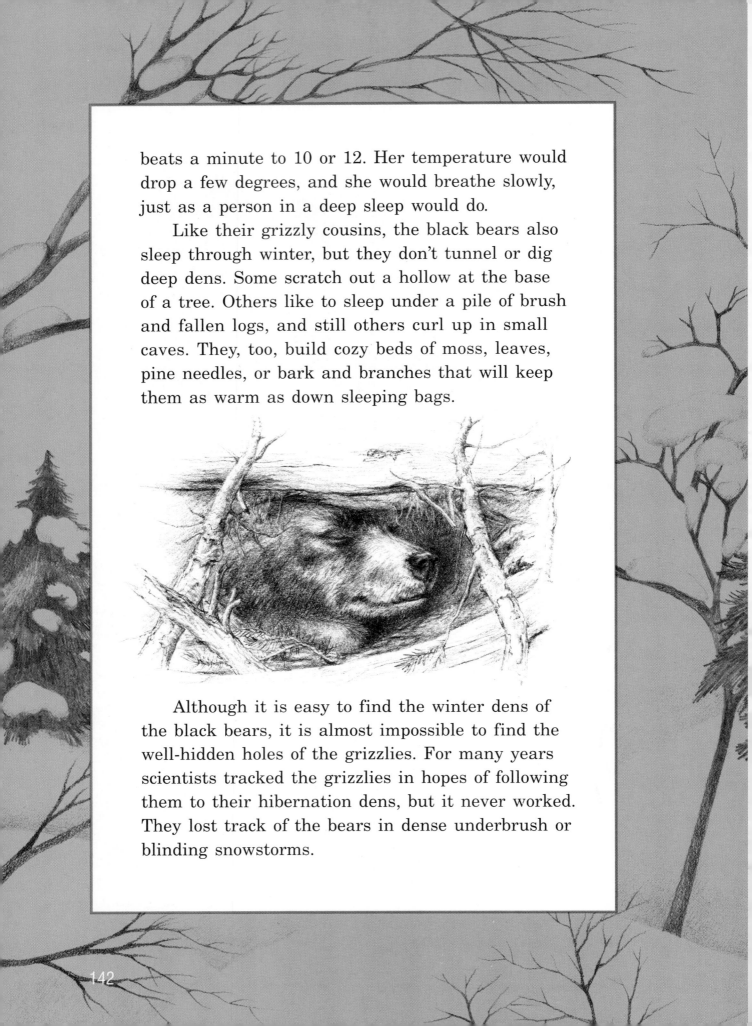

Although it is easy to find the winter dens of the black bears, it is almost impossible to find the well-hidden holes of the grizzlies. For many years scientists tracked the grizzlies in hopes of following them to their hibernation dens, but it never worked. They lost track of the bears in dense underbrush or blinding snowstorms.

Grizzlies are nearsighted. They can't easily recognize a person more than a hundred yards away, but they do have a keen sense of smell. If they catch the scent of a human, the bears may charge. Dr. Frank Craighead, Jr., who studies grizzlies with his brother Dr. John Craighead, had several close calls. "Our lives depended on detecting the bears before they detected us," he said.

The Craighead brothers, working in Yellowstone National Park, learned how to trap the bears and put them to sleep with tranquilizing drugs. Then they had to work fast in the short time a bear was unconscious. With a strong nylon rope net, they lifted and weighed the sleeping bear. One member of the team measured the bear while another took blood samples. They tattooed a number inside the bear's lip, checked its teeth, and attached a metal or plastic identification tag to the bear's ear. The Craighead team got to know the bears so well that they gave them names. There was Cutlip, Bigfoot, Scarface, Rip-nose, and Peg-leg, who limped on one stiff leg.

But no matter how carefully they watched these bears, they couldn't find their dens until they followed Marian. She was Number 40, and she became famous as the first grizzly to be tracked by radio.

In 1960 Marian was trapped and tranquilized. She weighed 300 pounds and was 65 inches long. The Craigheads put a bright red-and-yellow plastic collar around her 28-inch neck and attached a small battery-powered radio transmitter to the collar. The radio sent out beeps that the bear couldn't hear. But the Craigheads could hear the shrill beeping signal in the radio receivers they carried in their backpacks.

They followed Marian everywhere and finally solved the mystery of where grizzly bears hibernate. Since then, scientists have followed many bears and studied many dens. They found that bears, like people, have different ideas of comfort. The tunnel to Marian's den was only two feet long. One grizzly den in Alaska had an S-shaped tunnel 19 feet long, with a bedroom shaped like an ice-cream cone six feet across and nine feet high.

In the years since radio collars like Marian's were first used, newer ones have been made that work so well that bears can be tracked night and day in the most remote places. The continual beeping signal can be picked up by receivers in a satellite orbiting in space, in a helicopter flying overhead, or in a truck on a nearby road. Many of the bears' dens are even "bugged" with equipment that lets scientists know when the bear moves or when the temperature in the den changes.

One kind of transmitter is no bigger than a quarter. It can be easily implanted under the bear's skin after the animal has been tranquilized. When the bear wakes up, it doesn't seem to notice that it has become a walking radio station that sends messages every time its temperature or heart rate changes.

The Indians of the Northwest honored the grizzly bear and called it The Bear Who Walks Like a Man, Elder Brother, and Old Man with Claws. One of their legends says it was the grizzly who taught human beings how to survive in the woods.

And now it may be the grizzly who teaches humans how to survive in space. If people could learn how to hibernate, it would make long journeys beyond our galaxy safer and easier. Hibernating astronauts wouldn't have to eat. They wouldn't need to use precious fuel to heat the ship, and they wouldn't get bored.

But there are many questions and many years of research ahead before we find the answers. How does hibernation work? How can animals go without food and water for many months without starving to death? Why aren't they weak and sick when they wake up in the spring? Why don't they freeze in their snow-covered dens? What signals them to eat enough to add layers of fat for the winter? What tells them it's time to enter the den? And then how do they know it's time to wake up?

Do hibernating animals have some kind of "magic potion" that makes them hibernate?

MEET 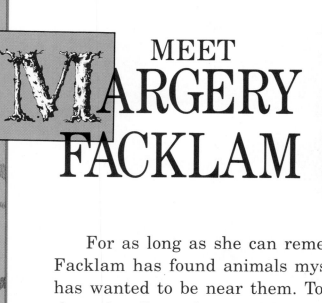 MARGERY FACKLAM

For as long as she can remember, Margery Facklam has found animals mysterious. And she has wanted to be near them. To work her way through college, she cared for a colony of porcupines. Later, she took jobs in zoos and science museums, where she taught others about animals.

As time passed, Facklam thought of another way to stay in touch with animals. She decided to write about them. In *Do Not Disturb: The Mysteries of Animal Hibernation and Sleep,* the author writes about animals that sleep through the winter. She wonders how hibernating animals can live without food or water for many months, why they don't freeze to death in even the coldest weather, and how they know when it's time to wake up. By writing about them, Facklam shares the mystery of animals with others.

Another book about animals by Margery Facklam that you might enjoy is *Partners for Life: The Mysteries of Animal Symbiosis.*

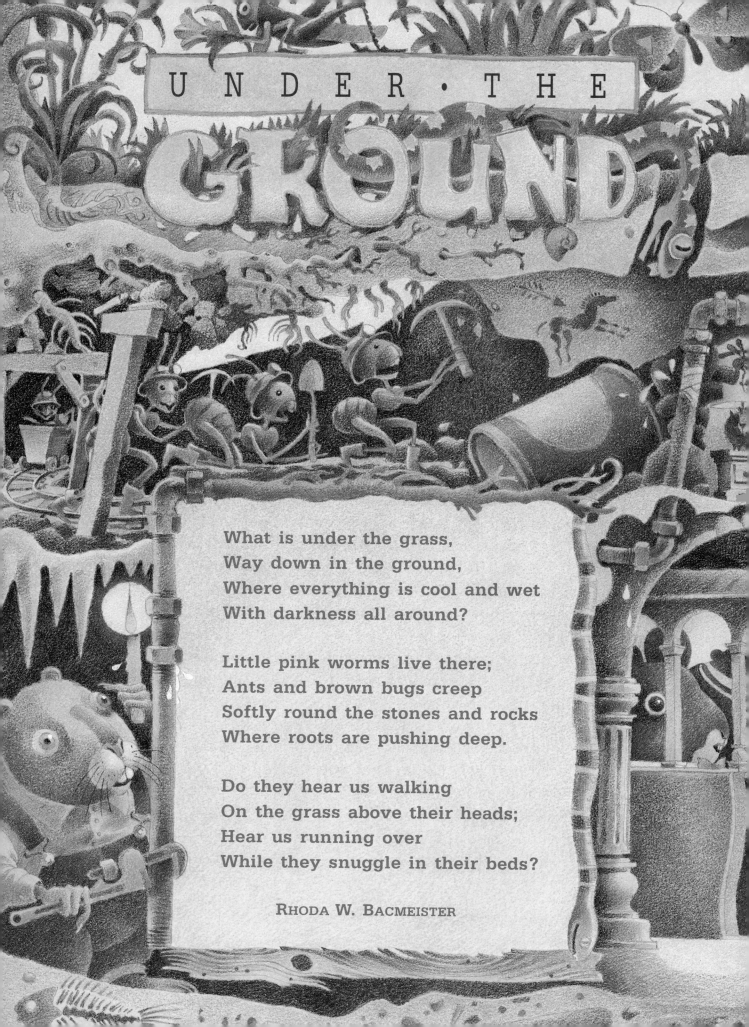

UNDER · THE GROUND

What is under the grass,
Way down in the ground,
Where everything is cool and wet
With darkness all around?

Little pink worms live there;
Ants and brown bugs creep
Softly round the stones and rocks
Where roots are pushing deep.

Do they hear us walking
On the grass above their heads;
Hear us running over
While they snuggle in their beds?

RHODA W. BACMEISTER

SECRETS AND SURPRISES

HER SEVEN BROTHERS

Written and illustrated by Paul Goble

Bradbury Press, 1988

WHAT DO ANIMALS SEE, HEAR,
SMELL, AND FEEL?

National Wildlife Federation, 1990

151

WHY FROG AND SNAKE NEVER PLAY TOGETHER

WRITTEN AND ILLUSTRATED BY

❖ ASHLEY BRYAN ❖

Mama Frog had a son. Mama Snake also had a son. One morning both children went out to play.

Mama Snake called after her child:

"Watch out for big things with sharp claws and teeth that gnaw. Don't lose your way in the bush, baby, and be back to the burrow before dark."

"Clawsangnaws," sang Snake as he went looping through the grass. "Beware of the Clawsangnaws."

Mama Frog called after her son:

"Watch out for things that peck or bite. Don't go into the bush alone, dear. Don't fight, and get home before night."

"Peckorbite," sang Frog as he went hopping from stone to stone. "Beware of the Peckorbite!"

Snake was singing his Clawsangnaws song, and Frog was singing of Peckorbites when they met along the way. They had never met before.

"Who are you?" asked Frog. "Are you a Peckorbite?" and he prepared to spring out of reach.

"Oh no! I'm Snake, called by my Mama 'Snakeson': I'm slick, lithe and slithery. Who are you? Are you a Clawsangnaws?" and he got ready to move, just in case.

"No no! I'm Frog, called by my Mama 'Frogchild.' I'm hip, quick and hoppy."

They stood and stared at each other, then they said together:

"You don't look anything like me."

Their eyes brightened. They did not look alike, that's true, but some of their customs were alike. Both knew what to do when two say the same thing at the same time.

They clasped each other, closed their eyes and sang:

> *"You wish a wish*
> *I'll wish a wish, too;*
> *May your wish and my wish*
> *Both come true."*

Each made a wish then let go.

Just then a fly flew by, right past Frog's eyes. Flip! out went his tongue as he flicked in the fly.

A bug whizzed past Snake's nose. Flash! Snake flicked out his tongue and caught the bug.

They looked in admiration at each other and smiled. The two new friends now knew something of what each other could do. They felt at ease with each other, like old friends.

"Let's play!" said Frog.

"Hey!" said Snake, "that was my wish. Let's play in the bush."

"The bush! In the bush!" cried Frog. "That was my wish. If you go with me, it's all right 'cause Mama said I shouldn't go alone."

Frog and Snake raced to the bush and started playing games.

"Watch this," said Frog. He crouched down and counted, "One a fly, two a fly, three a fly, four!"

He popped way up into the air, somersaulted and came down, whop!

"Can you do that Snake?"

Snake bounded for a nearby mound to try the Frog-Hop. He got to the top of the slope, stood on the tip of his tail and tossed himself into the air. Down he came, flop! a tangle of coils. He laughed and tried again.

ometimes Snake and Frog jumped together and bumped in midair. No matter how hard they hit, it didn't hurt. They had fun.

Then Snake said, "Watch this!" He stretched out at the top of the mound and counted, "One a bug, two a bug, three a bug, four!" Then swoosh! he slithered down the slope on his stomach.

"Try that Frog. It's called the Snake-Slither."

Frog lay on his stomach and slipped down the hill. His arms and legs flailed about as he slithered. He turned over at the bottom of the slope, *blump!* and rolled up in a lump.

Frog and Snake slithered down together, entangling as they went. Their calls and laughter could be heard all over the bush. One game led to another. They were having such a good time that the day passed swiftly. By late afternoon there were not two better friends in all the bush.

The sun was going down when Snake remembered his promise to his mother.

"I promised to be home before dark," he said.

"Me too," said Frog. "Good-bye!"

They hugged. Snake was so happy that he'd found a real friend that he forgot himself and squeezed Frog very tightly. It felt good, very, very good.

"Ow! easy!" said Frog. "Not too tight."

"Oh, sorry," said Snake loosening his hug-hold. "My! but you sure feel good, good enough to eat."

At that they burst out laughing and hugged again, lightly this time.

"I like you," said Frog. "Bye, Snake."

"Bye, Frog. You're my best friend."

"Let's play again tomorrow," they said together.

Aha! they clasped and sang once again:

> *"You wish a wish*
> *I'll wish a wish, too;*
> *May your wish and my wish*
> *Both come true."*

Off they went, Snake hopping and Frog slithering all the way home.

When Frog reached home, he knocked his knock, and Mama Frog unlocked the rock door. She was startled to see her child come slithering in across the floor.

"**N**ow what is this, eh?" she said. "Look at you, all covered with grass and dirt."

"It doesn't hurt," said Frog. "I had fun."

"Fun? Now what is this, eh? I can tell you haven't been playing in ponds or bogs with the good frogs. Where have you been all day? You look as if you've just come out of the bush."

"But I didn't go alone, Ma. I went with a good boy. He's my best friend."

"Best friend? Now what is this, eh?" said Mama Frog. "What good boy could that be, playing in the bush?"

"Look at this trick that he taught me, Ma," said Frogchild. He flopped on his stomach and wriggled across the floor, bungling up Mama Frog's neatly stitched lily-pad rug.

"That's no trick for a frog! Get up from there, child!" cried Mama Frog. "Now what is this, eh? Look how you've balled up my rug. Just you tell me, who was this playmate?"

"His name is Snakeson, Mama."

"Snake, son! Did you say Snake, son?"

"Yes. What's the matter, Mama?"

Mama Frog trembled and turned a pale green. She sat down to keep from fainting. When she had recovered herself, she said:

"Listen Frogchild, listen carefully to what I have to say." She pulled her son close. "Snake comes from the Snake family. They are bad people. Keep away from them. You hear me, child?"

"Bad people?" asked Frog.

"Bad, too bad!" said Mama Frog. "Snakes are sneaks. They hide poison in their tongues, and they crush you in their coils."

Frogchild gulped.

"You be sure to hop out of Snake's reach if ever you meet again. And stop this slithering foolishness. Slithering's not for frogs."

Mama Frog set the table muttering to herself: "Playing with Snake! Now what is this, eh?" She rolled a steaming ball of gleaming cornmeal onto Frogchild's plate.

"Sit down and eat your funji, child," said Mama Frog. "And remember, I'm not fattening frogs for snakes, eh?"

Snake too reached home. He rustled the braided twig hatch-cover to his home. His mother knew his rustle and undid the vine latch. Snake toppled in.

"I'm hungry, Ma," he said, hopping all about.

"Eh, eh! Do good bless you! What a sight you are!" said Mama Snake. "Just look at you. And listen to your panting and wheezing. Where have you been all day?"

"In the bush, Mama, with my new friend. We played games. See what he taught me."

Snakeson jumped up on top of the table and leaped into the air. He came down on a stool, knocking it over and entangling himself in its legs.

"Eh, eh! Do good bless you. What a dangerous game that is," said Mama Snake. "Keep it up and see if you don't break every bone in your back. What new friend taught you that?"

She bent over and untangled her son from the stool.

"My frog friend taught me that. His name's Frogchild. It's the Frog-Hop, Mama. Try it. It's fun."

"Frog, child?" Mama Snake's jaws hung open showing her fangs. "Did you say Frog, child?"

"Yes," said Snakeson. "He's my best friend."

"You mean you played all day with a frog and you come home hungry?"

"He was hungry too, Mama, after playing the Snake Slither game that I taught him."

"Eh, eh! Well do good bless you! Come, curl up here son and listen carefully to what I have to tell you."

Snakeson curled up on the stool.

"Don't you know, son, that it is the custom of our house to eat frogs? Frogs are delicious people!"

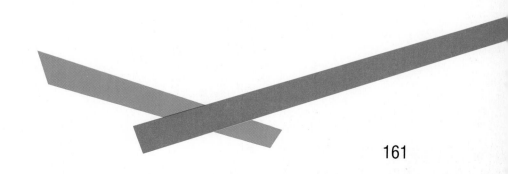

Snakeson's small eyes widened.

"Ah, for true!" said Mama Snake. "Eating frogs is the custom of our house, a tradition in our family. Hopping isn't, so cut it out, you hear me?"

"Oh, Mama," cried Snakeson. "I can't eat frogs. Frog's a friend."

"Frog a friend! Do good bless you!" said Mama Snake. "That's not natural. Now you listen to me, baby. The next time you play with Frog, jump, roll and romp all you like. But when you get hungry, his game is up. Catch him and eat him!"

The next morning Snakeson was up early. He pushed off his dry-leaf cover and stretched himself. He remembered his mother's words, and the delicious feel of his frog friend when they had hugged. He was ready to go.

Mama Snake fixed her son a light breakfast of spiced insects and goldfinch eggs. Snakeson was soon on his way.

"Now don't you forget my instructions about frogs, do good bless you," Mama Snake called out after him. "And don't let me have to tell you again to watch out for big things with sharp claws and teeth that gnaw."

"**C**lawsangnaw," sang Snakeson. "Clawsangnaw."

He reached the bush and waited for his friend. He looked forward to fun with Frog, and he looked forward to finishing the fun with a feast of his fine frog friend. He lolled about in the sun, laughing and singing:

> *"You wish a wish*
> *I'll wish a wish, too;*
> *Can your wish and my wish*
> *Both come true?"*

The sun rose higher and higher, but Frog did not come.

"What's taking Frogchild so long?" said Snakeson. "Perhaps too much slithering has given him the bellyache. I'll go and look for him."

Snake found Frog's rock home by the pond. He rolled up a stone in his tail and knocked on the rock door.

"Anybody home?"

"Just me," answered Frogchild.

"May I come in?"

"Ah, it's you Snakeson. Sorry, my Mama's out, and she said not to open the door to anyone."

"Come on out then and let's play," said Snakeson. "I waited all morning for you in the bush."

"I can't," said Frog, "not now, anyway."

"Oh, that's too bad," said Snake. "My mother taught me a new game. I'd love to teach it to you."

"I'll bet you would," said Frog.

"You don't know what you're missing," said Snake.

"But I do know what you're missing," said Frog, and he burst out laughing.

"Aha!" said Snake. "I see that your mother has given you instructions. My mother has given me instructions too."

Snake sighed. There was nothing more to say or do, so he slithered away.

Frog and Snake never forgot that day when they played together as friends. Neither ever again had that much fun with anybody.

Today you will see them, quiet and alone in the sun, still as stone. They are deep in thought remembering that day of games in the bush, and both of them wonder:

"What if we had just kept on playing together, and no one had ever said anything?"

But from that day to this, Frog and Snake have never played together again.

You wish a wish
I'll wish a wish, too;
May your wish and my wish
Both come true.

MEET ASHLEY BRYAN

Ashley Bryan has been drawing and painting for as long as he can remember. "My first books, made in kindergarten, were illustrated *ABC* and counting books," he says.

The writer also remembers listening to music as he was growing up. His father played the saxophone, guitar, and banjo. His mother, he says, "sang from one end of the day to the other."

To Bryan, it seems natural to combine art and music to create books, as he did in *Walk Together Children* and *I'm Going to Sing.* For these songbooks, he chose music that has special meaning for him—African-American spirituals. Then he created striking woodcuts to go along with the songs.

African-American music is not the only part of Ashley Bryan's heritage that has inspired him. He also loves African folk tales. By retelling these tales, he hopes to pass on to readers "something of the rich oral tradition of storytelling." "African tales," he says, "are a beautiful means of linking the living Africa, past and present, to our own present."

Meet Jim Arnosky

Jim Arnosky hopes the outdoors will jump off the page when you open one of his books. He wants to bring the world of animals and nature to his readers.

Arnosky thinks of himself as a naturalist as well as an artist and a writer. In the middle of nature, he learns about the subjects that he puts into his books.

Arnosky writes mainly about his own life. "My books are autobiographical," he says, and explains that he has difficulty thinking of a story that doesn't come from a personal experience.

The subjects of *A Kettle of Hawks and Other Wildlife Groups,* however, are not people but groups of animals found in nature. The author explains that the names we use for animal groups are important. Each name tells us something about the animals in that group.

A Kettle of Hawks

and other wildlife groups

WRITTEN AND ILLUSTRATED
BY JIM ARNOSKY

Many of the names
we use for groups of
animals describe
something interesting
about the animals in each
group. These names
can be a starting point
for learning more
about wildlife.

Jim Arnosky

A Kettle of Hawks

Hawks silently soaring,
circling, climbing,
high in a kettle of hot air.
A Kettle of Hawks in the sky.

Hawks fly alone much of the time, but in autumn and spring some travel great distances together. These seasonal movements are called migrations. To save energy, hawks will soar along using air currents or columns of hot air called thermals. The hot air in a thermal pushes the hawks high in the sky, giving them the altitude they need to peel away and glide for miles farther on their migration course.

When many hawks circle upward in the same thermal, they are said to be "kettling," because it looks as though the birds are boiling in a great kettle of air.

A Swarm of Bees

Bees in a ball—
humming, buzzing,
resting on a limb, then flying again,
following their queen to begin a new hive.
A Swarm of Bees in the orchard.

All activity in a beehive revolves around the queen bee. She is the mother of the hive, laying thousands of eggs that hatch into more bees—workers, drones, even new queen bees.

The worker bees are females. They gather pollen from flowers, bring it to the hive, and make it into beebread and honey. Worker bees also produce wax to make honeycomb.

Drones are male bees. They do not do any work. Drones mill about the hive, eating, growing fat, until one of them is singled out to mate with the queen. When that drone is chosen and mating is done, all the drones are driven from the hive. Since drones cannot feed themselves, they starve.

When the hive becomes over-crowded or a young queen takes control from an old queen, the bees will swarm. They leave the hive suddenly and go off, following one queen, to begin another hive in a new place. A swarm may contain thousands of bees—a buzzing cloud drifting through the air.

A School of Fish

Fish swimming,
darting together,
waving their fins in the water.
A School of Fish in the lake.

177

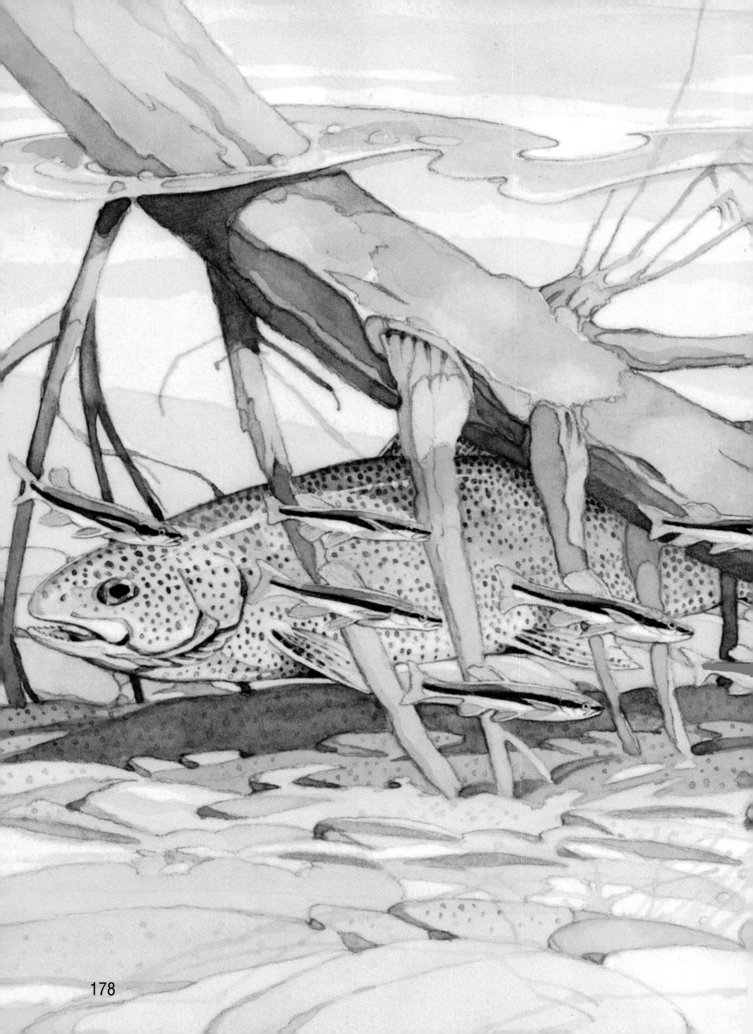

Minnows, bass, herring, and many other species of fish swim and feed in groups called schools. Imagine a group of classmates on a school trip, all facing in the same direction, staying close together. This gives you an idea of what a school of fish looks like underwater.

In the underwater world there is safety in numbers. A school of small fish may seem like one large fish to an enemy. Also, by grouping together, individual small fish are harder to locate than if they swam scattered all over.

Some species of fish swim in schools when they are very young and tiny and swim separately after they have grown bigger. Other species swim in schools all their lives.

A Gaggle of Geese

Geese in the distance,
honking, squawking,
landing in groups on the lake.
A Gaggle of Geese on a sandbar.

Even after a long journey geese are full of energy, flapping their wings, honking and gaggling noisily to one another. They are in top physical condition before, during, and after migration. This is due to their energy-saving system of flying in drafts. The leader of the flock breaks a trail through the air, and the rest of the geese follow behind. Each goose, flying a little to the side and rear of the goose ahead of it, is sucked along in the strong draft of air caused by the V-shaped flight formation. By "drafting" and taking turns leading the flock, the geese are able to pace themselves and conserve energy all through their long migration. And wherever they land, in a large flock or small groups called gaggles, they are never too tired to honk up a good goose conversation with their fellow travelers.

The next time you hear a name used to describe a group of animals, wonder about it. Find out if the name tells you something about the nature of the animals themselves. Anything you learn will add to the fun of watching wildlife.

Here are some other animal groups
you can think about:
A Bed of Clams
A Pod of Whales
A Paddle of Ducks
A Brood of Chickens
A Band of Coyotes
A Beaver Colony
A Wolf Pack

A member of the Yakima
Nation dressed for a
powwow in Fort Hall, Idaho.

I WONDER

I wonder how it feels to fly
high in the sky...
like a bird.
I wonder how it feels to sit
on a nest...
like a bird.
I wonder how it feels to catch
a worm in the morning...
like a bird.
I feel funny...
maybe he is wondering
how it feels to be like a man.

*Native American of the
Yakima Nation*

CONTENTS

SIDE BY SIDE

The only way to have a friend is to be one.

RALPH WALDO EMERSON
from "Friendship," *Essays*

189

Big Friend,

by Susan Sussman and Robert James

Why does the shark protect the remora fish instead of eating it? Symbiosis. Why does the red ant feed its young to the blue butterfly? Symbiosis. What makes the seeing-eye fish befriend the blind shrimp? Symbiosis.

Symbiosis is a Greek word meaning "life together." It is the word scientists use to describe the way two organisms help each other live. We see symbiosis in the lives of the tiniest ants and the biggest elephants. Sometimes two "symbionts" would die without each other. Other times they might be able to live, but would not be as healthy or as comfortable.

Studying symbiosis helps us understand some of the bizarre behavior we see in nature. There are thousands of symbiotic relationships. _Big Friend, Little Friend_ looks at a few of these.

Little Friend: A Book about Symbiosis

Big Friend: *African Buffalo*

Little Friend: *Red-Billed Oxpecker*

*D*id an insect ever bite you in a spot you couldn't reach? If so, you can understand how miserable even the largest animals are when they are bitten by tiny insects. We think of large animals as having skin too tough to be bothered by mosquitoes and flies. But although their skin is thick, it is sensitive. Fortunately, African animals have friends to help them out.

Red-billed and yellow-billed oxpeckers are often found on buffaloes, rhinoceros, elephants, antelopes, giraffes, and other large herbivores (plant-eating animals). These birds ride the backs of large animals, or hang woodpecker-style from their bodies. As they ride, the oxpeckers peck off ticks, leeches, flies, and other pests that bite and sometimes burrow into the skin of the big animals. The oxpeckers also scare off insects that might otherwise land.

Oxpeckers would die if they couldn't eat herbivore blood that has first passed through a tick. Nearly their entire life is spent on a herbivore. One of the few times oxpeckers ever leave their host is when they are startled or when they nest.

Oxpeckers have good eyesight and are extremely alert. They are usually the first to spot danger and call a warning. If a host is slow to react to the danger, the oxpecker flies to the animal's head and starts pecking and thumping on its skull.

You've heard of a seeing-eye dog, but did you know there is a seeing-eye fish?

The gobid fish cares for a shrimp that is completely blind. When the shrimp wants to go somewhere, it taps the gobid and then grabs a pectoral fin (located on the side, just behind the gills) with its claw. The gobid becomes a seeing-eye fish for the shrimp.

These friends live in the sandy bottoms of the Red Sea and the Indian and Pacific oceans. There is no coral or rock where they can hunt for food. There are no places to hide from enemies. To make a home, the blind shrimp digs a large cave in the sand. It always makes the home large enough for the gobid.

The blind shrimp has never been seen living away from the gobid. It could not survive without its friend. The gobid takes the shrimp out to find food. Sometimes the blind shrimp stays home and the gobid goes out, gets food, and brings it back.

Big Friend: *Gobid Fish*

Little Friend: *Blind Shrimp*

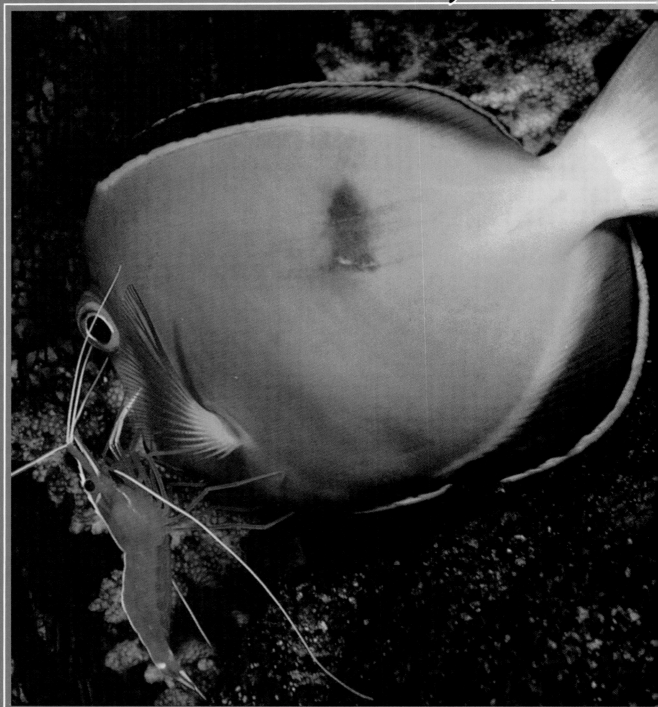

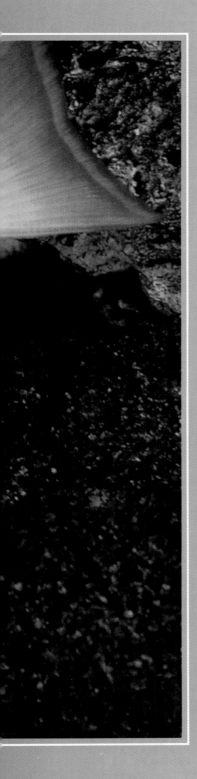

ave you ever seen a line of cars waiting to go into a car wash? This is how different species of fish line up to wait for the cleaner shrimp, the wrasse, and other cleaner fish.

Colonies of these tiny cleaners live in all the Earth's warm oceans. When a large fish swims into the colony, the cleaners swim over and around it. They pick and eat parasites off its skin, dig out pebbles stuck in its scales, and clean between its teeth. Sometimes the cleaners must bite the fish to remove a parasite that has dug into the fish's skin.

Fish that are being cleaned show some strange behavior. Even though they are usually fierce predators, these fish never attack the cleaners. They roll over, lie on their backs or sides, and open their gills and mouths so the cleaners can do their work. Fish usually keep moving to force water through their gills so they can breathe well. But they stop moving while they are being cleaned. If a grouper is being cleaned when danger threatens, it closes its mouth to prepare to swim away. If a cleaner is inside its mouth, the grouper leaves a small opening to allow the cleaner to escape.

Fish that migrate from one place to another line up at cleaning stations along the way. Once a fish is clean, it swims off and another fish moves into its place. If there were no cleaners, the large fish would be killed by the parasites and debris lodged in their bodies. And if there were no large fish, the cleaners would not have this steady supply of food.

The remora is an underwater hitchhiker. It looks like a miniature shark but has a specially shaped suction cup on the top of its head. When a shark, ray, turtle, or other creature swims by, the remora uses the cup to stick itself onto the larger animal.

As the big fish eats, the remora releases its suction cup and swims alongside, catching and eating scraps of food. The shark offers the remora protection from other predators. It also carries the remora from one place to another. The remora repays its hosts by nibbling parasites off a fish's skin or barnacles and leeches from under a turtle's flipper.

The remora's suction is so strong that some fishermen put this suckerfish on their lines. As soon as the remora attaches itself to another fish, the fisherman reels both of them in.

Meet

Susan Sussman and Robert James

Big Friend: *Shark*

Little Friend: *Remora*

Robert James has an unusual "office"—a traveling zoo in a huge brown truck. For many years, he and his zoo have traveled throughout North America to present his program "Animal Encounters, Inc." He wants to give young audiences a chance to learn about wild animals up close.

Susan Sussman loves words as much as Robert James loves animals. She cannot imagine not writing. Her mind writes constantly, even when she is far away from her computer. Books, plays, stories, and articles all come pouring out.

When Susan Sussman met Robert James and his wonderful traveling zoo, the two authors decided to write *Lies (People Believe) About Animals* to help clear up some common myths about animals. The partnership of the two writers continued with *Big Friend, Little Friend*.

It's a Small

Portland, Oregon, and Sapporo, Japan, are miles and miles apart. But they've become as close as sisters. Portland and Sapporo are, in fact, Sister Cities.

Sapporo, Japan

WORLD

Portland, Oregon

Students in Portland and Sapporo elementary schools send letters, art projects, musical tapes, and poems back and forth. They agree that learning about each other's holidays, customs, and language is very exciting. Sharing experiences helps the children in Sapporo and Portland become friends.

Many cities in the United States have found sisters all over the world. Some cities like the program so much that they have more than one Sister City. St. Louis, Missouri, has four—in France, Ireland, Germany, and Japan.

Would you like to know more about Sister Cities?

You can write to:

Sister Cities International
120 South Payne Street
Alexandria, Virginia 22314

Next time you look at a world map, think of all the children in other countries who could be your friends.

It is a small world, isn't it?

Dear Noriko,
Thank you for your letter. I've enclosed some pictures of Portland for you. I think you'll especially like the ones of the rose gardens. They are a lot like your Japanese gardens—filled with colorful flowers.
Imagine being the gardener who cares for all those plants? I don't think I could do it. I don't have much of a green thumb. I guess I should explain that in English green thumb means having a talent

JUSTIN and the BEST BISCUITS in the WORLD

by Mildred Pitts Walter

Ten-year-old Justin lives with his mother and two sisters. Justin's family expects him to help with the household chores, but he thinks cooking and cleaning are women's work. He would rather play ball with his friend Anthony. When Justin's cowboy grandfather invites him to visit his ranch, Justin is delighted. Justin is certain that he and his grandfather will do real men's work together, like riding the range. But Justin's grandfather is full of surprises. Before his visit is over, Justin learns a lot more from his grandfather than he ever imagined.

illustrated by Floyd Cooper

The smell of coffee and home-smoked ham woke Justin. His grandpa was already up and downstairs cooking breakfast. Justin jumped out of bed and quickly put on his clothes.

Grandpa had hot pancakes, apple jelly, and ham all ready for the table. Justin ate two stacks of pancakes with two helpings of everything else.

After breakfast, Grandpa cleared the table, preparing to wash the dishes. "Would you rather wash or dry?" he asked Justin.

"Neither," Justin replied, quickly thinking how little success he had with dishes.

Grandpa said nothing as he removed the dishes from the table. He took his time, carefully measuring liquid soap and letting hot water run in the sink. Then he washed each dish and rinsed it with care, too. No water splashed or spilled. Soapsuds were not all over. How easy it looked, the way Grandpa did it.

After washing the dishes, Grandpa swept the floor and then went upstairs.

Justin stood around downstairs. He had a strange feeling of guilt and wished he had helped with the dishes. He heard Grandpa moving about, above in his room. Justin thought of going outside, down into the meadow, but he decided to see what was going on upstairs.

When he saw his grandpa busy making his own big bed, Justin went into his room. His unmade bed and his pajamas on the floor bothered him. But he decided that the room didn't look too bad. He picked up his pajamas and placed them on the bed and sat beside them. He waited.

Finally Grandpa came in and said, "Are you riding fence with me today?"

"Oh yes!"

"Fine. But why don't you make your bed? You'll probably feel pretty tired tonight. A well-made bed can be a warm welcome."

Justin moved slowly, reluctant to let Grandpa see him struggle with the bed. He started. What a surprise! Everything was tightly in place. He only had to smooth the covers. The bed was made. No lumps and bumps. Justin looked at Grandpa and grinned broadly. "That was easy!" he shouted.

"Don't you think you should unpack your clothes? They won't need ironing if you hang them up. You gotta look razor sharp for the festival." He gave Justin some clothes hangers.

"Are we *really* going to the festival every day?" Justin asked.

"You bet, starting with the judging early tomorrow and the dance tomorrow night." Grandpa winked at him.

Justin's excitement faded when he started unpacking his rumpled shirts. "They sure are wrinkled, Grandpa," he said.

"Maybe that's because they weren't folded."

"I can't ever get them folded right," Justin cried.

"Well, let's see. Turn it so the buttons face down." Grandpa showed Justin how to bring the sleeves to the back, turning in the sides so that the sleeves were on top. Then he folded the tail of the shirt over the cuffs, and made a second fold up to the collar. "Now you try it."

Justin tried it. "Oh, I see. That was easy, Grandpa." Justin smiled, pleased with himself.

"Everything's easy when you know how."

Justin, happy with his new-found skill, hurriedly placed his clothes on the hangers. He hoped the wrinkles would disappear in time for the festival.

"Now you'll look sharp," Grandpa said.

Justin felt a surge of love for his grandpa. He would always remember how to make a bed snug as a bug and fold clothes neatly. He grabbed Grandpa's hand. They walked downstairs, still holding hands, to get ready to ride fence.

Riding fence meant inspecting the fence all around the ranch to see where it needed mending. Riding fence took a great deal of a rancher's time. Justin and Grandpa planned to spend most of the day out on the plains. Grandpa said he'd pack a lunch for them to eat on the far side of the ranch.

Justin was surprised when Grandpa packed only flour, raisins, shortening, and chunks of smoked pork. He also packed jugs of water and makings for coffee.

The horses stood in the meadow as if they knew a busy day awaited them. While Grandpa saddled Pal, he let Justin finish the saddling of Black Lightning. Justin tightened the cinches on Black,

feeling the strong pull on his arm muscles. With their supplies in their saddlebags, they mounted Pal and Black, leaving Cropper behind to graze in the meadow.

The early sun shone fiery red on the hilltops while the foothills were cast in shades of purple. The dew still lingered heavily on the morning. They let their horses canter away past the house through the tall green grass. But on the outer edge of the ranch where the fence started, they walked the horses at a steady pace.

The fence had three rows of taut wire. "That's a pretty high fence," Justin said.

"We have to keep the cattle in. But deer sometimes leap that fence and eat hay with the cattle." When it got bitter cold and frosty, Grandpa rode around the ranch dropping bales of hay for the cattle. It took a lot of hay to feed the cattle during the winter months.

"I didn't think a cow could jump very high," Justin said.

"Aw, come on. Surely you know that a cow jumped over the moon." Grandpa had a serious look on his face.

"I guess that's a joke, eh?" Justin laughed.

Justin noticed that Grandpa had a map. When they came to a place in the fence that looked weak, Grandpa marked it on his map. Later, helpers who came to do the work would know exactly where to mend. That saved time.

Now the sun heated up the morning. The foothills were now varying shades of green. Shadows dotted the plains. Among the blackish green trees on the rolling hills, fog still lingered like lazy clouds. Insects buzzed. A small cloud of mosquitoes swarmed just behind their heads, and beautiful cardinals splashed their redness on the morning air. Justin felt a surge of happiness and hugged Black with his knees and heels.

Suddenly he saw a doe standing close to the fence. "Look, Grandpa!" he said. She seemed alarmed but did not run away. Doe eyes usually look peaceful and sad, Justin remembered. Hers widened with fear. Then Justin saw a fawn caught in the wire of the fence.

Quickly they got off their horses. They hitched them to a post and moved cautiously toward the fawn.

The mother rushed to the fence but stopped just short of the sharp wire. "Stay back and still," Grandpa said to Justin. "She doesn't know we will help her baby. She thinks we might hurt it. She wants to protect it."

The mother pranced restlessly. She pawed the ground, moving as close to the fence as she could. Near the post the fence had been broken. The wire curled there dangerously. The fawn's head, caught in the wire, bled close to an ear. Whenever it pulled its head the wire cut deeper.

Grandpa quickly untangled the fawn's head.

Blood flowed from the cut.

"Oh, Grandpa, it will die," Justin said sadly.

"No, no," Grandpa assured Justin. "Lucky we got here when we did. It hasn't been caught long."

The fawn moved toward the doe. The mother, as if giving her baby a signal, bounded off. The baby trotted behind.

As they mounted their horses, Justin suddenly felt weak in the stomach. Remembering the blood, he trembled. Black, too, seemed uneasy. He moved his nostrils nervously and strained against the bit. He arched his neck and sidestepped quickly. Justin pulled the reins. "Whoa, boy!"

"Let him run," Grandpa said.

Justin kicked Black's sides and off they raced across the plain. They ran and ran, Justin pretending he was rounding up cattle. Then Black turned and raced back toward Grandpa and Pal.

"Whoa, boy," Justin commanded. Justin felt better and Black seemed calm, ready now to go on riding fence.

The sun beamed down and sweat rolled off Justin as he rode on with Grandpa, looking for broken wires in the fence. They were well away from the house, on the far side of the ranch. Flies buzzed around the horses and now gnats swarmed in clouds just above their heads. The prairie resounded with songs of the bluebirds, the bobwhite quails, and the mockingbirds mimicking them all. The cardinal's song, as lovely as any, included a whistle.

Justin thought of Anthony and how Anthony whistled for Pepper, his dog.

It was well past noon and Justin was hungry. Soon they came upon a small, well-built shed, securely locked. Nearby was a small stream. Grandpa reined in his horse. When he and Justin dismounted, they hitched the horses, and unsaddled them.

"We'll have our lunch here," Grandpa said. Justin was surprised when Grandpa took black iron pots, other cooking utensils, and a table from the shed. Justin helped him remove some iron rods that Grandpa carefully placed over a shallow pit. These would hold the pots. Now Justin understood why Grandpa had brought uncooked food. They were going to cook outside.

First they collected twigs and cow dung. Grandpa called it cowchips. "These," Grandpa said, holding up a dried brown pad, "make the best fuel. Gather them up."

There were plenty of chips left from the cattle that had fed there in winter. Soon they had a hot fire.

Justin watched as Grandpa carefully washed his hands and then began to cook their lunch.

"When I was a boy about your age, I used to go with my father on short runs with cattle. We'd bring them down from the high country onto the plains."

"Did you stay out all night?"

"Sometimes. And that was the time I liked most. The cook often made for supper what I am going to make for lunch."

Grandpa put raisins into a pot with a little water and placed them over the fire. Justin was surprised when Grandpa put flour in a separate pan. He used his fist to make a hole right in the middle of the flour. In that hole he placed some shortening. Then he added water. With his long delicate fingers he mixed the flour, water, and shortening until he had a nice round mound of dough.

Soon smooth circles of biscuits sat in an iron skillet with a lid on top. Grandpa put the skillet on the fire with some of the red-hot chips scattered over the lid.

Justin was amazed. How could only those ingredients make good bread? But he said nothing as Grandpa put the chunks of smoked pork in a skillet and started them cooking. Soon the smell was so delicious, Justin could hardly wait.

Finally Grandpa suggested that Justin take the horses to drink at the stream. "Keep your eyes open and don't step on any snakes."

Justin knew that diamondback rattlers sometimes lurked around. They were dangerous. He must be careful. He watered Black first.

While watering Pal, he heard rustling in the grass. His heart pounded. He heard the noise again. He wanted to run, but was too afraid. He looked around carefully. There were two black eyes staring at him. He tried to pull Pal away from the water, but Pal refused to stop drinking. Then Justin saw the animal. It had a long tail like a rat's. But it was as big as a cat. Then he saw something crawling on its back. They were little babies, hanging on as the animal ran.

A mama opossum and her babies, he thought, and was no longer afraid.

By the time the horses were watered, lunch was ready. *"M-mm-m,"* Justin said as he reached for a plate. The biscuits were golden brown, yet fluffy inside. And the sizzling pork was now crisp. Never had he eaten stewed raisins before.

"Grandpa, I didn't know you could cook like this," Justin said when he had tasted the food. "I didn't know men could cook so good."

"Why, Justin, some of the best cooks in the world are men."

Justin remembered the egg on the floor and his rice burning. The look he gave Grandpa revealed his doubts.

"It's true," Grandpa said. "All the cooks on the cattle trail were men. In hotels and restaurants they call them chefs."

"How did you make these biscuits?"

"That's a secret. One day I'll let you make some."

"Were you a cowboy, Grandpa?"

"I'm still a cowboy."

"No, you're not."

"Yes, I am. I work with cattle, so I'm a cowboy."

"You know what I mean. The kind who rides bulls, broncobusters. That kind of cowboy."

"No, I'm not that kind. But I know some."

"Are they famous?"

"No, but I did meet a real famous Black cowboy once. When I was eight years old, my grandpa took me to meet his friend Bill Pickett. Bill Pickett was an old man then. He had a ranch in Oklahoma."

"Were there lots of Black cowboys?"

"Yes. Lots of them. They were hard workers, too. They busted broncos, branded calves, and drove cattle. My grandpa tamed wild mustangs."

"Bet they were famous."

"Oh, no. Some were. Bill Pickett created the sport of bulldogging. You'll see that at the rodeo. One cowboy named Williams taught Rough Rider Teddy Roosevelt how to break horses; and another one named Clay taught Will Rogers, the comedian, the art of roping." Grandpa offered Justin the last biscuit.

When they had finished their lunch they led the horses away from the shed to graze. As they watched the horses, Grandpa went on, "Now, there were some more very famous Black cowboys. Jessie Stahl. They say he was the best rider of wild horses in the West."

"How could he be? Nobody ever heard about him. I didn't."

"Oh, there're lots of famous Blacks you never hear or read about. You ever hear about Deadwood Dick?"

Justin laughed. "No."

"There's another one. His real name was Nate Love. He could outride, outshoot anyone. In Deadwood City in the Dakota Territory, he roped, tied, saddled, mounted, and rode a wild horse faster than anyone. Then in the shooting match, he hit the bull's-eye every time. The people named him Deadwood Dick right on the spot. Enough about cowboys, now. While the horses graze, let's clean up here and get back to our men's work."

Justin felt that Grandpa was still teasing him, the way he had in Justin's room when he had placed his hand on Justin's shoulder. There was still the sense of shame whenever the outburst about women's work and the tears were remembered.

As they cleaned the utensils and dishes, Justin asked, "Grandpa, you think housework is women's work?"

"Do you?" Grandpa asked quickly.

"I asked you first, Grandpa."

"I guess asking you that before I answer is unfair. No, I don't. Do you?"

"Well, it seems easier for them," Justin said as he splashed water all over, glad he was outside.

"Easier than for me?"

"Well, not for you, I guess, but for me, yeah."

"Could it be because you don't know how?"

"You mean like making the bed and folding the clothes."

"Yes." Grandpa stopped and looked at Justin. "Making the bed is easy now, isn't it? All work is that way. It doesn't matter who does the work, man or woman, when it needs to be done. What matters is that we try to learn how to do it the best we can in the most enjoyable way."

"I don't think I'll ever like housework," Justin said, drying a big iron pot.

"It's like any other kind of work. The better you do it, the easier it becomes, and we seem not to mind doing things that are easy."

With the cooking rods and all the utensils put away, they locked the shed and went for their horses.

"Now, I'm going to let you do the cinches again. You'll like that."

There's that teasing again, Justin thought. "Yeah. That's a man's work," he said, and mounted Black.

"There are some good horsewomen. You'll see them at the rodeo." Grandpa mounted Pal. They went on their way, riding along silently, scanning the fence.

Finally Justin said, "I was just kidding, Grandpa." Then without planning to, he said, "I bet you don't like boys who cry like babies."

"Do I know any boys who cry like babies?"

"Aw, Grandpa, you saw me crying."

"Oh, I didn't think you were crying like a baby. In your room, you mean? We all cry sometime."

"You? Cry, Grandpa?"

"Sure."

They rode on, with Grandpa marking his map. Justin remained quiet, wondering what could make a man like Grandpa cry.

As if knowing Justin's thoughts, Grandpa said, "I remember crying when you were born."

"Why? Didn't you want me?"

"Oh, yes. You were the most beautiful baby. But, you see, your grandma, Beth, had just died. When I held you I was flooded with joy. Then I thought, *Grandma will never see this beautiful boy.* I cried."

The horses wading through the grass made the only sound in the silence. Then Grandpa said, "There's an old saying, son. 'The brave hide their fears, but share their tears.' Tears bathe the soul."

Justin looked at his grandpa. Their eyes caught. A warmth spread over Justin and he lowered his eyes. He wished he could tell his grandpa all he felt, how much he loved him.

meet
MILDRED PITTS WALTER

Mildred Pitts Walter wrote her first book, *Lillie of Watts*, when she was a teacher in Los Angeles. Since then she has written a number of award-winning books about African-American children, including *Justin and the Best Biscuits in the World*, which won the Coretta Scott King Award.

African-American traditions are often a part of Walter's stories. In *Have a Happy . . .* , for example, Chris, a boy whose birthday falls on December 25 and whose father is looking for work, fears his birthday won't seem very important to anyone. But as the family prepares for Kwanzaa, the seven-day celebration of African-American heritage, Chris begins to feel that his birthday may not be so disappointing after all.

Speaking about her stories, Walter says, "I like to think that the images I create will make all young people thoughtful and African Americans aware of themselves as well."

A Time to Talk

When a friend calls to me from the road
And slows his horse to a meaning walk,
I don't stand still and look around
On all the hills I haven't hoed,
And shout from where I am, "What is it?"
No, not as there is a time to talk.
I thrust my hoe in the mellow ground,
Blade-end up and five feet tall,
And plod: I go up to the stone wall
For a friendly visit.

Robert Frost

Young Corn, a painting by Grant Wood, 1931.
Courtesy of the Cedar Rapids, Iowa, Community School District.

In the Year of the Boar and Jackie Robinson

by Bette Bao Lord

illustrated by Marc Simont

Harper Trophy, 1986

IN COMPANY

**Girders and Cranes:
A Skyscraper Is Built**

by Lee Balterman
Albert Whitman, 1991

Nicholasa Mohr

Nicholasa Mohr studied to be an artist, not a writer. "Writing," she says, "just happened."

Maybe writing seems natural to Mohr because she creates stories out of her own experiences. Like the girl in *Felita*, Nicholasa Mohr grew up in New York City's El Barrio. Like Felita, too, she moved away from a neighborhood and then moved back to it. Mohr also based parts of *Felita* on other memories she had of growing up, such as problems she had with her best friend.

Not all of Mohr's characters are based on real people, however. Some come entirely from her imagination. One of these is Abuelita, the grandmother in *Felita*.

Nicholasa Mohr didn't know her grandmother, but she did grow up respecting older people. "It is part of my culture," she says. "I would love someday to be a grandmother like Abuelita—to have that kind of wisdom."

Felita

by
Nicholasa Mohr

When Felita and her family move back to their old neighborhood, she is thrilled to be reunited with her best friend, Gigi. Although there have not been many changes in the neighborhood itself, Felita soon learns that people, even best friends, can change. With her grandmother Abuelita's help, Felita works to make her friendship with Gigi survive these changes.

ILLUSTRATED BY RUDY GUTIERREZ

227

wonderful thing happened this new school year. Gigi, Consuela, Paquito, and I were all going into the fourth grade, and we were put in the same class. It had never happened before. Once I was in the same class with Consuela, and last year Gigi and Paquito were together. But this—it was too good to be true! Of course knowing Gigi and I were in the same class made me the happiest.

Our teacher, Miss Lovett, was friendly and laughed easily. In early October, after we had all settled into our class and gotten used to the routine of school once more, Miss Lovett told us that this year our class was going to put on a play for Thanksgiving. The play we were going to perform was based on a poem by Henry Wadsworth Longfellow, called "The

Courtship of Miles Standish." It was about the Pilgrims and how they lived when they first landed in America.

We were all so excited about the play. Miss Lovett called for volunteers to help with the sets and costumes. Paquito and I agreed to help with the sets. Consuela was going to work on makeup. Gigi had not volunteered for anything. When we asked her what she was going to do, she shrugged and didn't answer.

Miss Lovett said we could all audition for the different parts in the play. I was really interested in being Priscilla. She is the heroine. Both

Captain Miles Standish and the handsome, young John Alden are in love with her. She is the most beautiful maiden in Plymouth, Massachusetts. That's where the Pilgrims used to live. I told my friends how much I would like to play that part. Everyone said I would be perfect . . . except Gigi. She said that it was a hard part to do, and maybe I wouldn't be able to play it. I really got annoyed and asked her what she meant.

"I just don't think you are right to play Priscilla. That's all," she said.

"What do you mean by right?" I asked. But Gigi only shrugged and didn't say another word. She was beginning to get on my nerves.

Auditions for the parts were going to start Tuesday. Lots of kids had volunteered to audition. Paquito said he would try out for the brave Captain Miles Standish. Consuela said she was too afraid to get up in front of everybody and make a fool of herself. Gigi didn't show any interest in the play and refused to even talk to us about it. Finally the day came for the girls to read for the part of Priscilla. I was so excited I could hardly wait. Miss Lovett had given us some lines to study. I had practiced real hard. She called out all the names of those who were going to read. I was surprised when I heard her call out "Georgina Mercado." I didn't even know Gigi wanted to try out for Priscilla. I looked at Gigi, but she ignored me. We began reading. It was my turn. I was very nervous and kept forgetting my lines. I had to look down at the script a whole lot. Several other girls were almost as nervous as I was. Then it was Gigi's turn. She recited the part almost by

heart. She hardly looked at the script. I noticed that she was wearing one of her best dresses. She had never looked that good in school before. When she finished, everybody clapped. It was obvious that she was the best one. Miss Lovett made a fuss.

"You were just wonderful, Georgina," she said, "made for the part!" Boy, would I have liked another chance. I bet I could have done better than Gigi.

Why hadn't she told me she wanted the part? It's a free country, after all. She could read for the same part as me. I wasn't going to stop her! I was really angry at Gigi.

After school everyone was still making a fuss over her. Even Paquito had to open his stupid mouth.

"Oh, man, Gigi!" he said. "You were really good. I liked the part when John Alden asked you to marry Captain Miles Standish and you said, 'Why don't you speak for yourself, John?' You turned your head like this." Paquito imitated Gigi and closed his eyes. "That was really neat!" Consuela and the others laughed and agreed.

I decided I wasn't walking home with them.

"I have to meet my brothers down by the next street," I said. "I'm splitting. See you." They hardly noticed. Only Consuela said goodbye. The rest just kept on hanging all over Gigi. Big deal, I thought.

Of course walking by myself and watching out for the tough kids was not something I looked forward to. Just last Friday Hilda Gonzales had gotten beat up and had her entire allowance stolen. And at the beginning of the term Paquito had been walking home by himself and gotten mugged. A bunch of big bullies had taken his new schoolbag complete with pencil and pen case, then left him with a swollen lip. No, sir, none of us ever walked home from school alone if we could help it. We knew it wasn't a safe thing to do. Those mean kids never bothered us as long as we stuck together. Carefully I looked around to make sure none of the bullies were in sight. Then I put some speed under my feet, took my chances, and headed for home.

Just before all the casting was completed, Miss Lovett offered me a part as one of the Pilgrim women. All I had to do was stand in the background like a zombie. It wasn't even a speaking part.

"I don't get to say one word," I protested.

"Felicidad Maldonado, you are designing the stage sets and you're assistant stage manager. I think that's quite a bit. Besides, all the speaking parts are taken."

"I'm not interested, thank you," I answered.

"You know"—Miss Lovett shook her head—"you can't be the best in everything."

I turned and left. I didn't need to play any part at all. Who cared?

Gigi came over to me the next day with a great big smile all over her face. I just turned away and made believe she wasn't there.

"Felita, are you taking the part of the Pilgrim woman?" she asked me in her sweetest voice, just like nothing had happened.

"No," I said, still not looking at her. If she thought I was going to fall all over her like those dummies, she was wasting her time.

"Oh," was all she said, and walked away. Good, I thought. I don't need her one bit!

At home Mami noticed something was wrong.

"Felita, what's the matter? You aren't going out at all. And I haven't seen Gigi for quite a while. In fact I haven't seen any of your friends."

"Nothing is the matter, Mami. I just got lots of things to do."

"You're not upset because we couldn't give you a birthday party this year, are you?" Mami asked. "You know how hard the money situation has been for us."

My birthday had been at the beginning of November. We had celebrated with a small cake after dinner, but there had been no party.

"No. It's not that," I said and meant it. Even though I had been a little disappointed, I also knew Mami and Papi had done the best they could.

"We'll make it up to you next year, Felita, you'll see."

"I don't care, Mami. It's not important now."

"You didn't go having a fight with Gigi or something? Did you?"

"Now why would I have a fight with anybody!"

"Don't raise your voice, miss," Mami said. "Sorry I asked. But you just calm down."

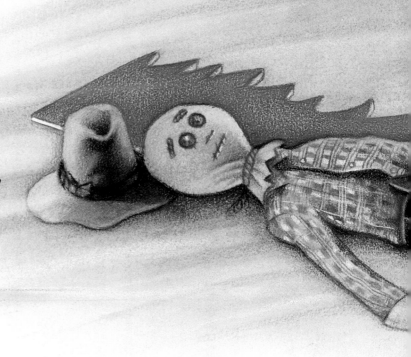

234

The play was going to be performed on the day before Thanksgiving. I made the drawings for most of the scenery. I made a barn, a church, trees and grass, cows, and a horse. I helped the others make a real scarecrow. We used a broom and old clothes. Paquito didn't get the part of Captain Miles Standish, but he made a wonderful fence out of cardboard. It looked just like a real wooden fence. Consuela brought in her mother's old leftover makeup. She did a good job of making up everybody.

By the time we set up the stage, everything looked beautiful. Gigi had tried to talk to me a few times. But I just couldn't be nice back to her. She acted like nothing had happened, like I was supposed to forget she hadn't told me she was going to read for the part! I wasn't going to forget that just because she was now Miss Popularity. She could go and stay with all her newfound friends for all I cared!

The morning of the play, at breakfast, everybody noticed how excited I was.

"Felita," Papi exclaimed, "stop jumping around like a monkey and eat your breakfast."

"She's all excited about the school play today," Mami said.

"That's right. Are you playing a part in the play?" Papi asked.

"No," I replied.

"But she's done most of the sets. Drawing and designing. Isn't that right, Felita?"

"Mami, it was no big deal."

"That's nice," said Papi. "Tell us about it."

"What kind of sets did you do?" Johnny asked.

"I don't know. Look, I don't want to talk about it."

"Boy, are you touchy today," Tito said with a laugh.

"Leave me alone!" I snapped.

"Okay." Mami stood up. "Enough. Felita, are you finished?" I nodded. "Good. Go to school. When you come back, bring home a better mood. Whatever is bothering you, no need to take it out on us." Quickly I left the table.

"Rosa," I heard Papi say, "sometimes you are too hard on her."

"And sometimes you spoil her, Alberto!" Mami snapped. "I'm not raising fresh kids."

I was glad to get out of there. Who needs them, I thought.

The play was a tremendous hit. Everybody looked wonderful and played their parts really well. The stage was brilliant with the color I had used on my drawings. The background of the countryside, the barn, and just about everything stood out clearly. Ernesto Bratter, the stage manager, said I was a good assistant. I was glad to hear that, because a couple of times I'd had to control my temper on account of his ordering me around. But it had all worked out great.

No doubt about it. Gigi was perfect as Priscilla. Even though the kids clapped and cheered for the entire cast, Gigi got more applause than anybody else. She just kept on taking a whole lot of bows.

Afterward Miss Lovett had a party for our class. We had lots of treats. There was even a record player and we all danced. We had a really good time.

Of course Priscilla, alias Gigi, was the big star. She just couldn't get enough attention. But not from me, that was for sure. After the party Gigi spoke to me.

"Your sets were really great. Everybody said the stage looked wonderful."

"Thanks." I looked away.

"Felita, are you mad at me?"

"Why should I be mad at you?"

"Well, I did get the leading part, but . . ."

"Big deal," I said. "I really don't care."

"You don't? But . . . I . . ."

"Look," I said, interrupting her, "I gotta go. I promised my mother I'd get home early. We have to go someplace."

I rushed all the way home. I didn't know why, but I was still furious at Gigi. What was worse was that I was unhappy about having those feelings. Gigi and I had been real close for as far back as I could remember. Not being able to share things with her really bothered me.

We had a great Thanksgiving. The dinner was just delicious. Abuelita brought her flan. Tío Jorge brought lots of ice cream. He always brings us kids a treat when he visits. Sometimes he even brings each one of us a small gift—a nature book or crayons for me and puzzles or sports magazines for my brothers. He's really very nice to us. One thing about him is that he's sort of quiet and doesn't talk much. Papi says that Tío Jorge has been like that as far back as he can remember.

Abuelita asked me if I wanted to go home with her that evening. Boy, was I happy to get away from Mami. I just couldn't face another day of her asking me questions about Gigi, my friends, and my whole life. It was getting to be too much!

It felt good to be with Abuelita in her apartment. Abuelita never questioned me about anything really personal unless I wanted to talk about it.

She just waited, and when she sensed that I was worried or something, then she would ask me. Not like Mami. I love Mami, but she's always trying to find out every little thing that happens to me. With my abuelita sometimes we just sit and stay quiet, not talk at all. That was nice too. We fixed the daybed for me. And then Tío Jorge, Abuelita, and I had more flan as usual.

"Would you like to go to the park with me this Sunday?" Tío Jorge asked me.

"Yes."

"We can go to the zoo and later we can visit the ducks and swans by the lake."

"Great!" I said.

Whenever Tío Jorge took me to the zoo, he would tell me stories about how he, Abuelita, and their brothers and sisters had lived and worked as youngsters taking care of farm animals. These were the only times I ever heard him talk a whole lot.

"It's not just playing, you know," he would say. "Taking care of animals is hard work. Back on our farm in Puerto Rico we worked hard, but we had fun too. Every one of us children had our very own favorite pets. I had a pet goat by the name of Pepe. He used to follow me everywhere." No matter how many times he told me the same stories, I always enjoyed hearing them again.

"Well." Tío Jorge got up. "It's a date then on Sunday, yes?"

"Yes, thank you, Tío Jorge."

"Good night," he said and went off to bed.

Abuelita and I sat quietly for a while, then Abuelita spoke.

"You are getting to be a big girl now, Felita. You just turned nine years old. My goodness! But I still hope you will come to bed with your abuelita for a little while, eh?"

I got into bed and snuggled close to Abuelita. I loved her the best, more than anybody. I hadn't been to stay with her since the summer, and somehow this time things felt different. I noticed

how tired Abuelita looked. She wasn't moving as fast as she used to. Also I didn't feel so little next to her anymore.

"Tell me, Felita, how have you been? It seems like a long time since we were together like this." She smiled her wonderful smile at me. Her dark, bright eyes looked deeply into mine. I felt her warmth and happiness.

"I'm okay, Abuelita."

"Tell me about your play at school. Rosa tells me you worked on the stage sets. Was the play a success?"

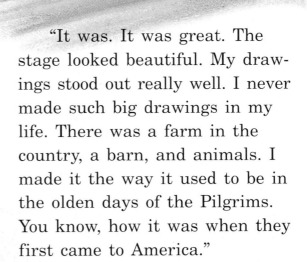

"It was. It was great. The stage looked beautiful. My drawings stood out really well. I never made such big drawings in my life. There was a farm in the country, a barn, and animals. I made it the way it used to be in the olden days of the Pilgrims. You know, how it was when they first came to America."

"I'm so proud of you. Tell me about the play. Did you act in it?"

"No." I paused. "I didn't want to."

"I see. Tell me a little about the story."

I told Abuelita all about it.

"Who played the parts? Any of your friends?"

"Some."

"Who?"

"Well, this boy Charlie Martinez played John Alden. Louie Collins played Captain Miles Standish. You don't know them. Mary Jackson played the part of the narrator. That's the person who tells the story. You really don't know any of them."

I was hoping she wouldn't ask, but she did.

"Who played the part of the girl both men love?"

"Oh, her? Gigi."

"Gigi Mercado, your best friend?" I nodded. "Was she good?"

"Yes, she was. Very good."

"You don't sound too happy about that."

"I don't care." I shrugged.

"But if she is your best friend, I should think you would care."

"I . . . I don't know if she is my friend anymore, Abuelita."

"Why do you say that?"

I couldn't answer. I just felt awful.

"Did she do something? Did you two argue?" I nodded. "Can I ask what happened?"

"Well, it's hard to explain. But what she did wasn't fair."

"Fair about what, Felita?"

I hadn't spoken about it before. Now with Abuelita it was easy to talk about it.

"Well, we all tried out for the different parts. Everybody knew what everybody was trying out

for. But Gigi never told anybody she was going to try out for Priscilla. She kept it a great big secret. Even after I told her that I wanted to try for the part, she kept quiet about it. Do you know what she did say? She said I wasn't right for it . . . it was a hard part and all that bunch of baloney. She just wanted the part for herself, so she was mysterious about the whole thing. Like . . . it was . . . I don't know." I stopped for a moment, trying to figure this whole thing out. "After all, I am supposed to be her best

friend . . . her very best friend. Why shouldn't she let me know that she wanted to be Priscilla? I wouldn't care. I let her know my plans. I didn't go sneaking around."

"Are you angry because Gigi got the part?"

It was hard for me to answer. I thought about it for a little while. "Abuelita, I don't think so. She was really good in the part."

"Were you as good when you tried out for Priscilla?"

"No." I looked at Abuelita. "I stunk." We both laughed.

"Then maybe you are not angry at Gigi at all."

"What do you mean?"

"Well, maybe you are a little bit . . . hurt?"

"Hurt?" I felt confused.

"Do you know what I think? I think you are hurt because your best friend didn't trust you. From what you tell me, you trusted her, but she didn't have faith in you. What do you think?"

"Yes." I nodded. "Abuelita, yes. I don't know why. Gigi and I always tell each other everything. Why did she act like that to me?"

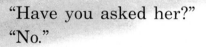

"Have you asked her?"

"No."

"Why not? Aren't you two speaking to each other?"

"We're speaking. Gigi tried to be friendly a few times."

"Don't you want to stay her friend?"

"I do. Only she came over to me acting like . . . like nothing ever happened. And something did happen! What does she think? That she can go around being sneaky and I'm going to fall all over her? Just because she got the best part, she thinks she's special."

"And you think that's why she came over. Because she wants to be special?"

"I don't know."

"You should give her a chance. Perhaps Gigi acted in a strange way for a reason."

"She wasn't nice to me, Abuelita. She wasn't."

"I'm not saying she was. Or even that she was right. Mira, Felita, friendship is one of the best things in this whole world. It's one of the few things you can't go out and buy. It's like love. You can buy clothes, food, even luxuries, but there's no place I know of where you can buy a real friend. Do you?"

I shook my head. Abuelita smiled at me and waited. We were both silent for a long moment. I wondered if maybe I shouldn't have a talk with Gigi. After all, she had tried to talk to me first.

"Abuelita, do you think it's a good idea for me to . . . maybe talk to Gigi?"

"You know, that's a very good idea." Abuelita nodded.

"Well, she did try to talk to me a few times. Only there's just one thing. I won't know what to say to her. I mean, after what's happened and all."

"After so many years of being close, I am sure you could say 'Hello, Gigi. How are you?' That should be easy enough."

"I feel better already, Abuelita."

"Good," Abuelita said. "Now let's you and I get to sleep. Abuelita is tired."

"You don't have to tuck me in. I'll tuck you in instead." I got out of bed and folded the covers carefully over my side. Then I leaned over her and gave her a kiss. Abuelita hugged me real tight.

"My Felita has become a young lady," she whispered.

I kept thinking of what Abuelita had said, and on Monday I waited for Gigi after school. It was as if she knew I wanted to talk. She came over to me.

"Hello, Gigi," I said. "How are you?"

"Fine." Gigi smiled. "Wanna walk home together?"

"Let's take the long way so we can be by ourselves," I said.

We walked without saying anything for a couple of blocks. Finally I spoke.

"I wanted to tell you, Gigi, you were really great as Priscilla."

"Did you really like me? Oh, Felita, I'm so glad. I wanted you to like me, more than anybody else. Of course it was nothing compared to the sets you did. They were something special. Everybody liked them so much."

"You were right too," I said. "I wasn't very good for the part of Priscilla."

"Look." Gigi stopped walking and looked at me. "I'm sorry about . . . about the way I acted. Like, I didn't say anything to you or the others. But, well, I was scared you all would think I was silly or something. I mean, you wanted the part too. So, I figured, better not say nothing."

"I wouldn't have cared, Gigi. Honest."

"Felita . . . it's just that you are so good at a lot of things. Like, you draw just fantastic. You beat everybody at hopscotch and kick-the-can. You know about nature and animals, much more than the rest of us. Everything you do is always better than . . . what I do! I just wanted this part for me. I wanted to be better than you this time. For once I didn't wanna worry about you. Felita, I'm sorry."

I was shocked. I didn't know Gigi felt that way. I didn't feel better than anybody about any-thing I did. She looked so upset, like she was about to cry any minute. I could see she was mis-erable and I wanted to comfort her. I had never had this kind of feeling before in my whole life.

"Well, you didn't have to worry. 'Cause I stunk!" We both laughed with relief. "I think I was the worst one!"

"Oh, no, you weren't." Gigi laughed. "Jenny Fuentes was the most awful."

"Worse than me?"

"Much worse. Do you know what she sounded like? She sounded like this. 'Wha . . . wha . . . why don't you . . . speeek for your . . . yourself *Johnnnn?*'" Gigi and I burst into laughter.

"And how about that dummy, Louie Collins? I didn't think he read better than Paquito."

"Right," Gigi agreed. "I don't know how he got through the play. He was shaking so much that I was scared the sets would fall right on his head."

It was so much fun, Gigi and I talking about the play and how we felt about everybody and everything. It was just like before, only better.

A LOT of kids

There are a lot of kids
Living in my apartment building
And a lot of apartment buildings on my street
And a lot of streets in this city
And cities in this country
And a lot of countries in the world.
So I wonder if somewhere there's a kid I've never met
Living in some building on some street
In some city and country I'll never know—
And I wonder if that kid and I might be best friends
If we ever met.

JEFF MOSS

TEAM

by Peter Golenbock

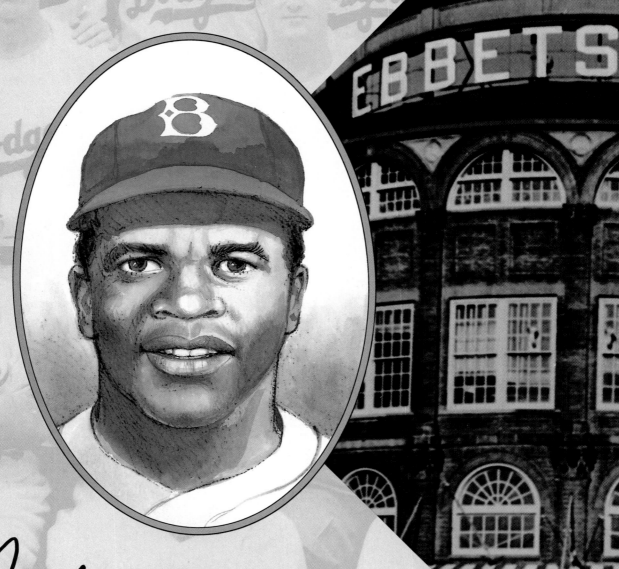

Jackie Robinson

MATES

illustrated by Paul Bacon

"Pee Wee" Reese

Jackie Robinson was more than just my teammate. He had a tremendous amount of talent, ability, and dedication. Jackie set a standard for future generations of ball players. He was a winner.

Jackie Robinson was also a man.

PEE WEE REESE
October 31, 1989

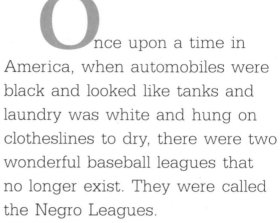

Once upon a time in America, when automobiles were black and looked like tanks and laundry was white and hung on clotheslines to dry, there were two wonderful baseball leagues that no longer exist. They were called the Negro Leagues.

The Negro Leagues had extraordinary players, and adoring fans came to see them wherever they played. They were heroes, but players in the Negro Leagues didn't make much money and their lives on the road were hard.

Laws against segregation didn't exist in the 1940s. In many places in this country, black people were not allowed to go to the same schools and churches as white people. They couldn't sit in the front of a bus or trolley car. They couldn't drink from the same drinking fountains that white people drank from.

Back then, many hotels didn't rent rooms to black people, so the Negro League players slept in their cars. Many towns had no restaurants that would serve them, so they often had to eat meals that they could buy and carry with them.

Life was very different for the players in the Major Leagues. They were the leagues for white players. Compared to the Negro League players, white players were very well paid. They stayed in good hotels and ate in fine restaurants. Their pictures were put on baseball cards and the best players became famous all over the world.

Many Americans knew that racial prejudice was wrong, but few dared to challenge openly the way things were. And many people were apathetic about racial problems. Some feared that it could be dangerous to object. Vigilante groups, like the Ku Klux Klan, reacted violently against those who tried to change the way blacks were treated.

The general manager of the Brooklyn Dodgers baseball team was a man by the name of Branch Rickey. He was not afraid of change. He wanted to treat the Dodger fans to the best players he could find, regardless of the color of their skin. He thought segregation was unfair and wanted to give everyone, regardless of race or creed, an opportunity to compete equally on ballfields across America.

To do this, the Dodgers needed one special man.

Branch Rickey launched a search for him. He was looking for a star player in the Negro Leagues who would be able to compete successfully despite threats on his life or attempts to injure him. He would have to possess the self-control not to fight back when opposing players tried to intimidate or hurt him. If this man disgraced himself on the field, Rickey knew, his opponents would use it as an excuse to keep blacks out of Major League baseball for many more years.

Rickey thought Jackie Robinson might be just the man.

BRANCH RICKEY

Jackie rode the train to Brooklyn to meet Mr. Rickey. When Mr. Rickey told him, "I want a man with the courage not to fight back," Jackie Robinson replied, "If you take this gamble, I will do my best to perform." They shook hands. Branch Rickey and Jackie Robinson were starting on what would be known in history as "the great experiment."

At spring training with the Dodgers, Jackie was mobbed by blacks, young and old, as if he were a savior. He was the first black player to try out for a Major League team. If he succeeded, they knew, others would follow.

Initially, life with the Dodgers was for Jackie a series of humiliations. The players on his team who came from the South, men who had been taught to avoid black people since childhood, moved to another table whenever he sat down next to them. Many opposing players were cruel to him, calling him nasty names from their dugouts. A few tried to hurt him with their spiked shoes. Pitchers aimed at his head. And he received threats on his life, both from individuals and from organizations like the Ku Klux Klan.

Despite all the difficulties, Jackie Robinson didn't give up. He made the Brooklyn Dodgers team.

Out making the Dodgers was only the beginning. Jackie had to face abuse and hostility throughout the season, from April through September. His worst pain was inside. Often he felt very alone. On the road he had to live by himself, because only the white players were allowed in the hotels in towns where the team played.

The whole time Pee Wee Reese, the Dodger shortstop, was growing up in Louisville, Kentucky, he had rarely even seen a black person, unless it was in the back of a bus. Most of his friends and relatives hated the idea of his playing on the same field as a black man. In addition, Pee Wee Reese had more to lose than the other players when Jackie joined the team.

Jackie had been a shortstop, and everyone thought that Jackie would take Pee Wee's job. Lesser men might have felt anger toward Jackie, but Pee Wee was different. He told himself, "If he's good enough to take my job, he deserves it."

When his Southern teammates circulated a petition to throw Jackie off the team and asked him to sign it, Pee Wee responded, "I don't care if this man is black, blue, or striped"—and refused to sign. "He can play and he can help us win," he told the others. "That's what counts."

Very early in the season, the Dodgers traveled west to Ohio to play the Cincinnati Reds. Cincinnati is near Pee Wee's hometown of Louisville.

The Reds played in a small ballpark where the fans sat close to the field. The players could almost feel the breath of the fans on the backs of their necks. Many who came that day screamed terrible, hateful things at Jackie when the Dodgers were on the field.

More than anything else, Pee Wee Reese believed in doing what was right. When he heard the fans yelling at Jackie, Pee Wee decided to take a stand.

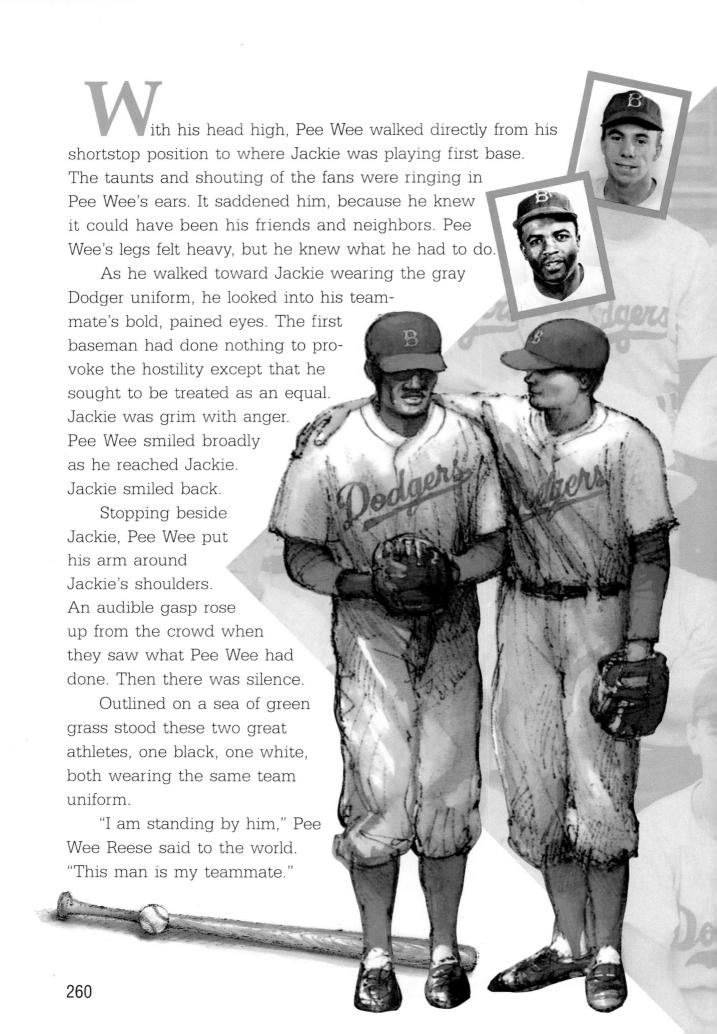

With his head high, Pee Wee walked directly from his shortstop position to where Jackie was playing first base. The taunts and shouting of the fans were ringing in Pee Wee's ears. It saddened him, because he knew it could have been his friends and neighbors. Pee Wee's legs felt heavy, but he knew what he had to do.

As he walked toward Jackie wearing the gray Dodger uniform, he looked into his teammate's bold, pained eyes. The first baseman had done nothing to provoke the hostility except that he sought to be treated as an equal. Jackie was grim with anger. Pee Wee smiled broadly as he reached Jackie. Jackie smiled back.

Stopping beside Jackie, Pee Wee put his arm around Jackie's shoulders. An audible gasp rose up from the crowd when they saw what Pee Wee had done. Then there was silence.

Outlined on a sea of green grass stood these two great athletes, one black, one white, both wearing the same team uniform.

"I am standing by him," Pee Wee Reese said to the world. "This man is my teammate."

260

MEET *Peter Golenbock*

When Peter Golenbock was thirteen, he met one of his heroes. After a World Series game between the Dodgers and the Yankees, he was introduced to Jackie Robinson. Meeting the great baseball player was quite an experience. "I was in awe of him," Golenbock remembers. "Robinson was huge. When I shook his hand, mine disappeared in his." Years later, Golenbock became a sportswriter and learned more about Robinson. Rex Barney, who had pitched for the Dodgers when Robinson was a player, told the writer a true story about two teammates—Jackie Robinson and Pee Wee Reese, the Dodgers' shortstop. Peter Golenbock never forgot that story.

When he was asked to write about baseball for young people, he thought about Jackie Robinson. He remembered Robinson's courage—as an athlete and as the first African-American player in the major leagues. He also remembered the story that Rex Barney had told him. In Teammates, Peter Golenbock wrote about baseball and how Robinson changed it. It is a story you, like the author, may never forget.

Oath of Friendship

This papercut was created by the Chinese artist Wang, Mei. Papercuts have been used as decorations in Chinese homes for centuries.

Shang ya!
I want to be your friend
For ever and ever without break or decay.
When the hills are all flat
And the rivers are all dry,
When it lightens and thunders in winter,
When it rains and snows in summer,
When Heaven and Earth mingle—
Not till then will I part from you.

Anonymous,
China, 1st century B.C.

CONTENTS

THE CHOICE IS OURS

We have not inherited the earth from our fathers, We are borrowing it from our children.

NATIVE AMERICAN

GOING

By JOHN ELKINGTON · JULIA HAILES · DOUGLAS HILL · JOEL MAKOWER

Illustrated by TONY ROSS

GREEN

A Kid's Handbook to Saving the Planet

You Can Do It!

All over the world, kids just like you are helping to save the Earth. Really. They may not feel powerful or important, but they are.

"How can this be?" you may be asking. "I'm just me, and even with all of my friends and neighbors and classmates it's not a very large group. After all, the world has billions of people!"

Well, a lot of those people are kids. And more and more kids are becoming aware of the environment. Many of them are doing something about it. You can be sure that when millions of kids all start doing the same thing, the entire world will sit up and take notice.

So, *you* have the power to change the world!

You've probably heard some things about the environment on the news or from your teachers or parents. Maybe you've heard about pollution, or the ozone layer, or the rainforests, or the greenhouse effect. You probably are confused about what some of these things mean. Don't worry—most grown-ups are confused, too.

Some of these problems sound so big and far away! The ozone layer is thousands of miles in the sky. The rainforests are mostly on other continents. How can you possibly do anything about these problems?

The fact is, when kids talk, grown-ups listen. And when kids do things, grown-ups pay attention. You don't have to be famous or rich or important to get grown-ups to listen. You just have to ask.

So, what are *you* going to do?

Air Pollution and Acid Rain

You may have some firsthand experience with air pollution, because almost every city—and even parts of the country—have polluted air. In fact, some of the most beautiful parts of the United States have polluted air, including the Grand Canyon in Arizona, the Everglades in Florida, and Yosemite National Park in California.

How did the air get this bad? Electricity production—the pollution generated by power plants—has contributed a lot to poor air quality. Cars are another big problem. While the cars made today pollute far less than cars made a few years ago, there are many more cars on the road today, and the typical car drives more miles each year than ever before. As a result, air pollution from cars hasn't decreased much.

In some areas, such as Los Angeles, air pollution has become so bad that the government has been forced to restrict many everyday activities, including driving a car, having a barbecue, even mowing the lawn with a power mower. All of these activities contribute to air pollution.

What's wrong with air pollution? When the air gets too dirty, it can be uncomfortable to breathe, and with every breath you may be inhaling substances that can make you sick. But even when the air is only a little polluted, the effects can still cause many illnesses, particularly among very young children and older adults like your grandparents.

That's not all. Air pollution also hurts plants and animals. It can poison trees and crops, and may even kill entire forests.

WHEN THE RAIN BECOMES POISON

We used to count on a good rainfall to cleanse the air of pollutants. Now, in some parts of the United States, even the rain is polluted. We call it "acid rain," even though the problem also pollutes the snow, sleet, hail, and even fog!

What turns the rain into poison? The problem comes primarily from the burning of fossil fuels, including gasoline burned in automobile engines and oil used for cooking and heating. The biggest source is the burning of coal—especially certain kinds of coal that contain high levels of sulfur—in electric-generating plants.

All of these sources release either sulfur dioxide or nitrogen oxides. Once in the air, these two substances mix with other chemicals and water to form sulfuric acid. When these chemicals mix with moisture, they fall to earth, where they can cause a great deal of harm.

What happens to acid rain when it reaches the ground? For one thing, it poisons fish and other things that live in rivers, lakes, and streams. It also kills trees. Buildings and monuments can also be affected. Some of the oldest and most treasured buildings in the world have been found to have damage caused by acid rain.

Acid rain also affects people. Some scientists see it as a threat to human health, causing lung disease and other serious problems. Babies, senior citizens, and people who have respiratory diseases such as asthma and bronchitis are among those most seriously affected by acid rain.

AMAZING FACT

About 110 million Americans live in areas with levels of air pollutants the federal government considers to be harmful.

A LITTLE EXPERIMENT

You can see the effects of acid rain for yourself. You'll need two houseplants, ideally the same kind. (Don't do this without permission from whoever is in charge of the plants.)

Place the plants side by side so they receive the same amount of sunlight. Then, whenever the plants need watering, give them the same amount, but add a few teaspoons of lemon juice or vinegar to one's water supply.

Watch the plants grow over the next two weeks. Chances are, the one which received the water and lemon juice or vinegar—both of which are highly acidic—isn't growing as well as the other plant. In fact, it will eventually die.

That's how acid affects plants. It also affects trees, insects, fish, animals, and humans.

WHAT CAN YOU DO?

The most important thing you can do is to conserve energy wisely. The less we use, the less we must generate through polluting power plants. As you'll see, there are many things you can do to reduce your energy use—without limiting the activities you've always done.

Too Much Trash

How many things will you throw away today? An empty cereal box? Your lunch bag? An empty soda can? Some papers from school? When you stop and think about it, you may be surprised at how much trash you toss out.

Every year, the typical American family throws out:

- **2,460 pounds of paper**
- **540 pounds of metals**
- **480 pounds of glass**
- **480 pounds of food scraps**

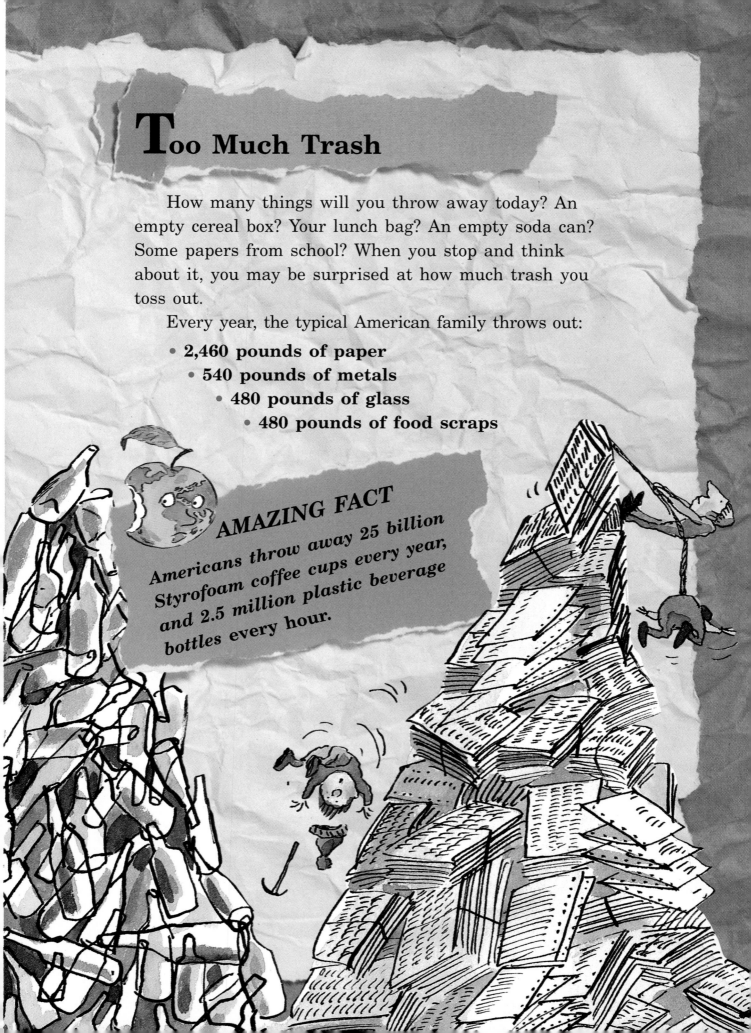

AMAZING FACT

Americans throw away 25 billion Styrofoam coffee cups every year, and 2.5 million plastic beverage bottles every hour.

All told, each of us throws away more than 1,200 pounds of trash per year, far more than people in most other countries. About 80 percent of that garbage ends up in landfills—dumps, as they are more commonly known. (Of the remaining 20 percent, about half is recycled and half is incinerated.) One big problem is that we are running out of landfill space—more than half of the nation's landfills will be full within ten years.

Where will we put all our garbage when we've run out of space?

But trash presents more than a space problem. Between 5 and 15 percent of what we throw away contains hazardous substances—substances that can seep into the ground and contaminate air, water, and soil, eventually injuring people and other living things. Batteries, plastics, inks used on packages, and disposable diapers are just some of the things we throw away that contain hazardous substances that can cause serious problems.

AMAZING FACT

Americans throw away enough glass bottles and jars to fill the 1,350-foot twin towers of New York's World Trade Center every two weeks.

THE PROBLEM OF PACKAGING

One of the things we throw away most often is packaging. Think about the products you and your family buy. From snack foods to compact discs, many products contain a great deal of packaging. Some have four or five layers, including several layers of plastic, far more than may be necessary. If your household is typical, about one-third of the packaging you buy will be thrown away immediately upon opening a package.

Some packaging is important—it protects products and ensures hygiene—but a lot of packaging is there simply to catch our eye, to make us buy this product rather than that one. Excessive packaging also adds to the cost of a product, so you pay extra for products that have a lot of packaging. We also pay for garbage in other ways—through higher taxes needed to create new landfills, for example, and through higher medical bills and health insurance costs required to cure the illnesses caused by pollution.

THE RECYCLING SOLUTION

The real tragedy behind the mountains of trash we produce is that a lot of what we throw away can be reused or recycled. Not everything is recyclable, and some materials are more easily recycled than others. But recycling makes perfect sense in any case. After all, why throw away what we can reuse?

What exactly can be recycled? Almost anything:

♻**Metals**—such as aluminum, steel, and tin. All of these metals must be mined from the ground, which can damage the local landscape and create water and air pollution. Most metals can be melted down and recycled again and again. This saves huge amounts of energy.

♻**Glass**—is made largely from sand, and there is hardly a shortage of that in the world. However, turning the sand into glass takes a large amount of energy. Much less energy (and much less sand) is used when glass is melted down and made into new bottles and jars. Every ton of crushed waste glass used saves the equivalent of about 30 gallons of oil.

♻**Paper**—is made from trees, of course, and cutting down trees can cause environmental problems. In the United States we cut down

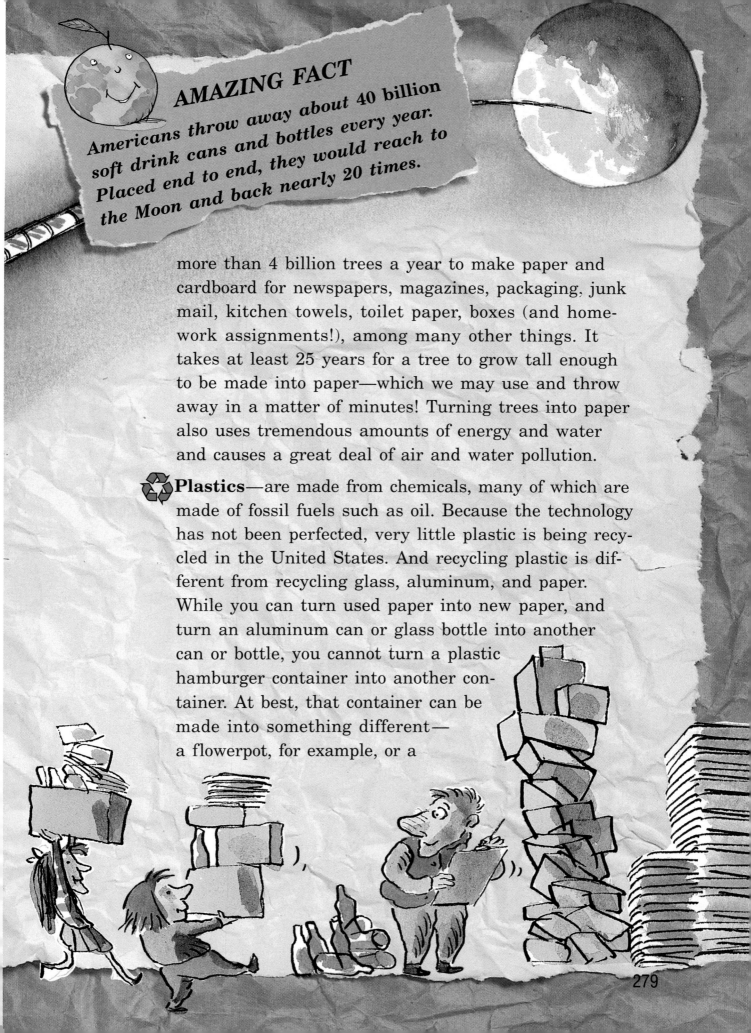

more than 4 billion trees a year to make paper and cardboard for newspapers, magazines, packaging, junk mail, kitchen towels, toilet paper, boxes (and homework assignments!), among many other things. It takes at least 25 years for a tree to grow tall enough to be made into paper—which we may use and throw away in a matter of minutes! Turning trees into paper also uses tremendous amounts of energy and water and causes a great deal of air and water pollution.

Plastics—are made from chemicals, many of which are made of fossil fuels such as oil. Because the technology has not been perfected, very little plastic is being recycled in the United States. And recycling plastic is different from recycling glass, aluminum, and paper. While you can turn used paper into new paper, and turn an aluminum can or glass bottle into another can or bottle, you cannot turn a plastic hamburger container into another container. At best, that container can be made into something different—a flowerpot, for example, or a

279

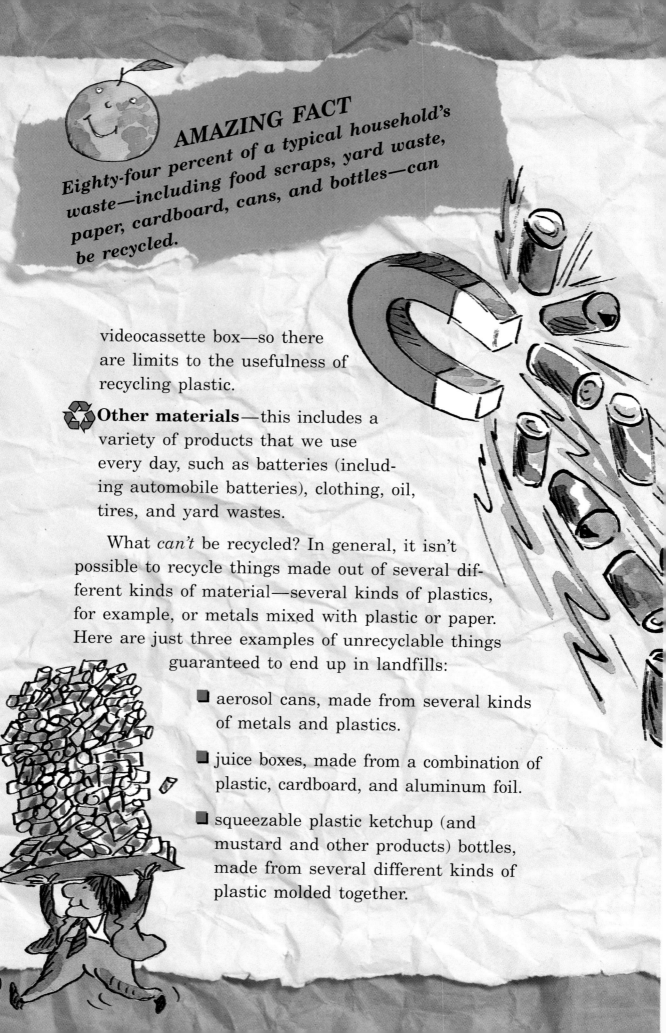

AMAZING FACT

Eighty-four percent of a typical household's waste—including food scraps, yard waste, paper, cardboard, cans, and bottles—can be recycled.

videocassette box—so there are limits to the usefulness of recycling plastic.

♻ **Other materials**—this includes a variety of products that we use every day, such as batteries (including automobile batteries), clothing, oil, tires, and yard wastes.

What *can't* be recycled? In general, it isn't possible to recycle things made out of several different kinds of material—several kinds of plastics, for example, or metals mixed with plastic or paper. Here are just three examples of unrecyclable things guaranteed to end up in landfills:

- aerosol cans, made from several kinds of metals and plastics.

- juice boxes, made from a combination of plastic, cardboard, and aluminum foil.

- squeezable plastic ketchup (and mustard and other products) bottles, made from several different kinds of plastic molded together.

THE MYTH OF DEGRADABILITY

We used to think that after we discarded something into a landfill it would eventually biodegrade—that is, it would rot and disappear completely. But we have come to learn that this doesn't really happen.

In a sense, everything in the world is biodegradable. Given enough time, air, sunlight, and other elements, your family's house, car, and possessions will all break down and wear away. It could take hundreds or even thousands of years for this to occur, but it will happen sooner or later.

But when things are buried in a landfill, where there is little if any air or sunlight, things do not break down. In fact, burying things in a landfill tends to *preserve* trash rather than *dispose* of it!

You have probably read or heard about the ancient Egyptians, who buried their leaders by wrapping them tightly in cloth and placing them in boxes stored in cool, dark places—mummies. Burying trash in landfills works in a similar way.

So, counting on trash to break down (sometimes referred to as biodegradability or photodegradability) is not a solution to our mountains of trash.

AMAZING FACT
Using recycled paper for one print run of the Sunday edition of The New York Times would save 75,000 trees.

How to Tell What's Recycled

There are several ways to identify products made of recycled material. Some products state on their labels "Made of recycled material." But some labels don't disclose *how much* of the material is recycled. Is it 5 percent or 100 percent? There may be no way of knowing.

Look for the recycled symbol to the right. But be careful: sometimes the symbol means that the product *can be recycled,* not that it is made from recycled material.

If the product or package is made from cardboard, such as a box of cereal or crackers, there is an easy way to tell whether it has been recycled. Peek under the top flap. If the *underside* of the cardboard is gray or dark brown, the box is made from recycled material. If the underside is white, it is made from virgin (unrecycled) material.

Whenever you have a choice, always choose the product made from recycled material.

AMAZING FACT

If every American recycled just one-tenth of his or her newspapers, we would save about 25 million trees a year.

WHAT CAN YOU DO?

You probably already know about the "three Rs"—reading, 'riting, and 'rithmetic. But there are three more Rs you should know to help you become a Green Consumer:

Refuse to buy things that are excessively packaged, that are made of plastics or other materials that are not fully recyclable, that are wasteful in other ways, or that you don't really need.

Reuse whatever you can. And buy products made of or packaged in reused (recycled) material.

Recycle as much as you can. This allows us to get the most use out of our precious resources.

MEET

**John Elkington,
Julia Hailes,
Douglas Hill** (*not shown*),
and Joel Makower

Commitment to preserving the environment brings people together from all over the world. When Joel Makower, a writer from Washington, D.C., read two handbooks for saving the earth by the British authors John Elkington, Julia Hailes, and Douglas Hill, he knew he wanted to team up with them. The result of their efforts is *Going Green*.

The authors of *Going Green* love to receive letters from young readers. "It's very satisfying to hear about young people doing the things we talk about in the book," says Makower. "The real power in environmental change rests with them," he explains. You can write to the authors at:

The Green Consumer
1526 Connecticut Avenue NW
Washington, DC 20036

LANDSCAPE

What will you find at the edge of the world?
A footprint,
a feather,
desert sand swirled?
A tree of ice,
a rain of stars,
or a junkyard of cars?

What will there be at the rim of the earth?
A mollusc,
a mammal,
a new creature's birth?
Eternal sunrise,
immortal sleep,
or cars piled up in a rusty heap?

WHA

By Seymour Simon

LES

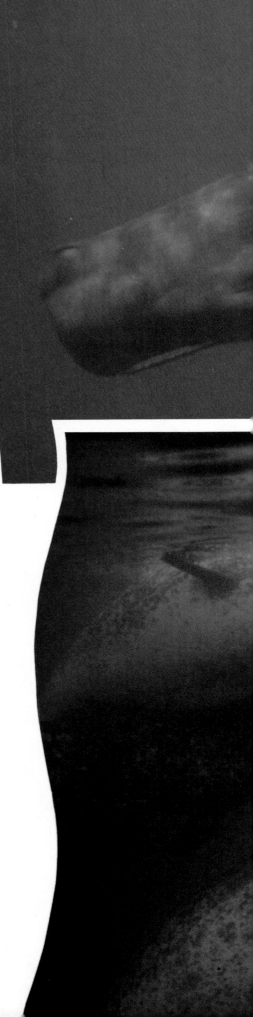

There are about ninety kinds of whales in the world. Scientists divide them into two main groups: toothed whales and baleen whales.

Toothed whales have teeth and feed mostly on fish and squid. They have only one blowhole and are closely related to dolphins and porpoises.

The **sperm whale** is the only giant among the toothed whales. It is the animal that comes to mind when most people think of a whale. A sperm whale has a huge, squarish head, small eyes, and a thin lower jaw. All the fist-sized teeth, about fifty of them, are in the lower jaw. The male grows to sixty feet long and weighs as much as fifty tons. The female is smaller, reaching only forty feet and weighing less than twenty tons.

A sperm whale's main food is squid, which it catches and swallows whole. A sperm whale is not a very fast swimmer, but it is a champion diver. It dives to depths of a mile in search of giant squid and can stay underwater for more than an hour.

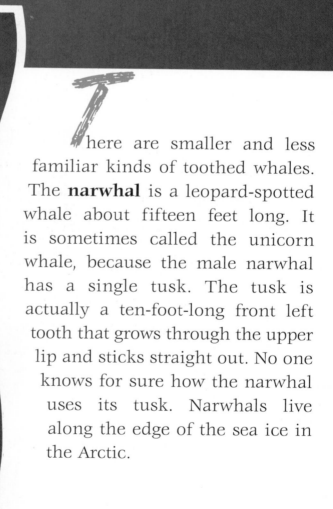

There are smaller and less familiar kinds of toothed whales. The **narwhal** is a leopard-spotted whale about fifteen feet long. It is sometimes called the unicorn whale, because the male narwhal has a single tusk. The tusk is actually a ten-foot-long front left tooth that grows through the upper lip and sticks straight out. No one knows for sure how the narwhal uses its tusk. Narwhals live along the edge of the sea ice in the Arctic.

Narwhals

289

Perhaps the best known of the toothed whales is the killer whale, or **orca**. That's because there are killer whales that perform in marine parks around the country. A killer whale is actually the largest member of the dolphin family. A male can grow to over thirty feet and weigh nine tons.

rcas are found in all of the world's oceans, from the poles to the tropics. They hunt for food in herds called pods. Orcas eat fish, squid, and penguins, as well as seals, sea lions, and other sea mammals, including even the largest whales. Yet they are usually gentle in captivity, and there is no record that an orca has ever caused a human death.

Orcas

Baleen whales differ from toothed whales. They have a two-part nostril or blowhole; and, instead of teeth, they have food-gathering baleen plates. Each whale has several hundred baleen plates, which hang down from the whale's upper jaw. The plates can be two to seven feet long and hang about one quarter of an inch apart. The inside edge of each plate is frayed and acts like a filter.

Baleen whales are the biggest whales of all, yet they feed on small fish and other very small sea animals, such as the shrimplike animals called krill. Krill, which are only as big as your little finger, occur in huge amounts in the Antarctic Ocean. In northern waters, baleen whales eat different kinds of small shrimplike animals.

Some baleen whales, such as the right whale, skim open-mouthed through the water. The frayed inner edges of the baleen trap the food animals while the water pours out through the gaps. In this way a right whale can filter thousands of gallons of seawater and swallow two tons of food each day.

The **right whale** was once very common in the North Atlantic Ocean. It was given its name by early whalers who regarded it as the "right whale" to catch, because it swam slowly, had lots of baleen and blubber, and floated when dead. So many right whales were killed that they are now quite rare.

Right whales may reach more than fifty feet and weigh more than seventy tons. They have large flippers and a long lower lip that covers and protects their baleen plates. Each right whale has its own pattern of strange bumps along its head called callosities. Scientists sometimes identify individual whales by the patterns of their callosities.

Right Whale

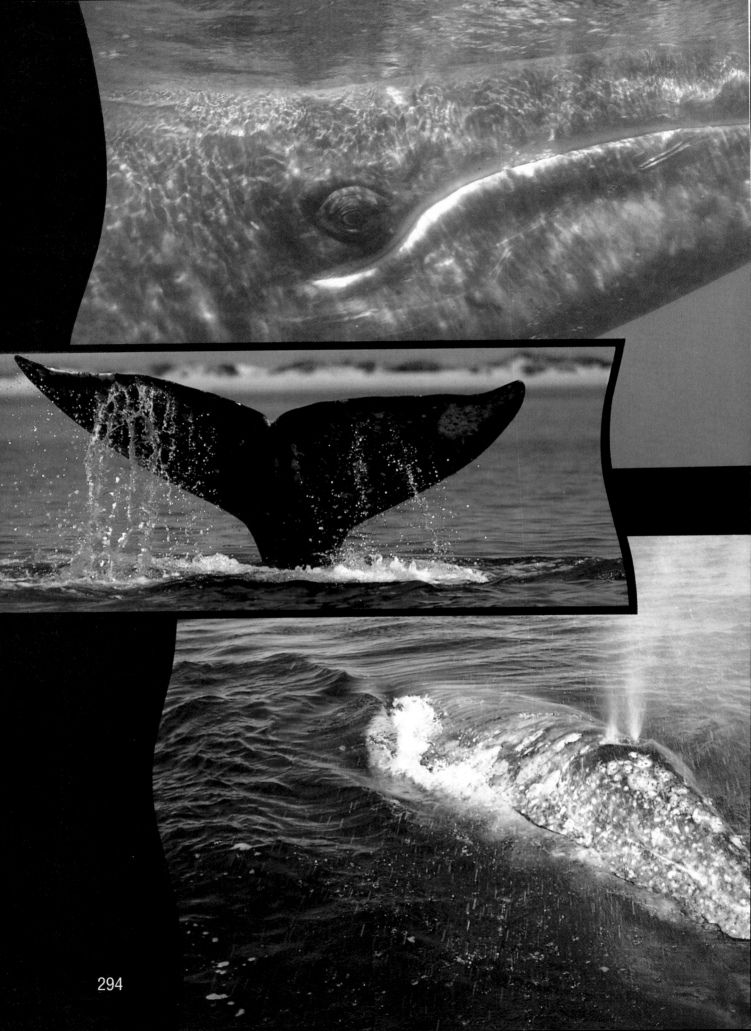

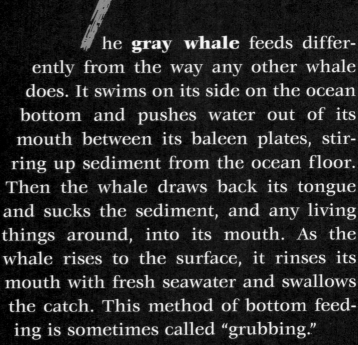

The **gray whale** feeds differently from the way any other whale does. It swims on its side on the ocean bottom and pushes water out of its mouth between its baleen plates, stirring up sediment from the ocean floor. Then the whale draws back its tongue and sucks the sediment, and any living things around, into its mouth. As the whale rises to the surface, it rinses its mouth with fresh seawater and swallows the catch. This method of bottom feeding is sometimes called "grubbing."

Gray whales once swam, in both the North Atlantic and North Pacific oceans, in the shallow waters along the coasts. Now, because of whaling in the Atlantic, they live only in the North Pacific and Arctic seas.

In the summer, the gray whales feed in the cold waters of the Arctic. In the winter, they travel about ten thousand miles to Mexican waters. There, the females give birth in the warm, protected lagoons along the Baja California peninsula. The journey of the gray whales is the longest known yearly migration for any mammal.

With its long, streamlined body, its pointed head, and its thin flukes, the **fin whale** has the right shape to be a fast and nimble swimmer—and it is. The long grooves on its throat allow the throat to expand while the whale is feeding. Whales that have these grooves, such as the fin, minke, humpback, and blue, are called rorquals, from the Norwegian word for groove or furrow.

Fin whales often work in pairs to round up and eat schools of fish. Fin whales are second only to blue whales in size. They can reach seventy to nearly ninety feet in length and weigh eighty tons.

The **blue whale** is bigger than the largest dinosaur that ever lived. The largest known dinosaur may have been 100 feet long and weighed 100 tons. But the biggest blue whales are over 110 feet long and weigh more than 150 tons. That's the weight of twenty-five full-grown elephants. The heart of a blue whale is the size of a small car.

A blue whale swims along the surface of the ocean up to a cloud of krill, opens its mouth wide, and sucks in fifty or more tons of water in one gulp. Then it opens its lips and strains out the krill through its baleen plates. In one day a blue whale eats more than four tons of krill, about forty *million* of these animals.

Blue whales have been hunted for many years. Even though they are now protected, only small numbers of blue whales are found in the Antarctic or anywhere else in the world.

Blue Whale

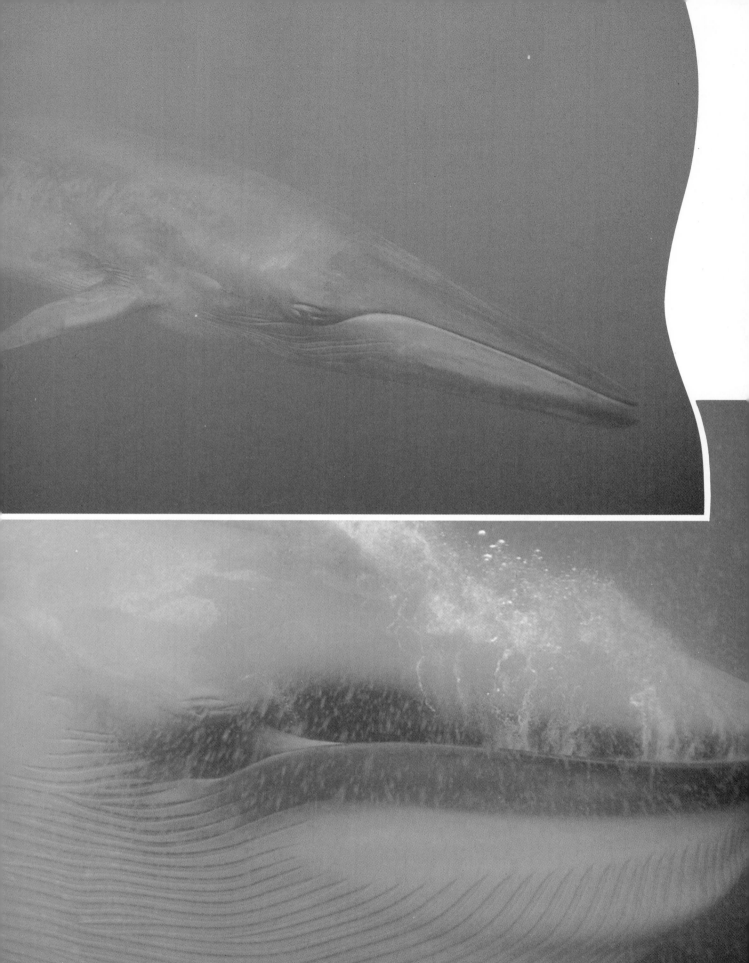

Humpback whales appear to be curious and seem to be accustomed to whale-watching boats. The whales show no hostility to the boats and are careful to avoid collisions.

Many whales make sounds, but the most famous are the songs of the humpbacks. They are sung only by the males. Some scientists think the songs may help to attract females or to keep other males from coming too close.

Whatever the reasons the whales have for singing them, the songs are strange and beautiful. Each one lasts as long as twenty or thirty minutes and is sung over and over again. The songs have patterns that repeat, but are different from one whale to another and from one year to the next. The song of a humpback can be heard from miles away.

Humpbacks feed in different ways. One way is called "bubble netting." A humpback sends out clouds of bubbles in a circle beneath a school of small fish or other food animals. When the fish are trapped by the bubbles, the whale lunges up inside the circle with its mouth open, swallowing huge amounts of water and food. A humpback's throat expands to make lots of room for the food and water. Sometimes several humpbacks feed together in the circle of bubbles.

Humpback Whales

In 1946, the International Whaling Commission (IWC) was set up to establish rules to limit whaling. Despite the rules, the numbers of whales steadily shrank. Some kinds of whales may be about to become extinct. Because of a worldwide movement to save the whales, the IWC banned all commercial whaling, beginning in 1985. But the governments of a few countries still allow their citizens to hunt whales.

Whales are one of the few wild animals that are commonly friendly to humans they encounter. Many people feel that we have an obligation to preserve these intelligent and special animals.

Will whales be allowed to remain to share the world with us? The choice is ours.

Meet Seymour Simon

From a very young age, Seymour Simon has been fascinated by whales. Simon's interest in the giant creatures has led him on whale watching expeditions from New York to Hawaii, and even to Alaska. "Whales are the greatest things going," he says.

The author of more than one hundred books, Simon has had more than forty of his books named as Outstanding Science Trade Books for Children. To Simon, a former teacher, science is a way of finding out about the world. Many of his books contain projects and questions that help readers find things out for themselves.

Simon enjoys receiving letters from readers who have answered a question using one of his books. For him, sharing a reader's experience is "as much fun as the first time I found out something myself."

Morgan's Zoo
by James Howe
illustrated by
Leslie Morrill
Atheneum, 1984

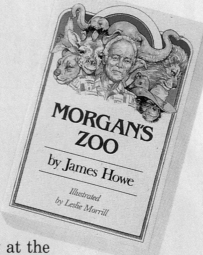

"Come to the party at the
zoo," Morgan echoed quietly.
He shook his head in amaze-
ment at the thought. "We're
going to do it!" he said, excitement overtaking him. "We're
going to save the zoo. I just
know we are. And it's going to
be every bit as wonderful as
the old days!"

Turtle Watch
Written and photographed
by George Ancona
Macmillan, 1987

Suddenly, above the roar of the
wind and the motor, Julio
shouts, *"Tartaruga!"* Neca
slams on the brakes and
switches off the motor.
Dousing the lights, they both
jump out into the darkness
and scramble silently down the
slope to the dark shape
on the beach.

You Can Make It So!

As usual, Walter stopped at the bakery on his way home from school. He bought one large jelly-filled dough-nut. He took the pastry from its bag, eating quickly as he walked along. He licked the red jelly from his fingers. Then he crumpled up the empty bag and threw it at a fire hydrant.

JUST A DREAM

Written and Illustrated by
Chris Van Allsburg

At home Walter saw Rose, the little girl next door, watering a tree that had just been planted. "It's my birthday present," she said proudly. Walter couldn't understand why anyone would want a tree for a present. His own birthday was just a few days away, "And I'm not getting some dumb plant," he told Rose.

After dinner Walter took out the trash. Three cans stood next to the garage. One was for bottles, one for cans, and one for everything else. As usual, Walter dumped everything into one can. He was too busy to sort through garbage, especially when there was something good on television.

The show that Walter was so eager to watch was about a boy who lived in the future. The boy flew around in a tiny airplane that he parked on the roof of his house.

He had a robot and a small machine that could make any kind of food with the push of a button.

Walter went to bed wishing he lived in the future. He couldn't wait to have his own tiny plane, a robot to take out the trash, and a machine that could make jelly doughnuts by the thousands. When he fell asleep, his wish came true. That night Walter's bed traveled to . . .

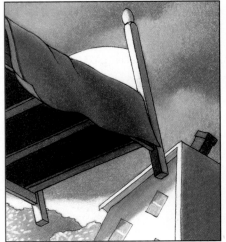

the future.

Walter woke up in the middle of a huge dump. A bulldozer was pushing a heap of bulging trash bags toward him. "Stop!" he yelled.

The man driving the bulldozer put his machine in neutral. "Oh, sorry," he said. "Didn't see you."

Walter looked at the distant mountains of trash and saw half-buried houses. "Do people live here?" he asked.

"Not anymore," answered the man.

A few feet from the bed was a rusty old street sign that read

FLORAL AVENUE. "Oh no," gasped Walter. He lived on Floral Avenue.

The driver revved up his bulldozer. "Well," he shouted, "back to work!"

Walter pulled the covers over his head. This can't be the future, he thought. I'm sure it's just a dream. He went back to sleep.

But not for long . . .

Walter peered over the edge of his bed, which was caught in the branches of a tall tree. Down below, he could see two men carrying a large saw. "Hello!" Walter yelled out.

"Hello to you!" they shouted back.

"You aren't going to cut down this tree, are you?" Walter asked.

But the woodcutters didn't answer. They took off their jackets, rolled up their sleeves, and got to work. Back and forth they pushed the saw, slicing through the trunk of Walter's tree. "You must need

this tree for something important," Walter
called down.

"Oh yes," they said, "very important."
Then Walter noticed lettering on the woodcutters' jackets. He could just make out the
words: QUALITY TOOTHPICK COMPANY. Walter
sighed and slid back under the blankets.

Until . . .

Walter couldn't stop coughing. His bed was balanced on the rim of a giant smokestack. The air was filled with smoke that burned his throat and made his eyes itch. All around him, dozens of smokestacks belched thick clouds of hot, foul smoke. A workman climbed one of the stacks.

"What is this place?" Walter called out.

"This is the Maximum Strength Medicine Factory," the man answered.

"Gosh," said Walter, looking at all the smoke, "what kind of medicine do they make here?"

"Wonderful medicine," the

workman replied, "for burning throats and itchy eyes."

Walter started coughing again.

"I can get you some," the man offered.

"No thanks," said Walter. He buried his head in his pillow and, when his coughing stopped, fell asleep.

But then . . .

Snowflakes fell on Walter. He was high in the mountains. A group of people wearing snowshoes and long fur coats hiked past his bed.

"Where are you going?" Walter asked.

"To the hotel," one of them replied.

Walter turned around and saw an enormous building. A sign on it read HOTEL EVEREST. "Is that hotel," asked Walter, "on the top of Mount Everest?"

"Yes," said one of the hikers. "Isn't it beautiful?"

"Well," Walter began. But the group didn't wait for his answer. They waved goodbye and marched away. Walter stared at the flashing yellow sign, then crawled back beneath his sheets.

But there was more to see . . .

Walter's hand was wet and cold. When he opened his eyes, he found himself floating on the open sea, drifting toward a fishing boat. The men on the boat were laughing and dancing.

"Ship ahoy!" Walter shouted.

The fishermen waved to him.

"What's the celebration for?" he asked.

"We've just caught a fish," one of them yelled back. "Our second one this week!" They held up their small fish for Walter to see.

"Aren't you supposed to throw the little ones back?" Walter asked.

But the fishermen didn't hear him.
They were busy singing and dancing.
Walter turned away. Soon the rocking
of the bed put him to sleep.

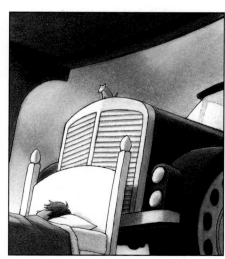

But only for a moment . . .

317

A loud, shrieking horn nearly lifted Walter off his mattress. He jumped up. There were cars and trucks all around him, horns honking loudly, creeping along inch by inch. Every driver had a car phone in one hand and a big cup of coffee in the other.

When the traffic stopped completely, the honking grew even louder. Walter could not get back to sleep.

Hours passed, and he wondered if he'd be stuck on this highway forever. He pulled his pillow tightly around his head.

318

This can't be the future, he thought. Where are the tiny airplanes, the robots? The honking continued into the night, until finally, one by one, the cars became quiet as their drivers, and Walter, went to sleep.

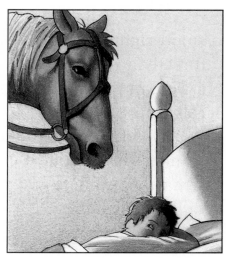

But his bed traveled on . . .

Walter looked up. A horse stood right over his bed, staring directly at him. In the saddle was a woman wearing cowboy clothes. "My horse likes you," she said.

"Good," replied Walter, who wondered where he'd ended up this time. All he could see was a dull yellow haze.

"Son," the woman told him, spreading her arms in front of her, "this is the mighty Grand Canyon."

Walter gazed into the foggy distance.

"Of course," she went on, "with all this smog, nobody's gotten a good look at it for years." The woman offered to sell Walter some

postcards that showed the canyon in the old days. "They're real pretty," she said.

But he couldn't look. It's just a dream, he told himself. I know I'll wake up soon, back in my room.

But he didn't . . .

Walter looked out from under his sheets. His bed was flying through the night sky. A flock of ducks passed overhead. One of them landed on the bed, and to Walter's surprise, he began to speak. "I hope you don't mind," the bird said, "if I take a short rest here." The ducks had been flying for days, looking for the pond where they had always stopped to eat.

"I'm sure it's down there somewhere," Walter said, though he suspected something awful might have happened. After a

while the duck waddled to the edge of the bed, took a deep breath, and flew off. "Good luck," Walter called to him. Then he pulled the blanket over his head. "It's just a dream," he whispered, and wondered if it would ever end.

Then finally . . .

Walter's bed returned to the present. He was safe in his room again, but he felt terrible. The future he'd seen was not what he'd expected. Robots and little airplanes didn't seem very important now. He looked out his window at the trees and lawns in the early morning light, then jumped out of bed.

He ran outside and down the block, still in his pajamas. He found the empty jelly doughnut bag he'd thrown at the fire hydrant the day before. Then Walter went back home and, before the sun came up, sorted all the trash by the garage.

A few days later, on Walter's birthday, all his friends came over for cake and ice cream. They loved his new toys: the laser gun set, electric yo-yo, and inflatable dinosaurs. "My best present,"

Walter told them, "is outside." Then he
showed them the gift that he'd picked out
that morning—a tree.

After the party, Walter and his dad
planted the birthday present. When he
went to bed, Walter looked out his window.
He could see his tree and the tree Rose had
planted on her birthday. He liked the way
they looked, side by side. Then he went to
sleep, but not for long, because that night
Walter's bed took him away again.

When Walter woke up, his bed was standing in the shade of two tall trees. The sky was blue. Laundry hanging from a clothes-line flapped in the breeze. A man pushed an old motorless lawn mower. This isn't the future, Walter thought. It's the past.

"Good morning," the man said. "You've found a nice place to sleep."

"Yes, I have," Walter agreed. There was something very peaceful about the huge trees next to his bed.

The man looked up at the rustling
leaves. "My great-grandmother planted
one of these trees," he said, "when she
was a little girl."

Walter looked up at the leaves too, and realized where his bed had taken him. This was the future, after all, a different kind of future. There were still no robots or tiny airplanes. There weren't even any clothes dryers or gas-powered lawn mowers. Walter lay back and smiled. "I like it here," he told the man, then drifted off to sleep in the shade of the two giant trees—the trees he and Rose had planted so many years ago.

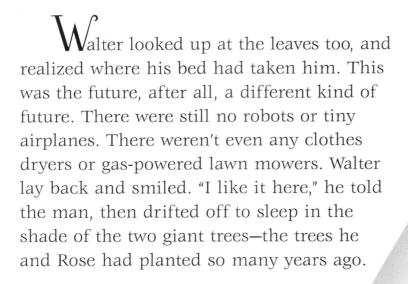

MEET

Chris Van Allsburg

Chris Van Allsburg is often asked where he gets the ideas for his books. Sometimes he says they are sent through the mail or beamed in from outer space. The truth, admits Van Allsburg, is that he isn't sure where he gets them. They just seem to arrive.

For Van Allsburg, who is both an artist and a writer, a story often begins with an image. He had just such an image in mind when he began *The Polar Express,* a book that won the Caldecott Medal. Van Allsburg pictured a boy looking at a train in front of his house and then taking trips on the train. Eventually, the train rolled all the way to the North Pole.

For *Just a Dream,* Van Allsburg pictured a polluted environment. How could he make this real problem into a good story? He decided to have a boy named Walter travel in his bed to various places. "Bed, with the covers up, is supposed to be a safe place," says the author. "But it's not safe to be in bed in a garbage dump."

Van Allsburg writes before he draws pictures for his stories. He can usually see the pictures in his mind as he writes, though. Creating a story, he says, is a little like making a film. He has to decide which parts to show in his drawings.

A full-grown tree is about 50 years old ~ that's when it's cut down. It takes about

The Lifeline of a Tree

YEARS

1 2   15   30

seedling   sapling   young tree

One edition of a Sunday newspaper can use 140 acres of pulpwood timber.

330

WHO CARES ABOUT TREES?

Who cares about trees
except beetles and bees,
fruit eaters, book readers,
and garden lovers galore,
bat shakers, box makers,
boat builders, woodcarvers,
and carpenters by the score?

Who cares?

What's special 'bout trees
except that they take
years to grow through rain
and through snow
and only a day to cut down.

And does anyone care
that trees clean the air, give shelter
and shade, and . . . what else?

And who'd want a tree
to plant in the yard, to
hold down the soil, hold up
a swing, bear sweet fruit, and
make your heart sing,
"Oh thank you, Tree!"

Who cares about trees?
You! Me!

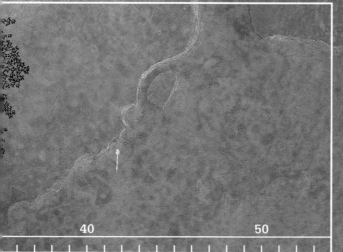

40   50

cut down/
made into paper/
used/paper trash

SHUMATE

Hail, Polluters

Motor exhaust
Chimney smoke
Oil refiners
Chemical plants
Burning garbage
Tobacco fumes—

You give

The air

An edge

That hurts

Whenever

I try

To breathe it.

Robert Froman

332

Meet
Virginia Evarts Wadsworth

Virginia Evarts Wadsworth grew up loving books. But she didn't spend all her time reading. The author has always enjoyed being outdoors, too.

Because of her love for books and nature, it's not surprising that Wadsworth became a writer—or that she decided to write about Rachel Carson. Carson, the writer and scientist who loved nature and fought to protect the environment, seems the perfect subject for Virginia Evarts Wadsworth. "I found her to be a fascinating person," Wadsworth says. "She accomplished things in her time that were unheard of for a woman. I wanted to share her extraordinary accomplishments with others."

Rachel Carson

Protector of Planet Earth

by
Virginia
Evarts
Wadsworth

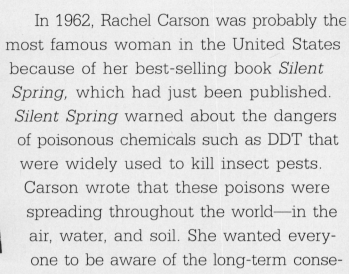

In 1962, Rachel Carson was probably the most famous woman in the United States because of her best-selling book *Silent Spring,* which had just been published. *Silent Spring* warned about the dangers of poisonous chemicals such as DDT that were widely used to kill insect pests. Carson wrote that these poisons were spreading throughout the world—in the air, water, and soil. She wanted everyone to be aware of the long-term consequences of spraying crops and orchards with chemicals.

How did Rachel Carson come to write about pesticides and pollution, little known subjects more than twenty-five years ago? From an early age, Carson loved nature. Born in 1907, she grew up on a farm in Pennsylvania. At the age of ten, she had a story published in *St. Nicholas,* a children's magazine. She planned to become a writer when she grew up.

When she graduated from college in 1928, however, her degree was in zoology, the study of animals. She felt that work in the world of nature was more important to her than writing fiction. That summer, Carson saw the ocean for the first time when she did research at the U.S. Biological Laboratory on Cape Cod, Massachusetts. For the rest of her life, Carson was rarely far away from the ocean.

Carson continued her education in marine biology, the study of the sea and its animal life. She landed a job with the Bureau of Fisheries and wrote factual articles about the ocean that were adapted for radio broadcasts. Carson later collected her articles into one manuscript and sold it to the *Atlantic Monthly.* This article grew into Carson's first book, *Under the Sea Wind,* which describes the sea's living creatures in relation to their surroundings and each other. Reviewers loved

Carson's writing, but *Under the Sea Wind* came out just as World War II began, and the book got lost in the shuffle.

After World War II, Carson wrote *The Sea Around Us,* which describes the sea's size, depths, currents, animal life, and underwater land formations. Writing about science with a poet's hand, Carson taught the American public to look at nature in a new way. *The Sea Around Us* stayed on the best-seller list for a year and a half, making Carson famous. Fan mail poured in, as readers wanted to meet her and read more of her writing. Although she made public appearances, she wrote a friend, "I'm much more at home barefoot in the sand . . . than on hardwood floors in high heels."

Carson won the National Book Award for *The Sea Around Us.* Newspaper editors named her Woman of the Year in Literature. She quit her government job and bought a house on the coast of Maine, where she wrote full-time. Her next book, *The Edge of the Sea,* which is about animal life along the seashore, also became a best seller.

A few years later, one of Carson's friends told her that a plane had sprayed her property with DDT to kill mosquitoes. Ten songbirds had died, she said, noting that she had "emptied and scrubbed the birdbath after the spraying, but you can never kill DDT."

Carson knew she must write about the dangers of pesticides and told fellow scientists and friends that "knowing what I do, I have no choice but to set it down to be read." Years of research, writing, and rewriting went into this book. Carson wanted to be sure that she had scientific proof of her allegations. She expected to be challenged by the powerful chemical companies and even the U.S. Department of Agriculture, which recommended the use of pesticides.

During those years, Carson battled cancer. She continued her project while undergoing tests and treatments because she so strongly believed in the subject. In a letter, she wrote, "Now my body falters and I know there is little time left."

The fruit of her labor, *Silent Spring,* opens in a beautiful fictitious town. When a white powder is sprayed from the sky, the "shadow of death" falls upon the town, and "only silence lay over the fields and wood and marsh." Carson's message—that the destruction of any part of the web of life threatens the human race—was a far cry from her gentle books about the sea.

Millions of copies of *Silent Spring* were sold. The book was discussed in newspapers and magazines across the country. Some people demanded that the government do something about the evils Carson had exposed. Others did not believe her, and still others labeled her a Communist. Critics accused her of being a sentimental bird watcher who would rather see people starve because their crops were destroyed by insects than kill a few birds. The chemical industry attacked her and advertised the importance of chemicals.

Because of the uproar over *Silent Spring,* John F. Kennedy formed the President's Science Advisory Committee to investigate the situation. A year after her book came out, the government issued a report that confirmed Carson's findings about pesticides.

As a result of her work, Carson received many honors. She became the first woman to receive the National Audubon Society Medal and was one of only a handful of women elected to the American Academy of Arts and Letters. Modest about her accomplishments, she reportedly said, "I could never again listen happily to a thrush song if I had not done all I could."

Carson died on April 14, 1964, at the age of fifty-seven. Eight years later, the U.S. government banned the use of DDT and some other chemical pesticides in the United States. In 1980, President Jimmy Carter posthumously awarded Carson the Presidential Medal of Freedom, the government's highest civilian award.

Rachel Carson was ahead of her time when she wrote that the songbirds would no longer sing in the spring unless people stopped polluting the environment. A gifted writer and scientist, she changed the way the world looks at planet Earth.

340

We sang songs that carried in their melodies
all the sounds of nature—
the running of waters, the sighing of winds,
and the calls of the animals.
Teach these to your children,
that they may come to love nature as we love it.

Native Americans Representing Many Nations

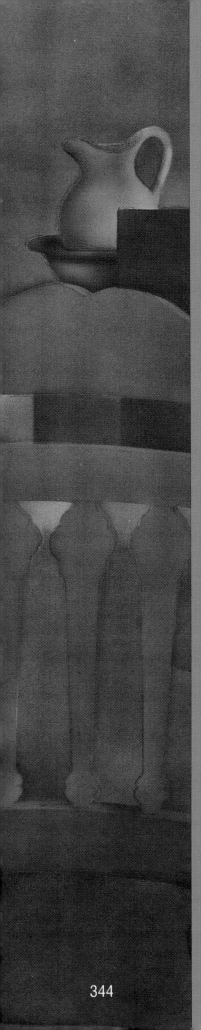
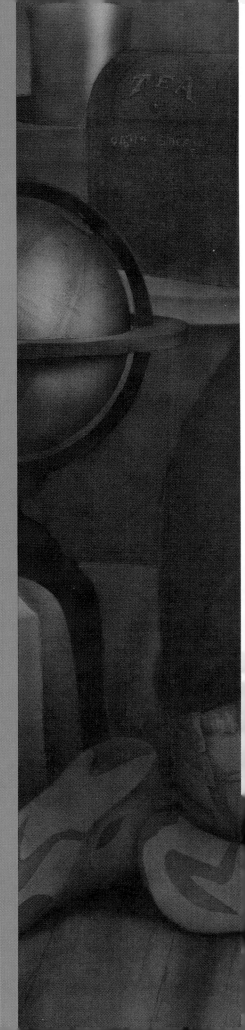

CONTENTS

Remember When...

Being human means
we can remember and
tell stories and pretend
and write and hope
and share...
We need to turn back
and celebrate our lives.

LUCY McCORMICK CALKINS
from *Living Between the Lines*

MEET
Lucille Clifton

It's not hard to get ideas for stories when you have six children, as Lucille Clifton does. But sometimes her children aren't the ones to give her ideas. Their friends are. Clifton based Jacob, in *My Friend Jacob*, on the boy next door. *Everett Anderson's Friend* is another book that the author wrote by paying attention to children around her. She also gets ideas for stories from another source. "I have such a good memory of my own childhood, my own time," she says.

Lucille Clifton's own memories and her experiences with young people make her characters seem very real. That's exactly what she wants. "I wish to have children see people like themselves in books," she explains. Clifton also wants readers to find joy in her stories. She writes books, she says, "that tend to celebrate life. I'm about that."

The LUCKY STONE

by Lucille Clifton

ILLUSTRATED BY JIM HAYS

When I was a girl we lived all together in a house with a big wrap-around porch: me, my Mama and Daddy and my Great-grandmother, Mrs. Elzie F. Pickens. The F. stood for Free. She was about seventy some years old, my Great-grand. We used to sit out on that porch in good weather, and she would tell me stories about when she was a girl and the different things that used to happen and such as that.

Oh, I loved it so, I loved her so! Tee, she would call me. Sweet Baby Tee. Some of my favorite stories were her favorites too. Oh, how we both loved telling and hearing about the Lucky Stone!

Mrs. Elzie F. Pickens was rocking slowly on the porch one afternoon when her Great-grand-

daughter brought her a big bunch of dogwood blooms, and that was the beginning of that story.

"Ahhh, now that dogwood reminds me of the day I met your Great-granddaddy, Mr. Pickens, Sweet Tee.

"It was just this time, spring of the year, and me and my best friend Ovella Wilson, who is now gone, was goin to join the Silas Greene. Usta be a kinda show went all through the South, called it the Silas Greene show. Somethin like the circus. Me and Ovella wanted to join that thing and see the world. Nothin wrong at home or nothin, we just wanted to travel and see new things and have high times. Didn't say nothin to nobody but one another. Just up and decided to do it.

"Well, this day we plaited our hair and put a dress and some things in a crokasack and started out to the show. Spring day like this.

"We got there after a good little walk and it was the world, Baby, such music and wonders as we never had seen! They had everything there, or seemed like it.

"Me and Ovella thought we'd walk around for a while and see the show before goin to the office to sign up and join.

"While we was viewin it all we come up on this dancin dog. Cutest one thing in the world next to you, Sweet Tee, dippin and movin and head bowin to that music. Had a little ruffly skirt on itself and up on two back legs twistin and movin to the music. Dancin dancin dancin till people started throwin pennies out of they pockets.

"Me and Ovella was caught up too and laughin so. She took a penny out of her pocket and threw it to the ground where that dog was dancin, and I took two pennies and threw 'em both.

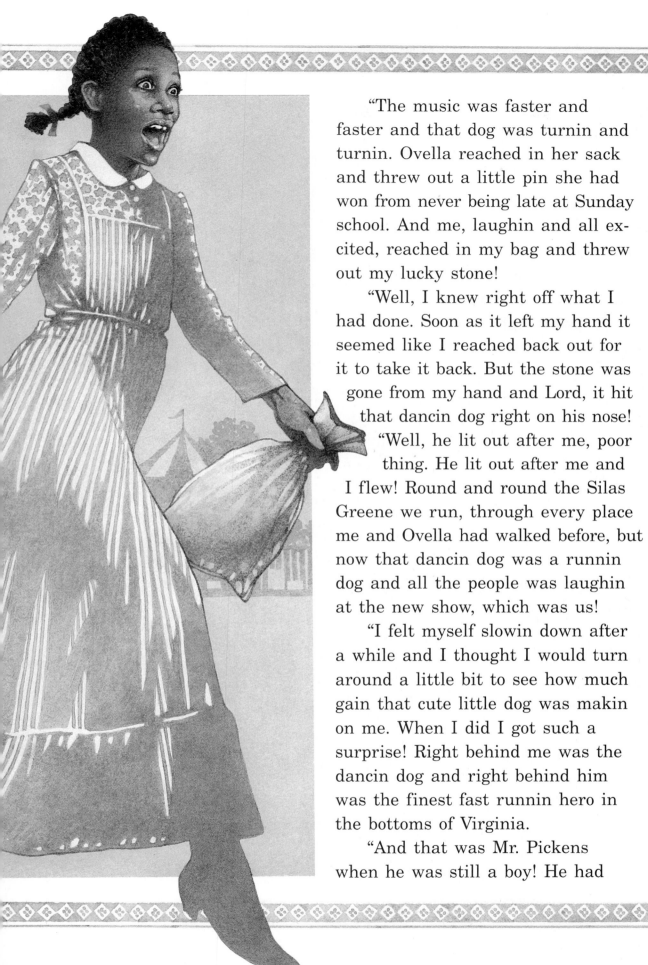

"The music was faster and faster and that dog was turnin and turnin. Ovella reached in her sack and threw out a little pin she had won from never being late at Sunday school. And me, laughin and all excited, reached in my bag and threw out my lucky stone!

"Well, I knew right off what I had done. Soon as it left my hand it seemed like I reached back out for it to take it back. But the stone was gone from my hand and Lord, it hit that dancin dog right on his nose!

"Well, he lit out after me, poor thing. He lit out after me and I flew! Round and round the Silas Greene we run, through every place me and Ovella had walked before, but now that dancin dog was a runnin dog and all the people was laughin at the new show, which was us!

"I felt myself slowin down after a while and I thought I would turn around a little bit to see how much gain that cute little dog was makin on me. When I did I got such a surprise! Right behind me was the dancin dog and right behind him was the finest fast runnin hero in the bottoms of Virginia.

"And that was Mr. Pickens when he was still a boy! He had

a length of twine in his hand and
he was twirlin it around in the air
just like the cowboy at the Silas
Greene and grinnin fit to bust.

"While I was watchin how the
sun shined on him and made him
look like an angel come to help a
poor sinner girl, why, he twirled
that twine one extra fancy twirl
and looped it right around one hind
leg of that dancin dog and brought
him low.

"I stopped then and walked slow
and shy to where he had picked up
that poor dog to see if he was hurt,
cradlin him and talkin to him soft
and sweet. That showed me how
kind and gentle he was, and when
we walked back to the dancin dog's
place in the show he let the dog
loose and helped me to find my
stone. I told him how shiny black
it was and how it had the letter *A*
scratched on one side. We searched
and searched and at last he spied it!

"Ovella and me lost heart for
shows then and we walked on
home. And a good little way, the
one who was gonna be your Great-
granddaddy was walkin on behind.
Seein us safe. Us walkin kind of
slow. Him seein us safe. Yes." Mrs.
Pickens' voice trailed off softly and

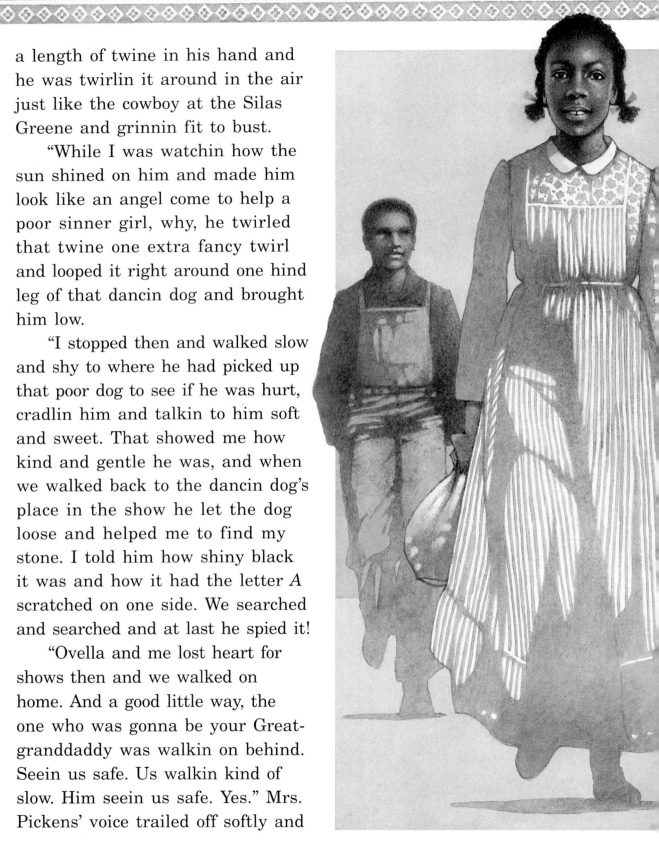

Tee noticed she had a little smile on her face.

"Grandmama, that stone almost got you bit by a dog that time. It wasn't so lucky that time, was it?"

Tee's Great-grandmother shook her head and laughed out loud.

"That was the luckiest time of all, Tee Baby. It got me acquainted with Mr. Amos Pickens, and if that ain't luck, what could it be! Yes, it was luckier for me than for anybody, I think. Least mostly I think it."

Tee laughed with her Great-grandmother though she didn't exactly know why.

"I hope I have that kind of good stone luck one day," she said.

"Maybe you will someday," her Great-grandmother said.

And they rocked a little longer and smiled together.

Children by a Brook, by the 19th Century painter, Francis Danby.

Grandmother's Brook

Grandmother tells me about a brook
    She used to pass on her way to school;
A quick, brown brook with a rushing sound,
    And moss-green edges, thick and cool.

When she was the age that I am now
    She would cross over it, stone by stone.
I like to think how she must have looked
    Under the greenery, all alone.

Sometimes I ask her: "Is it there,
    That brook you played by—the same, today?"
And she says she hasn't a doubt it is—
    It's children who change and go away.

RACHEL FIELD

Creation of a California Tribe

Grandfather's Maidu Indian Tales

Travis could see his grandfather from
a distance, as the older man leaned against a
giant oak tree in the front yard. Looking younger than
his sixty years, Grandfather was a wiry man
of average height. His black hair was still untouched
by gray. Grandfather was a Maidu Indian who was
greatly respected by the Maidu people. As a
tribal historian, Grandfather was the
keeper of their traditions. He was also a teacher of
the tribe's past here in California. He knew all
of the Maidu stories, and he often shared them
with his children and grandchildren.

BY LEE ANN SMITH-TRAFZER & CLIFFORD E. TRAFZER
ILLUSTRATED BY CLIFFORD BECK

The sky above Grandfather's head was deep blue, except for billowy white clouds forming around the Sierra Nevada Mountains. It was a beautiful fall day, but the wind had a touch of winter in it. Deep in thought, Travis pulled his jacket closer as he walked down the road to Grandfather's house. By the time he reached his grandfather, Travis knew exactly what he wanted to say.

"Hello, Grandfather!" the boy called out as he approached the gate. Grandfather raised his hand to wave in reply.

"Hello, Travis," he responded with his slight accent. "How was school today?"

Grandfather was always interested in his grandchildren's schoolwork, so his question was not a surprise to Travis. But today the boy was delighted to hear this familiar question. He explained to Grandfather that Ms. Smith, his fourth grade teacher at Newcastle Elementary School, had given the class a history assignment. The children had to write a paper on the history of California, and Travis really wanted Grandfather's help on this project.

"You know, Grandfather," Travis said, "most of the kids think that history began with the coming of the Spanish people and the missions." Grandfather nodded his head to show he understood. "But that's just not true! You are always telling us about our history, the history of the Maidu people. I want my paper to be different. I want to write about the time when no one lived in California except the Indians and the animal people."

Grandfather smiled his wide, toothy smile. "How can I help you, Travis?" he asked.

"I want to use what you have told me about the Maidu people to write my paper," Travis explained. "I've written a first draft of my paper. I used a story you told me about the creation of the land the Maidu lived on here in California. Can I read you this story?"

Grandfather nodded his head in agreement. The boy excitedly pulled out his white lined paper and began to read out loud.

People all over the earth have stories to explain the creation of the world. Maidu Indians have creation stories, too, and these stories are handed down by parents and grandparents to their children. To this very day the Maidu Indians remember these stories and share them with others.

The Maidu say that long ago the earth was filled with water. The blue water and sky blended together into a magnificent scene, melting together so that it was impossible to say where the water ended and the sky began. Earth Maker and Coyote floated about seeing nothing but sky and water. Earth Maker grew tired of floating and wanted to find a place to call his own. This idea impressed Coyote.

As Earth Maker and Coyote traveled in the water, they took turns singing a powerful song:

"Little world, where are you?
Little world, where are you?"

Over and over they sang this song. Eventually, it occurred to them that this song was not working. So Earth Maker and Coyote changed their song. Now they took turns singing:

"My world of great mountains, where are you?
My foggy mountains, where are you?"

Coyote grew tired and stopped singing these songs. "You can sing those power songs," he said to Earth Maker, "but I'm not going to sing any more."

Nevertheless, Earth Maker was convinced that one day they would find a country to call their own. When they did, they would arrange the land in a fine way! Meanwhile, they continued to float in the vast water.

Then one day, the travelers came upon another floating object. It looked like a bird's nest. Although it was very small, Earth Maker was convinced that he could transform it into a place for his country. The nest would have to be stretched and expanded if it were to become a country. Earth Maker thought about this for a long time. Then an idea struck him.

"I will take this strong rope," Earth Maker said to Coyote, "and extend it to the west, the north, and the northwest." Then Earth Maker went to work.

He extended the ropes to the west, the north, and the northwest, just as he had told Coyote he would. Then Earth Maker called upon the Robin to pack mud all around the nest. The Robin happily complied, singing a beautiful song of creation as she worked. It took many days for the Robin to complete her job, but she continued to sing until the land was finally made. If you listen today, the Robin still sings that wonderful creation song.

Earth Maker now asked Coyote to sing his creation song. Coyote sang a powerful song about the land he wanted created. Coyote sang in a loud voice:

"My world, where one will travel by the valley's edge, by great foggy mountains, by the zigzag paths through range after range. I sing of the country I shall travel in. In this world I shall wander."

This song was so beautiful that Earth Maker joined Coyote in chorus after chorus. Slowly, the Maidu world took shape. The only problem was that this world was very small.

Earth Maker decided to make the world larger, so he used his mighty foot to stretch the earth far to the east, the west, the north, and the south. In every direction the earth became larger. The movement and force of the stretching caused the mountains and the valleys to form. Although the Maidu world was becoming larger, it was not stable, because the earth rested on the various ropes.

"Now and then," Earth Maker warned, "when the ropes move back and forth, this earth will shake and tremble." Earth Maker was warning that earthquakes would shake the earth now and then.

Earth Maker was pleased with his country, but it was a lonely land because it was devoid of life. For this reason, he and Coyote created living things. Animals, plants, and human beings were formed and placed on the land. Coyote decided to paint the earth red, since blood was the life-giving source of humans and animals. Even today the rocks and soil of Maidu country are a little bit red in color.

Earth Maker and Coyote gave to human beings their separate lands, languages, and physical traits. Earth Maker traveled in every direction of the world, placing white people in one location, black people in another, Asians in still another, and so on. Earth Maker finally returned to his home at the center of the earth. This is where he placed the Maidu people.

When Earth Maker created human beings, he gave them intelligence, wisdom, and the means of survival. But most importantly to the Maidu Indians, he instructed them to be kind to one another and to be hospitable to strangers.

People all over the world have their own stories about the beginnings of this planet, as does each of the Indian tribes in America. This Maidu creation story is just one example of the rich variety of such stories. There are actually many other parts to the Maidu story of creation, but this is the main story about the origins of one California Indian tribe—the Maidu.

367

When Travis finished reading Grandfather his report, he waited for the older man to speak. The Maidu people teach their children to respect their elders and to have patience. Grandfather gazed off toward the Sierras, and his mind seemed to be miles away. Finally he turned his attention to Travis.

"Grandson," he said, "you have done well."

Travis smiled, feeling both pleased and relieved. He was happy that he had remembered the creation story accurately.

"You have captured on paper much of what we have taught through the spoken word for generations." Grandfather's face seemed to brighten with his smile. "Travis,

you have remembered the creation story well," he continued, placing his arm around the boy's shoulders. "I hope you will be able to share it with the other children in your class."

Although Grandfather said nothing more, Travis knew what he meant. He was pleased with the way his grandson had written the story. But Grandfather believed that it was especially important to tell the Maidu stories. Telling the stories, discussing them, and having the stories repeated time and again was the traditional way of passing on tribal history.

Grandfather and Travis walked together up the path by the large oak tree and into the older man's house. Grandfather's approval of the paper made Travis feel warm inside. He was looking forward to the next school day. Perhaps it would even be possible to tell the Maidu creation story to the rest of the class. Normally Travis would be scared to talk in front of the class, but Grandfather's pride in being a Maidu Indian made Travis proud, too. How nice it would be to share some of the Maidu tribal heritage with his friends at school!

Travis had not thought much about his paper on the Maidu creation story since he placed it on the teacher's desk. Then, nearly a week after he handed in the story, Ms. Smith announced that she had finished reading all of the papers.

"Overall I am very pleased," she said with a smile. "A few of the essays are really outstanding. I'm going to read a few of them to you now."

Travis's early interest in this project came rushing back to him as he listened to Ms. Smith. Despite Grandfather's urging, Travis had not asked Ms. Smith if he could read his story to the class. Travis was ashamed that he had not followed through with Grandfather's suggestion. Now the boy sat tensely in his seat, hoping that his would be one of the papers read by Ms. Smith. More than anything else, he wanted to be able to tell Grandfather that the children in his class had heard the Maidu creation story.

First, Ms. Smith read Emily Martinez's paper about the Gold Rush. Then she read Steve Foley's work about

modern day mountain men in California. Both of the papers were interesting, full of historical facts and funny little stories. As Travis listened to Ms. Smith read these papers, he sank sadly into his chair. Perhaps he had missed the point of the assignment! His paper wasn't about this kind of history at all. Travis was suddenly sure that he would receive a failing grade on this project.

Suddenly, Ms. Smith was talking about Travis. "Travis Molma has written a different type of history paper," she said. "He chose to share a part of his history and that of the Maidu Indians. It is an excellent report."

Travis felt as though every pair of eyes in the classroom were staring right at him. Since he was really only an average student, Travis wasn't used to this kind of attention in school.

"The Maidu Indians lived here long before anyone else," Ms. Smith continued. "Travis has written down what is called an oral history. Indians did not write down their stories, but kept them alive by passing them on from parents and grandparents to children."

A hand shot up in the front row. "But what if the kids forgot what their parents told them? Then the stories would be lost forever!"

"Well, the grown-ups didn't just tell them a story once. They would tell it over and over again, over a long period of time. Then, as the children got older, they would tell the stories back to the grown-ups. If a child made a mistake, he or she was corrected. Then they would tell the story again later. Isn't that right, Travis?"

Travis felt himself nod his head weakly in agreement.

"It is a very good way to teach. We do the same thing here at school. We talk about assignments in class so that you will think about and remember them."

Ms. Smith must have noticed that many of the students were losing interest, because she immediately began reading the Maidu creation story that Travis had written.

Grandfather would be pleased, Travis thought. The students were really listening to the story and seemed to be enjoying it. Most of the children had never before heard a story created by Indians to explain their past. When Ms. Smith finished reading Travis's paper, many of the students raised their hands to ask questions.

"Why did the Maidu Indians have this story?" Melissa asked.

Ms. Smith thought for a moment before answering. "That's not an easy question to answer," she began slowly. "I suppose everyone, including Indians, looks for ways to explain how the earth came to exist. This creation story is the Maidu Indian explanation." Ms. Smith hesitated, then looked at Travis. "What would you say, Travis?"

Holding onto the back of his chair for support, Travis stood up and faced the class. "My Grandfather has told my brothers, sisters, cousins, and me many Maidu stories," he said. "Grandfather says that these stories are the history of the Maidu people. The stories are literature, too. They tell us about ourselves, and they teach us how to think and live."

Travis was surprised to find that it was easy to talk to his class about Maidu Indian traditions. He explained that Grandfather had told him that the stories of the Maidu taught the difference between right and wrong, and between good and bad. In many of the stories the Earth Maker teaches the Maidu people what is good, but Coyote goes the other way. He is often bad, and the people are taught not to act like Coyote.

At this point Caitlin Riley said, "But I thought history had to come from something written down. Who wrote down the Maidu stories?"

"Many people believe that Indians had no history until things were written down," Travis responded. "But like Ms. Smith said, our way of passing down our stories is reliable, too."

This time Travis's friend Michael had a question. "I'm not sure I know how the Maidu Indians lived. I mean, what did they eat and what kind of houses did they live in? Could you tell us, Travis?"

Grandfather had told Travis all about how the Maidu Indians had lived. "The Maidu ate fruits, vegetables, and meat just like we do today," he said. "Women gathered wild strawberries, blackberries, and currants. The Maidu ate these fruits fresh, but they also dried them in the sun so they could eat them in winter, too. All they had to do was add some water and they could be eaten.

"The Maidu also ate wild lettuce and carrots. They gathered roots of the tule and camas. These looked and tasted something like potatoes, and had lots of vitamin C."

"Didn't they do any hunting?" one of the boys asked.

"Sure," Travis said. "They hunted deer, bear, quail, rabbits, raccoons, squirrels, geese, and porcupine. The Indians didn't just use the meat from the animal, though. For example, they used animal skins for blankets and clothing. Porcupine spines were used for needles and to make jewelry."

One of the students asked if the Maidu lived in tipis like Indians they had seen on television.

"No," Travis said, shaking his head. "They lived in different kinds of houses. When the Maidu moved around hunting and gathering food, they built temporary homes made out of logs and brush mats. When they made their winter homes, they used the same materials but made their houses larger and warmer. Grandfather told me that the people spent a lot of the winter months inside, where they told stories.

"In fact, it was during the cold, rainy winter months that Grandfather's parents and grandparents had told him the Maidu Indian stories. After hearing the stories repeated over and over, Grandfather was able to learn his lessons very well."

Ms. Smith stood up at her desk. "You know, Travis," she said, "I think you have learned your lessons well, too. Thank you for teaching us so much about the Maidu Indians."

To Travis's surprise, Ms. Smith began to clap her hands, and the rest of the class joined in, too! Travis couldn't wait to tell his grandfather that the other children had enjoyed hearing the Maidu creation story.

As the bell rang to signal the end of the school day, Ms. Smith came over to Travis's desk to speak to him. "Please give this note to your grandfather," she said, handing him a folded piece of paper. "I just want him to know how much we enjoyed learning about Maidu history. Perhaps he would visit our class one day and share more of his stories."

Later Grandfather said he was proud of his grandson for speaking in class. But everything Travis told his classmates came from his grandfather. One day, Travis thought, he would tell these same things to his own children.

Meet Lee Ann Smith-Trafzer and Clifford E. Trafzer

Clifford Trafzer's advice to young people who want to write is, "Write what you know. And write." Trafzer has followed his own advice. Part Wyandot Indian, he studies and teaches about Native Americans. Along with his wife, Lee Ann Smith-Trafzer, he also writes about them.

In books like *Grandmother's Christmas Story: A True Quechan Indian Story*, Clifford Trafzer, under the pen name Richard Red Hawk, retells Native American stories. Many of them have been handed down for generations.

"We want to share stories told to us by elders. We want to preserve them for our children and all children," says Lee Ann Smith-Trafzer, who worked with her husband on *Creation of a California Tribe: Grandfather's Maidu Indian Tales.* "We want to capture the rich traditions of America's first people." Smith-Trafzer grew up listening to the oral traditions of her own family. She wove these stories into a book, *Making Tracks: A Photo-Cultural History of an Arkansas Farm Family.*

Native American stories may be funny, sad, or exciting, but they often have deep meaning as well. By reading and listening to the stories, we can learn to appreciate the heritage of Native Americans.

Some readers may be surprised by how much they have in common with the characters in these stories. In *Creation of a California Tribe: Grandfather's Maidu Indian Tales*, Clifford Trafzer says, Travis is like "every young person who wants to know about his or her own history."

377

WOMEN OF OUR TIME

LAURA INGALLS WILDER
GROWING UP IN THE LITTLE HOUSE

BY PATRICIA REILLY GIFF
ILLUSTRATED BY EILEEN McKEATING

**Laura Ingalls Wilder:
Growing Up in the
Little House**

by Patricia Reilly Giff
illustrated by
Eileen McKeating
Puffin, 1988

Laura began her book.
"Once upon a time, sixty
years ago," she wrote
across the pad, "a little
girl lived in the Big Woods
of Wisconsin, in a little
gray house made of logs."

HOME SWEET HOME

The Best Town in the World
by Byrd Baylor
illustrated by
Ronald Himler
Scribners, 1982

My father said it was the best town in the world and he just happened to be born there. How's that for being lucky?

The IRA Children's Book Award is presented annually to two new authors who show the most promise in writing for children. *No Star Nights* was the 1990 winner in the younger readers category.

By Anna Egan Smucker
Paintings by Steve Johnson

NO STAR NIGHTS

When I was little, we couldn't see the stars in the nighttime sky because the furnaces of the mill turned the darkness into a red glow. But we would lie on the hill and look up at the sky anyway and wait for a bright orange light that seemed to breathe in and out to spread across it. And we would know that the golden spark-spitting steel was being poured out of giant buckets into molds to cool.

Then we would look down on a train pulling cars
mounted with giant thimbles rocking back and forth.
They were filled with fiery hot molten slag that in the
night glowed orange. And when they were dumped,
the sky lit up again.

A loud steam whistle that echoed off the hills
announced the change of shifts, and hundreds of men

streamed out of the mill's gates. Everyone's dad worked in the mill, and carried a tin lunchbox and a big metal thermos bottle.

Work at the mill went on night and day. When Dad worked night shift, we children had to whisper and play quietly during the day so that we didn't wake him up. His job was too dangerous for him to go without sleep. He operated a crane that lifted heavy ingots of steel into a pit that was thousands of degrees hot.

When Dad worked the three-to-eleven shift, Mom made dinner early so we could all eat together. She made the best stuffed cabbage of anyone in the neighborhood. We sometimes tried to help fold the cabbage leaves around the meat and rice like she did, but our cabbage leaves always came unrolled.

During the school year days went by when we didn't see Dad at all because he was either at work or sleeping. When he changed shifts from daylight to night and back again it took him a while to get used to the different waking and sleeping times. We called these his grumpy times. We liked it best when he had daylight hours to spend with us. We played baseball until it was too dark to see the ball.

On a few very special summer afternoons he would load us all into the car for a hot, sweaty trip to Pittsburgh and a doubleheader Pirates game at Forbes Field. We sat in the bleachers way out in left field, eating popcorn and drinking lemonade that we brought from home, yelling our heads off for the Pirates. Our brother always wore his baseball glove, hoping to catch a foul ball that might come into the stands. Dad helped us mark our scorecards and bought us hot dogs during the seventh-inning stretch.

On our way home we passed the black silhouettes of Pittsburgh's steel mills, with their great heavy clouds of smoke billowing from endless rows of smokestacks. The road wound along as the river wound, and between us and the river were the mills, and on the other side of the road were the hills—the river, the mills, and the hills. And we sang as we rode home, "She'll be comin' round the mountain when she comes . . ."

July was just about the best month of the year. Everyone who worked in the mill got their vacation pay

then. We called it Christmas in July. All the stores had big sales. Even though it wasn't really Christmas, we each got a present.

And the Fourth of July parade was something everyone looked forward to. We were busy for weeks making flowers out of Kleenex to cover our Girl Scout float.

Some of our friends took baton lessons and were part of a marching unit called the Steel Town Strutters. They wore shiny black-and-gold-spangled leotards and threw their batons high up into the air and caught them! Something we sure couldn't do. But our favorites were the baby strutters. Some of them were only two years old. They did a good job just carrying their batons.

With all the bands and fire engines and floats, the parade
went on and on. There were convertibles with beauty queens
sitting on the back. Members of the Kennel Club marched
their dogs in circles and figure eights. Kids rode bikes
decorated with colored crepe paper, flags, and balloons.
The mayor drove an old-fashioned car, and his children
threw bubblegum and candies into the crowds.

We went to school across from the mill. The smokestacks towered above us and the smoke billowed out in great puffy clouds of red, orange, and yellow, but mostly the color of rust. Everything—houses, hedges, old cars—was a rusty red color. Everything but the little bits of graphite, and they glinted like silver in the dust. At recess when the wind whirled these sharp, shiny metal pieces around, we girls would crouch so that our skirts touched the ground and kept our bare legs from being stung.

We would squint our eyes when the wind blew to keep the graphite out. Once a piece got caught in my eye, and no matter how much I blinked or how much my eye watered it wouldn't come out. When the eye doctor finally took it out and showed it to me, I was amazed that a speck that small could feel so big.

We played on the steep street that ran up the hill beside our school. Our favorite game was dodge ball. The kids on the bottom row knew they had to catch the ball. If they didn't, it would roll down onto the busy county road that ran in front of the school. Too often a truck carrying a heavy roll of steel would run over it and with a loud *bang* the ball would be flattened.

The windows in our school were kept closed to try to keep the graphite and smoke out. On really windy

days we could hear the dry, dusty sound of grit hitting
against the glass. Dusting the room was a daily job. The
best duster got to dust the teacher's desk with a soft white
cloth and a spray that made the whole room smell like lemons.
It was always a mystery to us how the nuns who were our
teachers could keep the white parts of their habits so clean.

Some days it seemed as though there was a giant lid covering the valley, keeping the smoke in. It was so thick you couldn't see anything clearly. On days like that I felt as if we were living in a whirling world of smoke.

The road we took home from school went right through part of the mill. Tall cement walls with strands of barbed wire

at the top kept us on the sidewalk and out of the mill. But when we got to the bridge that spanned the railroad tracks, there was just a steel mesh fence. From there we could look straight down into the mill! There was always something wonderful to watch. Through a huge open doorway we could see the mammoth open-hearth furnace. A giant ladle would tilt to give the fiery furnace a "drink" of orange, molten iron. Sometimes we would see the golden, liquid steel pouring out the bottom of the open hearth into enormous bucketlike ladles. The workers were just small dark figures made even smaller by the great size of the ladles and the furnace. The hot glow of the liquid steel made the dark mill light up as if the sun itself was being poured out. And standing on the bridge we could feel its awful heat.

Warning sirens and the toots of steam whistles, the screeching sounds of train wheels and the wham-wham of cars being coupled and uncoupled—all these sounds surrounded us as we stood on the bridge. From the other side we could look into another part of the mill. Rows of lights hung from girders across the ceiling. White-hot steel bars glided smoothly over rollers on long tables. Men were using torches on the big slabs of steel. The torches gave off streaks of

burning, white light and showers of sparks that looked like our Fourth of July sparklers.

Behind the mill rose huge piles of black shiny coal and rich red iron ore, and a hill of rusting scrap metal. A crane that to us looked like a dinosaur with huge jaws was constantly at work picking up twisted, jagged pieces of metal and dropping them into railroad cars to be taken into the mill. Sometimes we would imagine that the mill itself was a huge beast, glowing hot, breathing heavily, always hungry, always needing to be fed. And we would run home, not stopping once to look back over our shoulders.

Not too far from our house was a hill made of boulders of slag from the mill. Our grandfather told us that long ago it had been a deep ravine. Over the years truckload after truckload of slag from the mill had been dumped into it until the hole had become a hill. Now it towered over the old houses that were near it.

For an adventure, my best friend and I once decided to climb the slag hill. We slipped and slid and sent the pitted rocks rolling down as we scrambled up. Our younger sisters spied us, by now near the top, and started climbing too. It was then that my friend and I saw the dump truck with a heavy load of slag from the mill slowly winding its way up the hill.

"Don't dump! Don't dump!" we screamed. But the deep
engine sounds of the truck straining under its great load
drowned out our cries. Chunks of slag fell onto the roadway.
The truck backed onto the flat place to dump its load.
Stumbling toward it, we waved our arms and screamed

again, "Don't dump! Please don't dump! Our sisters are down
there!" The driver finally heard us, and leaning out the window of the cab he saw the little girls. He nodded and waved
his hand, then the truck lurched forward back onto the road
and disappeared around the curve.

We sank exhausted to the ground, our hearts pounding
in our ears. The roar of the truck's engine became fainter
and fainter. The sky around us was turning red and orange
and gold. We looked down on the mill that seemed to go

on forever into the valley. From its long straight row of stacks, clouds of orange smoke swirled into the colors of the sunset. In the distance a whistle blew.

Many years have passed since then, and now the slag hill is covered with grasses and blackberry bushes and sumac trees. The night sky is clear and star filled because the mill is shut down. The big buckets no longer pour the hot, yellow steel. The furnaces whose fires lit up everything are rusting and cold.

Not many children live in the town now. Most of the younger people have moved away to other places to find work. The valley's steelworking way of life is gone forever. But whenever the grandchildren come back to visit, they love more than anything else to listen to stories about the days when all night long the sky glowed red.

MEET ANNA EGAN SMUCKER

Ever since she was a child, Anna Egan Smucker has been enchanted by books and writing. "I love words and how they strike you," she says. Today she works with words, teaching writing to West Virginia schoolchildren. Writing, Smucker believes, comes "from within," and our experiences allow us to write about anything.

No Star Nights came from her memories of growing up in Weirton, West Virginia, a steel mill town along the Ohio River. "I wrote the story when mills were closing all around the Pittsburgh area to try to preserve what I remembered about growing up in a steel mill town," she explains.

MEET STEVE JOHNSON

Steve Johnson never lets readers forget the steel mill's importance in *No Star Nights*. He never saw Weirton's steel mills, but he was able to imagine the reddish smoky skies. Here's what helped him: While he was preparing the paintings for the book, forest fires raged in Yellowstone. The smoke was carried to Minnesota, where he lives, and colored the air.

No Star Nights is Johnson's first picture book for children.

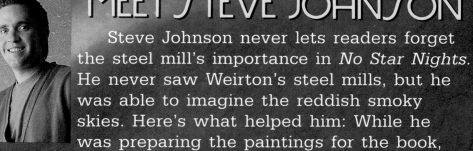

Can you guess what these are? Take a careful look. Then turn the book upside down. You might have one or two more modern ones in your own home!

FIRST THINGS FIRST

Would you believe that a motorcycle could run on wooden wheels? In the late 1800s, people were amazed by this strange, motorized machine.

Alexander Graham Bell used clock springs and magnets in his invention, the telephone. It was the first instrument that used electricity to send sounds over a distance.

Made in Germany in 1885, the pocket sewing machine stood only eight inches (twenty centimeters) high. It was attached to a table and operated by hand.

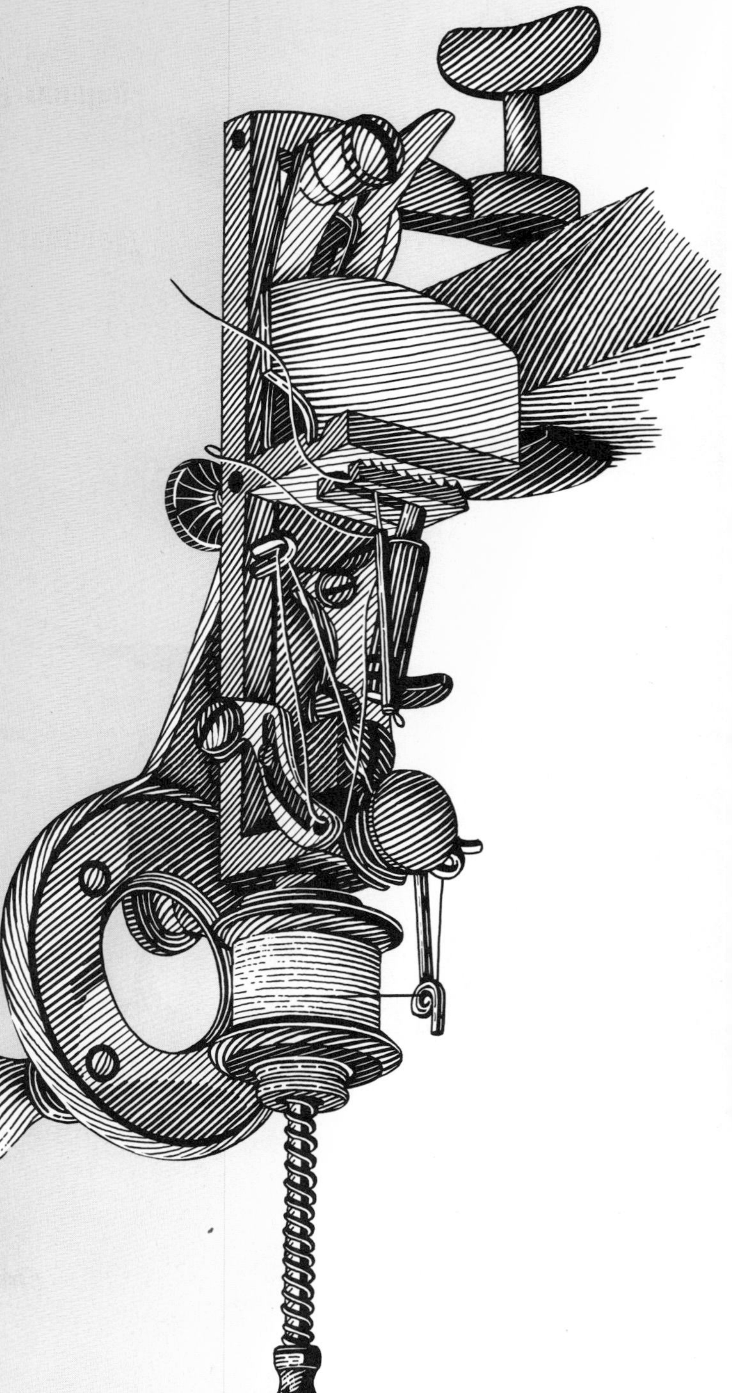

An early refrigerator, or icebox, contained a tin-lined compartment that held a block of ice. The ice was delivered several times a week.

That Was Summer

Have you ever smelled summer?
Sure you have.
Remember that time
When you were tired of running
Or doing nothing much
And you were hot
And you flopped right down on the ground?
Remember how the warm soil smelled—
And the grass?
That was summer.

Remember that time
When the storm blew up quick
And you stood under a ledge
And watched the rain till it stopped
And when it stopped
You walked out again to the sidewalk,
The quiet sidewalk?
Remember how the pavement smelled—
All steamy warm and wet?
That was summer.

Remember that time
When you were trying to climb
Higher in the tree
And you didn't know how
And your foot was hurting in the fork
But you were holding tight
To the branch?
Remember how the bark smelled then—
All dusty dry, but nice?
That was summer.

If you try very hard,
Can you remember that time
When you played outside all day
And you came home for dinner
And had to take a bath right away,
Right away?
It took you a long time to pull
Your shirt over your head.
Do you remember smelling the sunshine?
That was summer.

Marci Ridlon

407

ᐅᐱᐅᖅᑕᖅᑐᒥ

ARCTIC

Written and Illustrated by
NORMEE EKOOMIAK

Normee Ekoomiak is an Inuit artist from northern Quebec. He grew up in the Inuit settlement of Fort George, on James Bay, living the traditional life of his people. Although hearing-impaired, Normee Ekoomiak has not forgotten the

ᐃᖃᐅᒪᓂᖅ

MEMORIES

sounds of his happy days in the settlement. With his pictures and words he keeps the sounds and sights alive.

NORTHWEST TERRITORIES

Hudson Bay

MANITOBA

James Bay ● Fort George

ONTARIO

QUEBEC

NEW FOUNDLAND

CANADA

UNITED STATES OF AMERICA

Ottawa ●

Toronto ●

ATLANTIC OCEAN

NDRMEE EKOOMIAK.

ᐃᕝᓗ ᐃᓗᐊᓂ

ᓄᑕᖄᕐᔪᖕᒃᖑᓪᓗᖕ ᐃᕝᓗᒥᕐᔪᖁᓯᒋᐅᑉᖑᓗ ᐅᑭᐅᖅᑎᓐᒍ
ᐊᒪᓗ ᐅᑭᐅᖁᑦᑕᓂᕐᖑᓛᑦ ᑐᐱᕐᔪᑎᒃᖁᓘᑦ.
ᐃᕝᓗᓴᐅᑉᖄᑦ ᐃᕐᑐᐊᖁᑦᑐᑉᖑᖢᓂᒃ ᐊᐳᕐᖓᑦ.
ᐅᑭᐅᖅᑕᖅᒥ ᓯᐱᔪᖅᑐᖄ ᐅᑭᐅᕐᑉ. ᐃᕐᒥᓇᖢᓂ
ᐊᒪᓗ Ċᖁᓯᓂ. ᓯᐅᖓ ᑕᑦᖅᑎᑕᖄᑦ ᑭᕐᐊᓂ
ᐅᐱᑲᕐᔪᑲᖢᕝᒃ, ᖃᑐᓚᔪᐊᖃᖢᓂ ᐅᓇᓄᖅᑕᓄᖄᑦ
ᐅᑭᐅᖁᑦᑕᖄᑦ ᐊᓄᓕᖅᑲᕐᖓᒃ ᑭᕐᐊᖑ ᐱᑎᓇᖅᑕᔫᑦ
ᖁᑎᖃᖢᒋᓓ ᐃᕝᓗ ᐃᓗᐊᓂ. ᐅᔭᖄ ᐊᒐᒃ ᓇᖑᕐᐊᕐᒥᖑᖅ
ᐅᖕᓯᒋᑦ ᓇᖑᕐᐊᕐᐃᓂᖅ ᓄᐅᐱᖅᑕᐅᕐᖑᔭᖄᕐᓂᖑᖅ. ᐅᔭᖄᑦ
ᐊᓇᓇ ᒥᖁᖅᑐᖅ ᓇᓰᐅᑦ ᐊᕐᒦᓂᖕ ᑐᐱᓕᑕᐳᕐᓴᖓ.
ᐅᖃᐅᔨᓇᖕᓂᓂ ᑕᐊᖅᑲᖄᑦ Ċᖓ ᑐᐱᖅ. ᐃᕝᓗ ᐃᓗᐊᓂ
ᖅᑯᓕᖅᖅ ᓂᐅᖅᑲᖅᖑᖅ ᐱᖕᓕᕐᓂᖅ. Ċᖓᓕ ᑕᐊᖅᑲᖄᑦ
ᖅᑯᓕᖅᖅ ᐊᒪᓗ ᐅᐱᓇᖅĊᖅᑲᖢᓄᑦ ᓇᕐᓯᕐᒃ.
ᓯᓇᖕᑎᓇᖅᑕ ᖅᑯᓕᖅᖅ ᖃᒻᑕᑕᐅᕐᑲᖢᓄᑦ ᐃᕝᓗ
ᐅᖅᑯᐊᑎᕐᐊᑕᖢᕝᔪᖄᑦ. ᖃᐱᐅᖅᑯᑕᓄᑦ ᔪᖕᑦ ᐊᕐᒥᖑᓄᑦ ᑖᐅᕐᐊ
ᐅᖕᑯᒍᑦ ᓄᑕᖕᑦ ᐅᖅᖑᓇᖣᕐᒥᑦ ᐃᖓᖅᕕᑦ ᓯᖃᐊᒪᕐᒐ
ᐊᕝᕆᖃᕐᓇᖕᓂ ᐊᖁᐊᖕᓄᖅᑕᖤᓄᑦ.

IN THE IGLU

"Iglu" means house. When I was small, we used to live in a snow house in the winter and in a tent the rest of the year. During the long winter up North, there is little sun and it is always dark. We stay inside and do our work and play. Here the father is carving a soapstone sculpture for sale at the co-op. The mother is sewing together seal skins to cover a tent. When it starts to get warm, the snow house will melt. We will build a tent to live in, and we will move with it from place to place when we hunt for food. Inside the iglu there is an oil lamp on three legs. It is for light and for heat. But when we go to sleep, we put out the lamp, and then it gets cold, so we must all sleep together to keep warm. The kids sleep in the middle, between their parents.

ᖅᑎᒃᑐᑦ ᐊᒥᐅᕙᐱᕐᓂᕐᒥ

ᖅᑎᒍᒪᒌᑦᑫᖁᔪᑦ ᓯᓛᒥ. ᑕᕝᕓ ᐊᑕᑕᖕ ᖅᑎᖅᑕᑐᕆᕐᕿ
ᐸᓂᖕᒥᓂᖕ ᐊᒻᓗ ᐱᖕᒃᔨᑦ ᐃᓂᓂᖕᑎᖕ ᐊᒥᐅᕙᐱᕐᓂᕐᒥ.
ᓯᓚᒥ ᖅᑎᖕᑳᕿᑯᑦᖄᐃᑦ ᑎᒃᑎᖕ ᖂᓄᖕ ᐃᖕᓂᖅᓴᕆᐊᖅᖅᖅᓐᓂᓄᖕᑦ
ᐊᒻᓗ ᐸᖕᑦᒐᖕᑌᓗᓄ.

ᐃᖕᓄᖕᖕᑐᓐ ᐊᐳᕐᑦ ᐅᕐᓴᑎᐊᕐᑐᖕ ᐃᓄᐊᓂ.
ᐱᖕᕆᐊᖕᖕᖕᑦᖕᑦ ᐊᐳᑕᖕᓴᓄᒍ ᕑᖃ ᑭᕿᐊᓂ ᐊᓄᓇᖕᑐᖕ.

PLAYING ON A SNOWBANK

We love to go outside and play. Here three boys and a girl are playing with their father on a snowbank. They all slide down, and then race to get back to the top and do it all over again.

Inside an iglu there is not very much space. You cannot stay inside for a long time, not even during a snowstorm. But if you go outside to play, then your body will always be healthy and normal.

Also, someone has to go outside the iglu after a snowstorm to dig the people out.

ᓯᑯᒥ ᐃᖃᓗᑕᕐᓂᖅ

ᐃᓗᐊᓂᒃᑦ ᐱᖅᓯᐊᓂᖃᖅᓯᒃ ᐅᒪᔭᑦ ᑕᑯᐊ ᑐᑐᐊᑦ, ᓇᐅᑦ
ᐊᒻᒪᓗ ᐊᐃᐱᑦ ᓇᓂᓯᓂᖅ ᐊᕐᓱᐊᖅᑐᐊᑦ. ᓂᖃᓚᖅᑎᒍ
ᑭᕐᐊᓂ ᐱᑕᖅᓱᕼᓱᖕᑦ ᐃᖃᓗᖅᑑᓚᖅᑐᒍᑦ.
ᐊᖢᐊᑕᐅᖅᑕᓚᑕᐅᖅᐸᑦ ᐃᖃᓗᖕᓲᖅᑲᓗᖕᓂᖅ ᐃᖃᓗᖅᐱᓐᓱᓂᑦ.

ᐊᖅᓇᓗᖅ ᑕᖅᓇᓗᖅ ᐊᒪᖓᓂᑦ ᒃᓚᕐᓱ
ᐃᖃᓗᖅᓯᐊᖅᓴᐊᕙᖅᓗᖅ. ᑭᕐᐊᓂ ᐃᓗᐊᓂᒃᑦ
ᐃᖃᓗᖅᓱᕼᓇᓱᖅ.

ᐅᒪᕈᖅᐹᓄᖃᖅᓱᑦ ᓂᖃᖅᓱᖅᓯᑎᓂᖕ ᓄᐿᒦᒃ
ᑐᐱᖅᔭᐅᖅᑎᓇᐊᖅᑕᓚᖅᐸᑦᑐᒍᑦ. ᐊᖅᑐᓇᐼᐿᑦ ᓯᓚᑐᖅᓕᓄᑦ
ᖃᑐᕙᐴᖅᔭᑦ ᓇᓂᒪᖕᒃᑦ ᐅᒪᕐᐊᑦ.

ICE FISHING

After a snowstorm it is hard to
find caribou and seal and walrus.
All of the birds and animals are
gone. Sometimes months go by
before they come back. So the
whole family has to go out fishing,
to catch the arctic char, through
holes in the ice. Sedna is good,
and she makes sure there are
plenty of fish. But sometimes it
is hard to catch any fish, and
the birds and animals stay away
for a long time. Then the people
must move to a new camp if they
are strong enough. Or else they
will starve.

NORMEE EKOOMIAK

ᐅᖅᑯᐊᖅ

ᓇᓂᑦᓯᓇᑲᖅᑲᑕ ᓂᕐᔪᑎᑦ ᓂᕿᑐᑎᒃᓴᑉᑎᖕᓂ ᐊᖑᓇᓱᒃᑎᐊᕙᑐᑦ ᕐᑭᓂᕐᐸᒃᑐᐃᑦ ᐊᖑᓇᓱᒃᑎᐊᕙᐅᔪᒥᓇᕐᑐᓂ. ᑕᖅᒪᑐᐃᓐᓇᕐᓂᐊᕋᖅᑲᒥᒃ ᐃᒡᓗᓕᐅᕐᐸᒃᑐᑦ ᓯᓚᑦᓴᐅᖏᑐᐊᓇᐊᕋᖅᑲᑦ ᐃᒡᓗᓕᐅᕐᐸᒃᑐᑦ, ᑭᓯᐊᓂ ᓯᓚᐅᑦᓴᐅᔭᕋᖅᑲᑦ ᐅᕐᑯᐊᓕᐅᑐᐃᓐᓇᕐᓗᑎᒃ ᓴᓇᕙᒃᑐᑦ ᐊᐳᒻᒥᑦ.

ᓇᓂᓯᔭᕋᖅᑲᒥᒃ ᑐᐱᕐᕕᒃᓴᑦᓯᐊᒥᒃ ᐅᑎᕐᓗᑎᒃ ᐃᓚᒥᓄᑦ ᐅᖅᑲᓇᐊᑐᕐᐸᒃᑐᑦ ᒪᑦᑐᑦ ᐊᒡᒐᐃᑦ ᑕᒪᓂᕋᓚᒃ ᐃᓄᐃᑦ ᑐᐱᖅᑲᑎᒋᔫᑦ.

THE SHELTER

When it is hard to find animals and fish for food, then the two best hunters in the village go out to look for a better place. At the end of the day, they build a shelter for the night. If the weather is bad, they build a whole iglu. But when the weather is not bad, all they need is a windbreak made of two layers of snow blocks. At the end of the next day they build another shelter. This goes on every day until the hunters find a good spot for a new village. Then they go back home, and soon the other Inuit, ten or twenty people, will move to a new place.

ᖁᐱᖕᒧᑦ   ᐃᕐᕈᑦᕐᑕᐅᓂᖅ

ᖁᐱᖕᒧᑦ ᐃᕐᕈᑦᕐᑕᐅᓂᖅ ᖁᐱᐊᓇᕐᒧᑦ. ᑕᕝᕙ ᑕᖄ ᓂᐱᐊᕐᔪᖅ ᖁᐱᖕᒧᑦ ᐃᕐᕈᑦᕐᑕᐅᖁᖅ.
ᐊᓄᕆᖃᑦᑐᖅ ᓄᖕᒥᓄᑦ. ᑕᖄ ᖁᑎᐅᒻᔮᖅ ᓄᑦᕐᓄᑦ ᐱᔪᖕᓇᐅᕐᑐᖅ ᑭᕆᖓ ᖁᐱᐊᓇᐳᑕᐅᒍᐃᐊᕐᑐᖅ.

BLANKET-TOSS GAME

Blanket tossing is great fun. Here a girl is being tossed
up in the air. The wind is blowing through her long hair. This
game makes the children stronger, but it is just for fun, to
have a good time.

ᐊᔭᒐᖅ

ᐃᓄᐃᑦ ᐊᔭᒐᕈᒪᑦᑕᖅᑐᐃᑦ ᓱᓇᑐᐃᓐᓇᕐᓂᑦ ᐊᒻᒪᓗ ᐆᒪᔪᖑᐊᕐᓂᑦ ᐊᒃᓗᓴᒥᑦ. ᑕᒃᑯᓂ ᐊᔾᔨᒥᑦ ᐊᔭᒐᑎᐊᕆᔪᐃᑦ ᖃᔭᕐᒥᑦ. 22-ᖑᓇᕐᓗᓂ ᐊᔭᒐᑎᐊᓚᒃ ᑭᓯᐊᓂ ᐃᓄᒃᑐᐃᑦ ᐱᐊᓚᓂᖕᓴᐅᔪᐃᑦ ᐊᑯᓂᐅᓗᐊᖕᖏᑐᒥᑦ ᐱᐊᓂᒍᓴᒪᕐᑐᑦ. 200-ᓂᑦ ᐊᔾᔨᖕᖏᑐᐃᑦ ᖃᓄᐃᑦᑐᑐᐃᓐᓇᕐᓂᑦ ᐊᒻᒪᓗ ᕿᑎᒐᒃᓴᑦ ᐊᔭᒐᕐᑕᖅᑐᑦ.

THE STRING GAME

The Inuit like to make figures of things and animals with string. In this picture the boys are getting ready to make the shape of a kayak. It will take twenty-two separate steps, but the boys' fingers will move quickly and it won't take them long. In all, the people have over two hundred shapes to make and games to play with string.

ᒐᐳᕐᑎᐅᐸ ᐱᓂ%ᑲ

ᑕ°ᓇ ᒥ%ᕐᑕᐅᐸ<ᕐ ᓂ∧%ᕕᕐᑕ⊲% ᑐᓂᕐᕈᐅᖃᑦᑫ−ᔪ ᐃ−ᓄᖃᖃᑦᓂᓐ ᐅᑭᐅ%ᑕ%ᒥᒐᑕᓐᕐ ᑕᕐᓘ%ᑭ
ᒐᐳᕐᑎᒍᑦ 100−ᓂᑦ ᐊ−ᓪᑕᐅᓂᖁᒃ. ⊲ᕐᕈᕐᑐᐃᑦ ᑲᓴᕝᑦ ᑎᕝᕐ⊲ᑦ ᑐᑭᖃ%ᒍᑦ ⊲ᕐᕈᕐᑐᐃᑦ
ᕒᓇᖃᑐ∆ᓇᐃᑦ ∆ᓄᐃᑦ ᐅᑭᐅ%ᑕ%ᒍᒥ ⊲ᒥ⊲ᓚᑲ−ᖃᖃᑲᓂᓇᖃᕝᑦ ᑲᒍᕐᒥ⊲ᓯᔪᕐᓄ ᒐᐳᕐᑎᒥᓐ ⊲ᒪᓗ
%ᑯ∧⊲ᕈᑲᕐᒍᔍᕐᓄ. ᑕ°ᓇᔍ ᐅᖃᐱ ᐅᐃᒪᐃᖑᕈᑯᕐ%ᒍ%᎐ ᒐᐳᕐᑎᒐᓐᕐ, ᐅᖃᐸᐅᕐ ᐱᓂ%ᑲ, ᑕᐅᔍᖁᖅᖅ
ᐊᓂᒍᑕ∆ᓇᕐᓂᓐᕐ ⊲ᒪᓗ ᕒᓇᓂᖃᖃᓂᓐᕐ.

THE SPIRIT OF LIBERTY

I made this wall hanging as a gift from the native
people of North America when the Statue of Liberty was
one hundred years old. The different-colored geese flying
by stand for all of the races of man. They have all come to
North America to enjoy liberty and happiness. Watching over
them and the Statue of Liberty is Okpik, the spirit owl, who
sees everywhere and who sees everything.

MEET
NORMEE EKOOMIAK

Normee Ekoomiak, who wrote and made the illustrations for *Arctic Memories,* is an Inuit from northern Quebec in Canada. In his language, Inuktitut, the word *Inuit* means "people." Ekoomiak describes where he was born as "a place of magic."

Normee Ekoomiak grew up in his grandfather's tent, which had a wooden frame and was covered in canvas and seal skins. In this tent lived Normee, his parents, his six brothers, and his seven sisters. His grandfather taught him how to do felt appliqué and wool embroidery. Ekoomiak used his skill and talent to make wall hangings, some of which appear in the book. He also learned how to paint and draw.

The author and artist remembers his early life well, and through his art everybody is able to share in the traditional life of the Inuit.

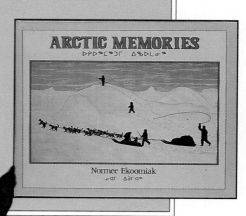

417

Memory

Memory is a tape recorder
And there's one in every head
Storing everything we've ever seen,
Or felt, or heard, or said.
The word, remember, simply means
We're playing back a part
Of all that's been recorded there
And lives close to our heart.
Sad thing, sweet thing,
Whatever it be,
The calling it back is a
Memory.

Mary O'Neill

PAR AVION
VIA AIR MAIL
VIA AEREA

POCKET MEMO

70 Sheets

CONTENTS

TWICE UPON A TIME

GOOD BOOKS, GOOD TIMES!

Good books.
Good times.
Good stories.
Good rhymes.
Good beginnings.
Good ends.
Good people.
Good friends.
Good fiction.
Good facts.
Good adventures.
Good acts.
Good stories.
Good rhymes.
Good books.
Good times.

LEE BENNETT HOPKINS

423

Yeh-Shen

A Cinderella Story from China

This story is older
than the Cinderella story as most
people know it. It predates
all European versions of the story by
at least 800 years.

retold by Ai-Ling Louie
illustrated by
Ed Young

425

In the dim past, even before the Ch'in and the Han dynasties, there lived a cave chief of southern China by the name of Wu. As was the custom in those days, Chief Wu had taken two wives. Each wife in her turn had presented Wu with a baby daughter. But one of the wives sickened and died, and not too many days after that Chief Wu took to his bed and died too.

Yeh-Shen, the little orphan, grew to girlhood in her stepmother's home. She was a bright child and lovely too, with skin as smooth as ivory and dark pools for eyes. Her stepmother was jealous of all this beauty and goodness, for her own daughter was not pretty at all. So in her displeasure, she gave poor Yeh-Shen the heaviest and most unpleasant chores.

The only friend that Yeh-Shen had to her name was a fish she had caught and raised. It was a beautiful fish with golden eyes, and every day it would come out of the water and rest its head on the bank of the pond, waiting for Yeh-Shen to feed it. Stepmother gave Yeh-Shen little enough food for

427

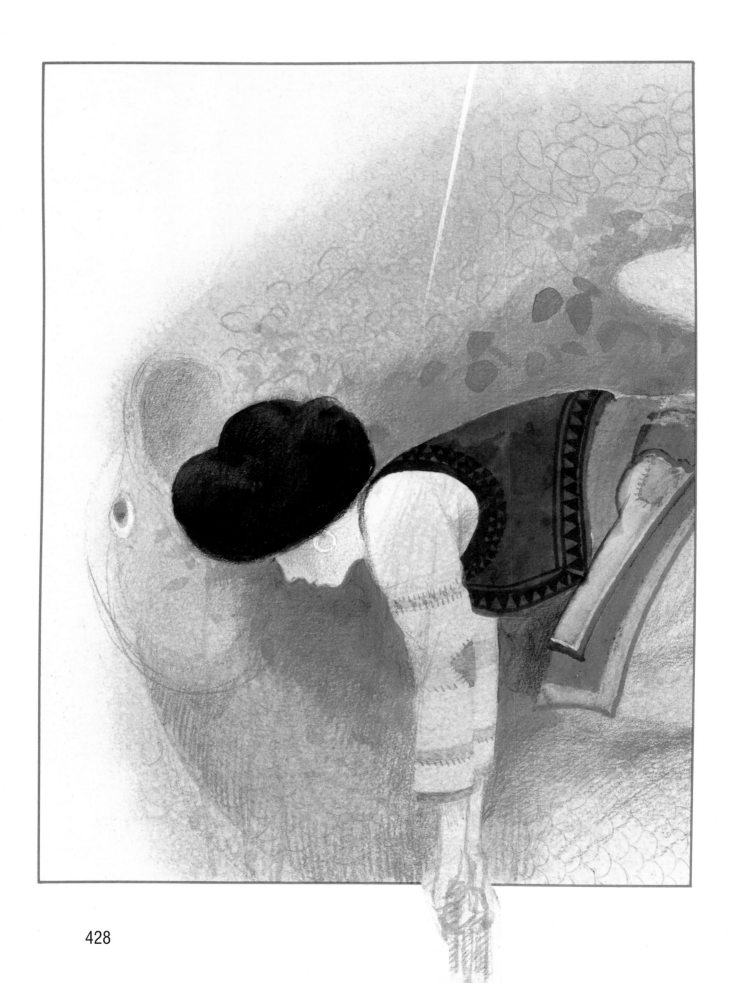

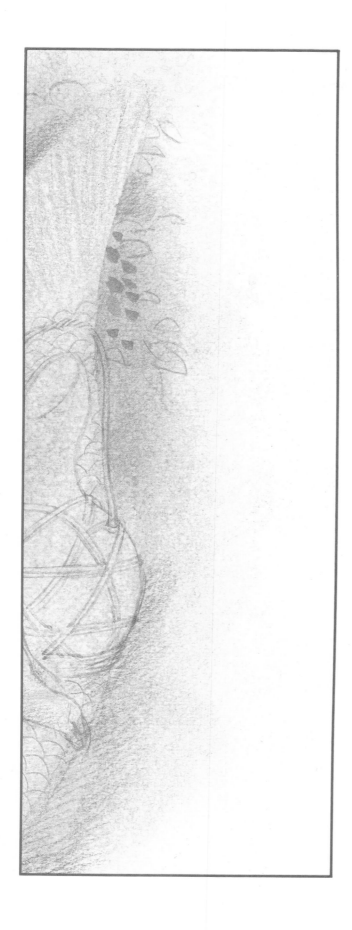

herself, but the orphan child always found something to share with her fish, which grew to enormous size.

Somehow the stepmother heard of this. She was terribly angry to discover that Yeh-Shen had kept a secret from her. She hurried down to the pond, but she was unable to see the fish, for Yeh-Shen's pet wisely hid itself. The stepmother, however, was a crafty woman, and she soon thought of a plan. She walked home and called out, "Yeh-Shen, go and collect some firewood. But wait! The neighbors might see you. Leave your filthy coat here!" The minute the girl was out of sight, her stepmother slipped on the coat herself and went down again to the pond. This time the big fish saw Yeh-Shen's familiar jacket and heaved itself onto the bank, expecting to be fed. But the stepmother, having hidden a dagger in her sleeve, stabbed the fish, wrapped it in her garments, and took it home to cook for dinner.

When Yeh-Shen came to the pond that evening, she found her pet had disappeared. Overcome with grief, the girl collapsed on the ground and dropped her tears into the still waters of the pond.

"Ah, poor child!" a voice said.

Yeh-Shen sat up to find a very old man looking down at her. He wore the coarsest of clothes, and his hair flowed down over his shoulders.

"Kind uncle, who may you be?" Yeh-Shen asked.

"That is not important, my child. All you must know is that I have been sent to tell you of the wondrous powers of your fish."

"My fish, but sir . . ." The girl's eyes filled with tears, and she could not go on.

The old man sighed and said, "Yes, my child, your fish is no longer alive, and I must tell you that your stepmother is once more the cause of your sorrow." Yeh-Shen gasped in horror, but the old man went on. "Let us not dwell on things that are past," he said, "for I have come bringing you a gift. Now you must listen carefully to this: The bones of your fish are filled with a powerful spirit. Whenever you are in serious need, you must kneel before them and let them know your heart's desire. But do not waste their gifts."

Yeh-Shen wanted to ask the old sage many more questions, but he rose to the sky before she could utter another word. With heavy heart, Yeh-Shen made her way to the dung heap to gather the remains of her friend.

Time went by, and Yeh-Shen, who was often left alone, took comfort in speaking to the bones of her fish. When she was hungry, which happened quite often, Yeh-Shen asked the bones for food. In this way, Yeh-Shen managed to live from day to day, but

she lived in dread that her step-mother would discover her secret and take even that away from her.

So the time passed and spring came. Festival time was approaching: It was the busiest time of the year. Such cooking and cleaning and sewing there was to be done! Yeh-Shen had hardly a moment's rest. At the spring festival young men and young women from the village hoped to meet and to choose whom they would marry. How Yeh-Shen longed to go! But her stepmother had other plans. She hoped to find a husband for her own daughter and did not want any man to see the beauteous Yeh-Shen first. When finally the holiday arrived, the stepmother and her daughter dressed themselves in their finery and filled their baskets with sweetmeats. "You must remain at home now, and watch to see that no one steals fruit from our trees," her stepmother told Yeh-Shen, and then she departed for the banquet with her own daughter.

As soon as she was alone, Yeh-Shen went to speak to the bones of her fish. "Oh, dear friend," she said, kneeling before the precious bones, "I long to go to the festival, but I cannot show myself in these rags. Is there somewhere I could borrow clothes fit to wear to the feast?" At once she found herself dressed in a gown of azure blue, with a cloak of kingfisher feathers draped around her shoulders. Best of all, on her tiny feet were the most beautiful slippers she had ever seen. They were

woven of golden threads, in a pattern like the scales of a fish, and the glistening soles were made of solid gold. There was magic in the shoes, for they should have been quite heavy, yet when Yeh-Shen walked, her feet felt as light as air.

"Be sure you do not lose your golden shoes," said the spirit of the bones. Yeh-Shen promised to be careful. Delighted with her transformation, she bid a fond farewell to the bones of her fish as she slipped off to join in the merrymaking.

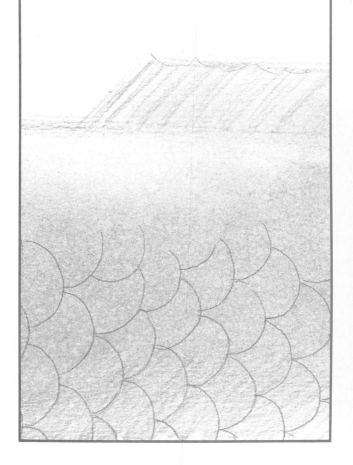

That day Yeh-Shen turned many a head as she appeared at the feast. All around her people whispered, "Look at that beautiful girl! Who can she be?"

But above this, Stepsister was heard to say, "Mother, does she not resemble our Yeh-Shen?"

Upon hearing this, Yeh-Shen jumped up and ran off before her stepsister could look closely at her. She raced down the mountainside, and in doing so, she lost one of her golden slippers. No sooner had the shoe fallen from her foot than all her fine clothes turned back to rags.

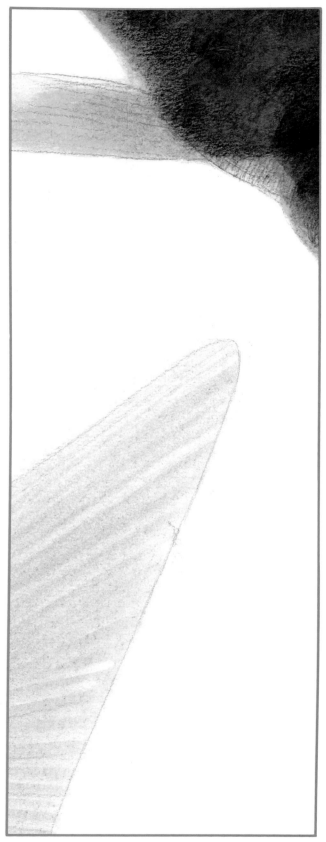
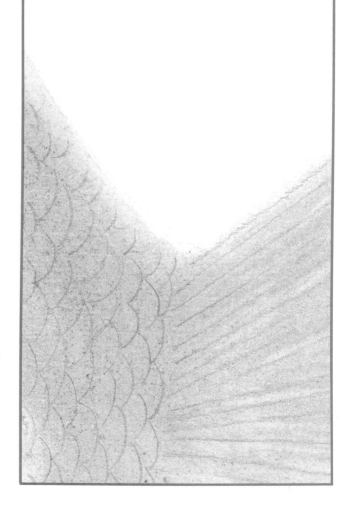

Only one thing remained—a tiny golden shoe. Yeh-Shen hurried to the bones of her fish and returned the slipper, promising to find its mate. But now the bones were silent. Sadly Yeh-Shen realized that she had lost her only friend. She hid the little shoe in her bedstraw, and went outside to cry. Leaning against a fruit tree, she sobbed and sobbed until she fell asleep.

The stepmother left the gathering to check on Yeh-Shen, but when she returned home she found the girl sound asleep, with her arms wrapped around a fruit tree. So thinking no more of her, the stepmother rejoined the party. Meantime, a villager had found the shoe. Recognizing its worth, he sold it to a merchant, who presented it in turn to the king of the island kingdom of T'o Han.

The king was more than happy to accept the slipper as a gift. He was entranced by the tiny thing, which was shaped of the most precious of metals, yet which made no sound when touched to stone. The more he marveled at its beauty, the more determined he became to find the woman to whom the shoe

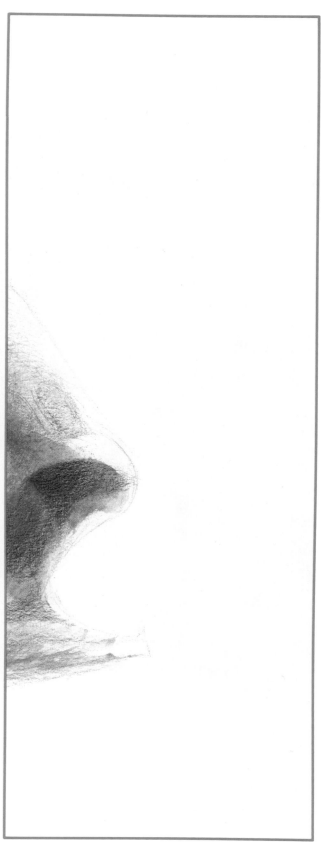

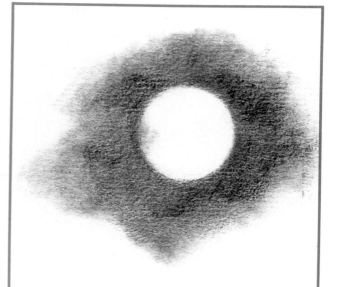

belonged. A search was begun among the ladies of his own kingdom, but all who tried on the sandal found it impossibly small. Undaunted, the king ordered the search widened to include the cave women from the countryside where the slipper had been found. Since he realized it would take many years for every woman to come to his island and test her foot in the slipper, the king thought of a way to get the right woman to come forward. He ordered the sandal placed in a pavilion by the side of the road near where it had been found, and his herald announced that the shoe was to be returned to its original owner. Then from a nearby hiding place, the king and his men settled down to watch and wait for a woman with tiny feet to come and claim her slipper.

All that day the pavilion was crowded with cave women who had come to test a foot in the shoe. Yeh-Shen's stepmother and stepsister were among them, but not Yeh-Shen—they had told her to stay home. By day's end, although many women had eagerly tried to put on the slipper, it still had not been worn. Wearily, the king continued his vigil into the night.

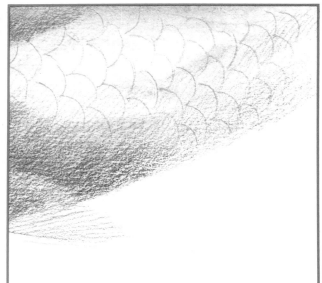

It wasn't until the blackest part of night, while the moon hid behind a cloud, that Yeh-Shen dared to show her face at the pavilion, and even then she tiptoed timidly across the wide floor. Sinking down to her knees, the girl in rags examined the tiny shoe. Only when she was sure that this was the missing mate to her own golden slipper did she dare pick it up.

At last she could return both little shoes to the fish bones. Surely then her beloved spirit would speak to her again.

Now the king's first thought, on seeing Yeh-Shen take the precious slipper, was to throw the girl into prison as a thief. But when she turned to leave, he caught a glimpse of her face. At once the king was struck by the sweet harmony of her features, which seemed so out of keeping with the rags she wore. It was then that he took a closer look and noticed that she walked upon the tiniest feet he had ever seen.

With a wave of his hand, the king signaled that this tattered creature was to be allowed to depart with the golden slipper. Quietly, the king's men slipped off and followed her home.

All this time, Yeh-Shen was unaware of the excitement she had caused. She had made her way home and was about to hide both sandals in her bedding when there was a pounding at the door. Yeh-Shen went to see who it was—and found a king at her doorstep. She was very frightened at first, but the king spoke to her in a kind voice and asked her to try the golden slippers on her feet. The maiden did as she was told, and as she stood in her golden shoes, her rags were transformed once more into the feathered cloak and beautiful azure gown.

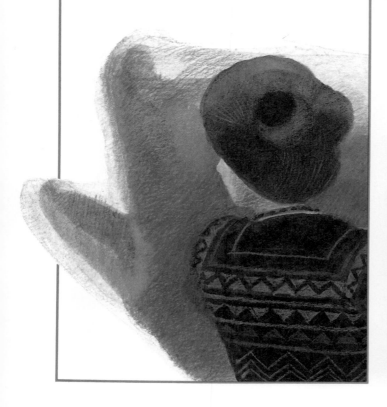
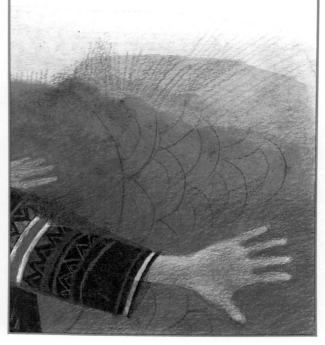

Her loveliness made her
seem a heavenly being, and
the king suddenly knew in his
heart that he had found his
true love.

Not long after this, Yeh-Shen
was married to the king. But fate
was not so gentle with her stepmother and stepsister. Since they
had been unkind to his beloved,
the king would not permit Yeh-
Shen to bring them to his pal-
ace. They remained in their cave
home, where one day, it is said,
they were crushed to death in
a shower of flying stones.

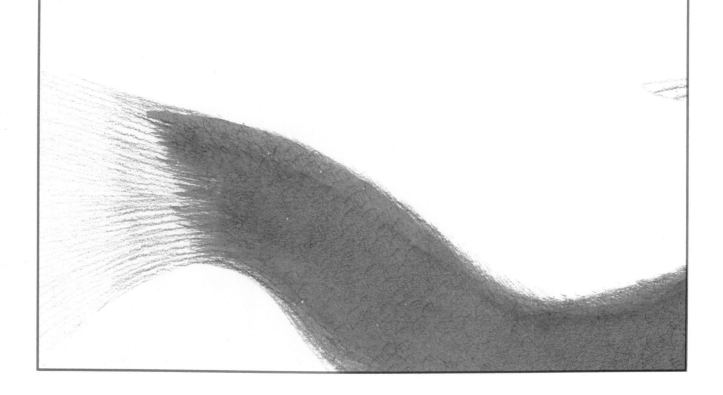

Meet Ed Young

In Shanghai, China, where Ed Young grew up, his father would entertain the family by reading and spinning endless tales. Young still remembers some of the scenes he imagined as he listened. He made his own drawings, too. "I drew everything that happened to cross my mind: airplanes, people, a tall ship. . . . I have always been happiest doing my own thing."

In some of his books, Young combines his love of storytelling and drawing. One of his best-known books, *Lon Po Po,* is his retelling of a Chinese Little Red-Riding Hood story, for which he won the Caldecott Medal. For both *Lon Po Po* and *Yeh-Shen,* Young set his art in colorful panels like those of Chinese folding screens. He also created hidden images. In *Lon Po Po,* the wolf's image is cleverly hidden in some drawings. Looking closely at the drawings in *Yeh-Shen,* you will see Yeh-Shen's fish hidden in the panels.

Meet Ai-Ling Louie

Books have always been a part of Ai-Ling Louie's life. "When I was a girl, it seemed I always had my nose in a book," she says. Ai-Ling Louie's career as a teacher brought out her desire to write. "I used to love to write stories to tell the children."

Louie wrote down *Yeh-Shen: A Cinderella Story from China* for one of her classes. She learned the story from her mother, who first heard it as a child in China.

IN SEARCH OF CINDERELLA

From dusk to dawn,
From town to town,
Without a single clue,
I seek the tender, slender foot
To fit this crystal shoe.
From dusk to dawn,
I try it on
Each damsel that I meet.
And I still love her so, but oh,
I've started hating feet.

Shel Silverstein

INVITATION

If you are a dreamer, come in,
If you are a dreamer, a wisher, a liar,
A hope-er, a pray-er, a magic bean buyer...
If you're a pretender, come sit by my fire
For we have some flax-golden tales to spin.
Come in!
Come in!

Shel Silverstein

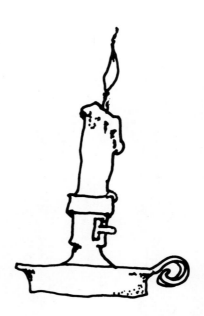

An Interview with Storyteller
WON-LDY PAYE
by Margaret H. Lippert

In a classroom filled with curious children, Won-Ldy Paye tells a story of the trickster Anansi. Paye becomes Anansi, sneaking as Anansi sneaks, dancing as Anansi dances. Soon everyone in the audience is drumming, dancing, or both. Afterward, Ms. Lippert, who lives in Washington near Paye, interviewed him.

Paye: I come from a family of "Griots"—storytellers. We tell stories when we work on the rice farm, at bedtime, or when the kids get together. My grandmother would tell us stories every evening. Before Grandmother would tell her story, she might say, "Won-Ldy, it's your turn to tell a story." As I repeated the story, she and the other kids would correct me. After a while, I learned the stories and added my own style and fun and movement to them. By seventh grade, I was already telling stories to big crowds. People would say, "The kid's a good storyteller."

Lippert: What makes a good storyteller?

Paye: You must be able to make people listen—that is the true quality of a storyteller. Just because people ask you to tell a story doesn't guarantee that they're going to sit and listen to you all night. . . . Storytelling is a profession—something that you learn, and study, and devote a lot of time to, and go to great people to learn from. I've learned storytelling because others have shared with me. It's important to me to tell my stories. So, anybody who wants to hear my story, I will tell them the story.

Lippert: You are a master storyteller and drummer. How did you develop these talents?

Paye: I grew up in rural Liberia, a country on the West Coast of Africa. I am from the Dan tribe, which is known for its artistic abilities, especially mask making and traditional dancing. I am an actor and a musician; storytelling is like a one-person play to me.

Lippert: How did you learn the art of storytelling?

453

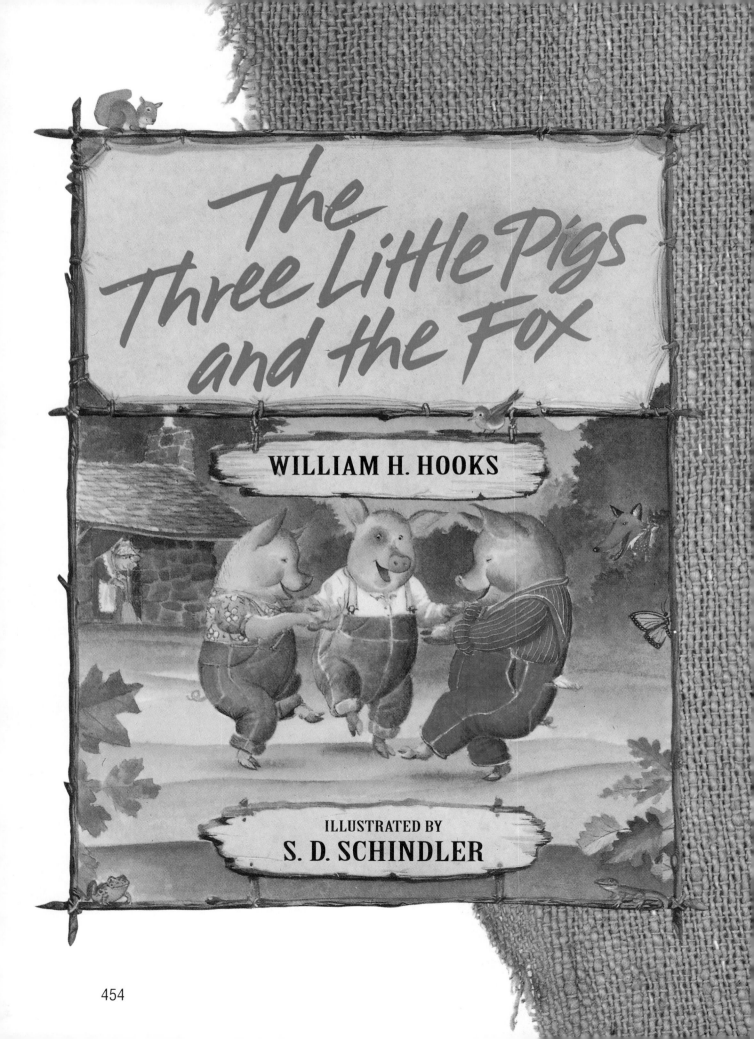

The Three Little Pigs and the Fox

WILLIAM H. HOOKS

ILLUSTRATED BY
S. D. SCHINDLER

AUTHOR'S NOTE

The art of storytelling is alive and well in Appalachia. It has flourished there since the earliest English, Scottish, and Irish settlers arrived more than three centuries ago. The classic folk and fairy tales have been preserved, but gradually in the telling they have changed until they seem to spring not from some fanciful, faraway place, but from the mountains and hollows of Appalachia itself.

Each storyteller is unique, adding local color and regional language to capture and enchant an audience. This rendition of The Three Little Pigs *is based on several oral versions I have heard over the years in the Great Smoky Mountains. In keeping with one of the truest roles of the storyteller, I have added a few flourishes of my own.*

This story happened a long time ago, way back when the animals could still talk around these parts. Back then they could say a whole lot more than *baa-baa, moo-moo, oink-oink,* and stuff like that. They could talk just like human folks.

Back then there was this humongous mama pig. She built herself a house out of rocks in a pretty green holler over Black Mountain way. As soon as she'd finished, she moved into her fine rock house with her three piglets.

The oldest piglet, Rooter, was a fair-sized shoat.
The middle piglet, Oinky, was a real mama's boy.
The baby piglet was a tiny little girl runt named
Hamlet.

Now, Rooter and Oinky and Hamlet had the finest
pig house in the holler. They even had a wallowing
hole right in the front yard. But all Rooter and Oinky
wanted to do was eat, eat, eat!
Baby Hamlet liked to eat, too—but not all the
time. Hamlet liked to roll around in the delicious mud

in the wallowing hole and look up at the pretty blue sky. She was a right smart piglet with more on her mind than eating.

It wasn't long 'fore Rooter and Oinky got so fat they just about filled up the whole house. What a squeeze it was to fit everybody in.

Finally it got so tight that Mama Pig spoke to Rooter. "Rooter, you're the oldest. Time's come for you to go out and seek your fortune."

"Oh, no!" Rooter squealed. "I'm still a piglet!"

"Look in that mud hole," said Mama Pig. "What do you see?"

Rooter looked in the muddy water. "I see a great big fat pig," he said.

"That big fat pig is you, Rooter. Time's come to go out and seek your fortune."

Well, Rooter hemmed and hawed and had an extra big helping of his mama's baked beans to settle his nerves. Oinky had some, too, just to keep Rooter company.

Meanwhile, Mama Pig gathered up some hoecakes and turnips, along with some dried beans and corn. She packed them in a big tow sack for Rooter to take along.

"Now, son," said Mama Pig, "you'll be fine if you remember three things."

"That's a lot to remember," said Rooter.

"Stop chewing and listen careful," said Mama Pig.

Rooter gulped. "I'm listening."

"One: You got to watch out for that mean, tricky old drooly-mouth fox.

"Two: Build yourself a safe, strong house out of rocks.

"Three: Come home to see your mama every single Sunday."

Mama and Oinky and baby Hamlet kissed Rooter on his fat, round jowls. And for good luck they kissed him again on his pink, trembly snout.

Then Rooter trotted on down the road, dragging his tow sack behind him. He walked and he walked. And what did all that walking do? It made him mighty hungry.

He didn't think about any mean, tricky old drooly-mouth fox.

He didn't think about any safe, strong rock house.

He didn't think about visiting his mama come Sunday.

All he could think about was the food his mama had put into the tow sack. So he set himself down on a rock and opened up the sack.

"Hoecakes!" He squealed and started gobbling them up.

Rooter felt a tap on the shoulder. He didn't look around, and he didn't miss a chew, just said between bites, "Don't bother me. I'm busy eating."

But the tapping went on. Rooter swallowed a big chunk of hoecake and looked around. There was mean, tricky old drooly-mouth fox grinning at him.

459

"Have some hoecake," said Rooter, real scared.

"Don't like hoecake," said the fox.

"Well, how about some turnips or corn?" said Rooter.

"Don't like none of them," said the fox.

"Well, what can I offer you?" asked Rooter.

"I love barbecued pig!" cried the fox. And he grabbed the tow sack and stuffed Rooter into it.

"Please don't eat me up," Rooter pleaded.

"I won't eat you right now," said mean, tricky old drooly-mouth fox. "I'm going to save you up for a cold winter's day. Nothing like hot barbecue on a cold winter's day."

So he took poor Rooter off to his den and locked him up.

Sunday rolled around. All day Mama Pig and baby Hamlet looked for Rooter to come visiting, while Oinky spent the Sabbath eating a double share of rutabagas and corn dumplings. But the night came on without Rooter ever showing up.

A month of Sundays passed, and they didn't see snout or tail of Rooter. Meanwhile, Oinky was growing so big the house was getting crowded again. They were having a hard time fitting in.

Finally Mama Pig said, "Oinky, it's time you set out to seek your fortune."

"No, Mama!" Oinky squealed. "I'm too little to leave my mama."

"Look in that mud hole and tell me what you see," said Mama Pig.

Oinky looked in the muddy water and saw how huge he had grown. He knew his mama was right.

Oinky didn't say a word, but two big tears rolled down his plump jowls.

Mama Pig said, "No need for tears, Oinky. All you have to do is remember three things.

"One: Watch out for that mean, tricky old drooly-mouth fox.

"Two: Build yourself a safe, strong house out of rocks.

"Three: Come home to see your mama every single Sunday."

Mama packed Oinky a tow sack full of his favorite food, rutabagas and corn dumplings.

Then baby Hamlet and Mama Pig kissed Oinky on his fat, round jowls. And for good luck they kissed him again on his pink, trembly snout.

Oinky went slowly on down the road till he was out of sight. He walked and he walked. And he kept thinking how much he was going to miss his mama. He felt so sad, he sat down on a rock to have a little nourishment and cheer himself. He didn't think once about the mean fox or building a safe house, although he did long for Sunday to visit his mama.

Oinky was just easing a tooth into a crusty, golden corn dumpling when he felt a tap on the shoulder. He whirled around so fast he dropped the dumpling. There was mean, tricky old drooly-mouth fox grinning at him.

"Would you like some of my dumplings?" stammered Oinky, scared to death.

"Never eat 'em," said the fox.

"How about some rutabagas?" asked Oinky.

"Can't stand the smell of 'em," said the fox.

"Well, what do you like?" asked Oinky.

"Pork with lima beans!" said the fox. And he snatched up the tow sack and stuffed poor Oinky inside.

"Please don't eat me," begged Oinky. "Please! Please! Please!"

"Oh, shut up," said mean, tricky old drooly-mouth fox. "I'm not going to eat you right now. I'm going to save you for a rainy day. There's nothing better than pork and beans on a rainy day."

So the fox took Oinky to his den and locked him up.

Sunday rolled around. Mama and baby Hamlet got up early and cooked a big mess of collard greens and wild onions. They wanted to have something special in case Rooter and Oinky remembered to come see their mama. But the night came on without either Rooter or Oinky ever showing up.

A month of Sundays passed, and they didn't see snout or tail of Rooter or Oinky. The leaves turned all red and gold, and the nights got real nippy.

Baby Hamlet—who didn't look so much like a little runt anymore—was getting restless. One day she spoke to her mama. "Mama, it's high time I set out to seek my fortune."

"No, no!" Mama Pig cried. "You're too young to leave your mama! Besides, none of my children ever come back to visit me on Sundays."

"Now, stop your worrying, Mama," said Hamlet. "I can take care of myself. All I've got to do is remember three things.

"One: Watch out for that mean, tricky old drooly-mouth fox.

"Two: Build myself a safe, strong house out of rocks.

"Three: Come home and visit my dear, sweet mama every Sunday."

So Mama Pig packed a tow sack with sweet potato pone, Hamlet's favorite food. She kissed baby Hamlet on her fat, round jowls, and for luck kissed her again on her pink, trembly snout.

Hamlet skipped on down the road. She walked and she walked. She looked all around to make sure no mean fox was sneaking up on her. She got tired and set herself down on a rock to rest.

"I think I'll just have a nibble on this sweet potato pone," she said.

Suddenly she felt a tap on the shoulder. It was mean, tricky old drooly-mouth fox grinning at her.

"What a surprise!" exclaimed Hamlet. She was thinking fast and stalling for time.

"I've got a real big surprise for you," said the fox.

"I mentioned *surprise* first," said Hamlet. "This tow sack is full of surprises."

The fox reached inside the sack and pulled out some sweet potato pone. "Umm," he mumbled, chewing away. "Only one thing I like better than sweet potato pone."

"What's that?" asked Hamlet.

"Pork chops to go with it!" cried the fox, grabbing for baby Hamlet.

But Hamlet was too sharp for him. She slapped the tow sack over the fox and tied it tight with a hard knot. Then she left that old fox rolling and squirming around on the ground inside the sack.

Hamlet skipped on down the road till she found a place with a fine bunch of rocks. She made herself a safe little rock house with a nice fireplace to keep warm by.

No sooner had Hamlet settled in than that mean, tricky old drooly-mouth fox came knocking at her door. "Please let me in, little pig," he begged. "I'm near freezing to death."

"Not on the fuzz of your bushy tail will I let you in," said Hamlet.

"Please, have mercy on a poor old fox. My nose is about frozen off. Just open the door a crack to let me warm my nose," he pleaded.

Hamlet cracked the door a mite. The fox shoved his nose in the crack.

Slam! Hamlet banged the door shut.

The fox thought his nose would really drop off, it hurt so. But he was thinking what nice pork chops Hamlet would make.

"My nose is warmer now," he called, "but my ears are freezing. Please open the door a little wider so I can warm my ears."

Hamlet opened the door a little more. The fox tried to push all the way in.

Slam! Hamlet banged the door shut, pretty

near knocking the breath out of mean, tricky old drooly-mouth fox.

But the fox still had his mind set on pork chops.

"Oh, that was much better, little pig." He gasped. "Now, if you would open the door a little bit more and let me get my hind feet warmed, I'll be on my way."

Hamlet opened the door wide. The fox sprang inside. But that smart little pig was too fast for him. *Slam!* She shut the door on his tail and stopped him in his tracks.

"Oh, oh, my tail!" cried mean, tricky old drooly-mouth fox.

"Shut up!" said Hamlet. "You're making so much racket I can't hear what's going on outside."

The fox lowered his voice to a moan. "Please, my tail. My tail."

"Just what I thought I heard," said Hamlet. "Dogs barking."

"Dogs? What kind of dogs?" asked the fox.

"Hunting dogs. I'm sure they're fox-hunting dogs, from the way they're barking."

"Please hide me," cried the fox. "Don't let the hounds catch me!"

Hamlet was thinking fast and sharp.

"I'll hide you if you tell me what you've done with Rooter and Oinky."

"They're locked up in my den. Please, hurry. Those dogs will be here any minute."

"First tell me where I can find your den."

Mean, tricky old drooly-mouth fox hated to give that away. But his tail was killing him, and the dogs were hot on his trail.

"It's under the big, rusty-colored rock over in Rattlesnake Holler." He groaned.

"Here, jump into this churn," said Hamlet. She pushed the door off mean, tricky old drooly-mouth fox's tail and lifted the lid from the big wooden churn.

The fox squeezed inside. Hamlet slammed the lid down on the churn and latched it tight.

"Are the dogs getting closer?" the fox mumbled from inside the churn.

"What dogs?" asked baby Hamlet. "I don't hear any dogs."

The old fox knew he'd been tricked. He gnashed his teeth and rattled and raved and shook the churn. But he couldn't get out.

Baby Hamlet rolled the churn down to the creek and right into the water. Downstream it floated like an ark. And that was the last mean, tricky old drooly-mouth fox was seen around the hollers of Black Mountain.

Baby Hamlet hurried on down to Rattlesnake Holler and searched all around till she found the fox den with her brothers, Rooter and Oinky.

It just happened to be on Sunday when she found them and set them free. So they all trotted right over to Mama Pig's house. And there was snorting and eating, and kissing and eating, and wallowing in the mud hole and more eating, the likes of which you've never seen.

Meet
WILLIAM H. HOOKS

As a youngster growing up in the North Carolina countryside, William H. Hooks heard many tales that the country folk had told for generations. Hooks has woven memories of those tales into the many books he has written for children.

During a visit to the Smokey Mountains of Tennessee, Hooks heard an old Appalachian version of *The Three Little Pigs*. Hooks turned that story into his book *The Three Little Pigs and the Fox*.

Hooks has this advice for youngsters who want to write: "Write. Do it. Keep doing it. It will get better and better."

Érase Una Vez

Érase una vez
un lobito bueno

al que maltrataban
todos los corderos.

Y había también
un príncipe malo,

una bruja hermosa
y un pirata honrado.

Todas estas cosas
había una vez
cuando yo soñaba
un mundo al revés.

Juan Goytisolo

Once Upon a Time

Once upon a time
there was a good little wolf

that all the sheep
used to bother.

And at the same time
there was an evil prince,

a beautiful witch
and an honest pirate.

And all of these things
were once upon a time
in a world of my dreams
that was upside down, it seems.

TALE SPINNERS

For me there is a special time at the end of every day. After the
work is finished and I am ready to go to bed, my grandmother and
grandfather tell me stories from the past. Sometimes they
tell about the legends of the pueblo people. Other times they
tell about things that happened in their own lives.

Pueblo Storyteller
by Diane Hoyt-Goldsmith
photographs by Lawrence Migdale
Holiday House, 1991

PUEBLO STORYTELLER

BY DIANE HOYT-GOLDSMITH
PHOTOGRAPHS BY LAWRENCE MIGDALE

The Cat's Purr

Written and illustrated
by Ashley Bryan
Atheneum, 1985

The **CAT'S PURR**

written & illustrated by Ashley Bryan

"That was different, Rat," Cat said. "My uncle said no one else plays this Cat drum. Anyway, this is not a time for drumming. Let's get to work in the fields."

Cat set the drum down on the bed.

"I must think of a good plan so that I can play Cat's drum," Rat thought. "I'll need time to think."

Meet John Steptoe

When John Steptoe wanted to write a book about his African ancestors, he decided to write a version of the Cinderella story. As he prepared to write by talking to Africans and reading about Africa, he found many reasons to be proud of his ancestors. Steptoe discovered that people of a thousand years ago behaved much the same as people do today. "My ancestors were probably very like my own family," he said. "Telling the story was easy once I knew who my characters were."

Mufaro's Beautiful Daughters is Steptoe's African Cinderella story. He used members of his family as models for some of the characters.

Steptoe hoped his books would lead children, especially African-American children, "to accomplish the dreams I know are in their hearts."

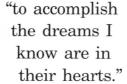

Mufaro's Beautiful Daughters

An African Tale

Written and Illustrated by John Steptoe

Mufaro's Beautiful Daughters *was inspired by a folktale collected by G. M. Theal and published in 1895 in his book, Kaffir Folktales. Details of the illustrations were inspired by the ruins of an ancient city found in Zimbabwe, and the flora and fauna of that region. The names of the characters are from the Shona language: Mufaro (moo-FAR-oh) means "happy man"; Nyasha (nee-AH-sha) means "mercy"; Manyara (mahn-YAR-ah) means "ashamed"; and Nyoka (nee-YO-kah) means "snake."*

A LONG TIME AGO, in a certain place in Africa, a small village lay across a river and half a day's journey from a city where a great king lived. A man named Mufaro lived in this village with his two daughters, who were called Manyara and Nyasha. Everyone agreed that Manyara and Nyasha were very beautiful.

anyara was almost always in a bad temper. She teased her sister whenever their father's back was turned, and she had been heard to say, "Someday, Nyasha, I will be a queen, and you will be a servant in my household."

"If that should come to pass," Nyasha responded, "I will be pleased to serve you. But why do you say such things? You are clever and strong and beautiful. Why are you so unhappy?"

"Because everyone talks about how kind *you* are, and they praise everything you do," Manyara replied. "I'm certain that Father loves you best. But when I am a queen, everyone will know that your silly kindness is only weakness."

Nyasha was sad that Manyara felt this way, but she ignored her sister's words and went about her chores. Nyasha kept a small plot of land, on which she grew millet, sunflowers, yams, and vegetables. She always sang as she worked, and some said it was her singing that made her crops more bountiful than anyone else's.

One day, Nyasha noticed a small garden snake resting beneath a yam vine. "Good day, little Nyoka," she called to him. "You are welcome here. You will keep away any creatures who might spoil my vegetables." She bent forward, gave the little snake a loving pat on the head, and then returned to her work.

From that day on, Nyoka was always at Nyasha's side when she tended her garden. It was said that she sang all the more sweetly when he was there.

*M*ufaro knew nothing of how Manyara treated Nyasha. Nyasha was too considerate of her father's feelings to complain, and Manyara was always careful to behave herself when Mufaro was around.

Early one morning, a messenger from the city arrived. The Great King wanted a wife. "The Most Worthy and Beautiful Daughters in the Land are invited to appear before the King, and he will choose one to become Queen!" the messenger proclaimed.

Mufaro called Manyara and Nyasha to him. "It would be a great honor to have one of you chosen," he said. "Prepare yourselves to journey to the city. I will call together all our friends to make a wedding party. We will leave tomorrow as the sun rises."

"But, my father," Manyara said sweetly, "it would be painful for either of us to leave you, even to be wife to the king. I know Nyasha would grieve to death if she were parted from you. I am strong. Send me to the city, and let poor Nyasha be happy here with you."

Mufaro beamed with pride. "The king has asked for the most worthy and the most beautiful. No, Manyara, I cannot send you alone. Only a king can choose between two such worthy daughters. Both of you must go!"

That night, when everyone was asleep, Manyara stole quietly out of the village. She had never been in the forest at night before, and she was frightened, but her greed to be the first to appear before the king drove her on. In her hurry, she almost stumbled over a small boy who suddenly appeared, standing in the path.

"Please," said the boy. "I am hungry. Will you give me something to eat?"

"I have brought only enough for myself," Manyara replied.

"But, please!" said the boy. "I am so *very* hungry."

"Out of my way, boy! Tomorrow I will become your queen. How dare you stand in my path?"

After traveling for what seemed to be a great distance, Manyara came to a small clearing. There, silhouetted against the moonlight, was an old woman seated on a large stone.

The old woman spoke. "I will give you some advice, Manyara. Soon after you pass the place where two paths cross, you will see a grove of trees. They will laugh at you. You must not laugh in return. Later, you will meet a man with his head under his arm. You must be polite to him."

"How do you know my name? How dare you advise your future queen? Stand aside, you ugly old woman!" Manyara scolded, and then rushed on her way without looking back.

Just as the old woman had foretold, Manyara
came to a grove of trees, and they did indeed seem
to be laughing at her.

"I must be calm," Manyara thought. "I will *not* be
frightened." She looked up at the trees and laughed
out loud. "I laugh at you, trees!" she shouted, and she
hurried on.

It was not yet dawn when Manyara heard the sound
of rushing water. "The river must be up ahead," she
thought. "The great city is just on the other side."

But there, on the rise, she saw a man with his head
tucked under his arm. Manyara ran past him without
speaking. "A queen acknowledges only those who please
her," she said to herself. "I will be queen. I will be
queen," she chanted, as she hurried on toward the city.

Nyasha woke at the first light of dawn. As she put on her finest garments, she thought how her life might be changed forever beyond this day. "I'd much prefer to live here," she admitted to herself. "I'd hate to leave this village and never see my father or sing to little Nyoka again."

Her thoughts were interrupted by loud shouts and a commotion from the wedding party assembled outside. Manyara was missing! Everyone bustled about, searching and calling for her. When they found her footprints on the path that led to the city, they decided to go on as planned.

As the wedding party moved through the forest, brightly plumed birds darted about in the cool green shadows beneath the trees. Though anxious about her sister, Nyasha was soon filled with excitement about all there was to see.

They were deep in the forest when she saw the small boy standing by the side of the path.

"You must be hungry," she said, and handed him a yam she had brought for her lunch. The boy smiled and disappeared as quietly as he had come.

Later, as they were approaching the place where the two paths crossed, the old woman appeared and silently pointed the way to the city. Nyasha thanked her and gave her a small pouch filled with sunflower seeds.

The sun was high in the sky when the party came to the grove of towering trees. Their uppermost branches seemed to bow down to Nyasha as she passed beneath them.

At last, someone announced that they were near their destination.

Nyasha ran ahead and topped the rise before the others could catch up with her. She stood transfixed at her first sight of the city. "Oh, my father," she called. "A great spirit must stand guard here! Just look at what lies before us. I never in all my life dreamed there could be anything so beautiful!"

Arm in arm, Nyasha and her father descended the hill, crossed the river, and approached the city gate. Just as they entered through the great doors, the air was rent by piercing cries, and Manyara ran wildly out of a chamber at the center of the enclosure. When she saw Nyasha, she fell upon her, sobbing.

"Do not go to the king, my sister. Oh, please, Father, do not let her go!" she cried hysterically. "There's a great monster there, a snake with five heads! He said that he knew all my faults and that I displeased him. He would have swallowed me alive if I had not run. Oh, my sister, please do not go inside that place."

It frightened Nyasha to see her sister so upset. But, leaving her father to comfort Manyara, she bravely made her way to the chamber and opened the door.

On the seat of the great chief's stool lay the little garden snake. Nyasha laughed with relief and joy.

"My little friend!" she exclaimed. "It's such a pleasure to see you, but why are you here?"

"I am the king," Nyoka replied.

And there, before Nyasha's eyes, the garden snake changed shape.

"I am the king. I am also the hungry boy with whom you shared a yam in the forest and the old woman to whom you made a gift of sunflower seeds. But you know me best as Nyoka. Because I have been all of these, I know you to be the Most Worthy and Most Beautiful Daughter in the Land. It would make me very happy if you would be my wife."

*A*nd so it was that, a long time ago, Nyasha agreed to be married. The king's mother and sisters took Nyasha to their house, and the wedding preparations began. The best weavers in the land laid out their finest cloth for her wedding garments. Villagers from all around were invited to the celebration, and a great feast was held. Nyasha prepared the bread for the wedding feast from millet that had been brought from her village.

Mufaro proclaimed to all who would hear him that he was the happiest father in all the land, for he was blessed with two beautiful and worthy daughters—Nyasha, the queen; and Manyara, a servant in the queen's household.

THE Stonecutter

An Indian folk tale retold and illustrated by Pam Newton

Once there was a poor stonecutter who lived in a small hut in the forest on the side of a mountain.

Every morning while the sun was still a yellow ribbon of promise in the eastern sky, the stonecutter picked up his tools and climbed the mountain path until he arrived at a big rock in the side of the mountain. Along the way trees waved morning greetings and calling birds soared across the mountainside. A tiger, hidden in his cave, yawned and curled up for a nap.

Before the stonecutter began to work he prayed to the mountain spirit for blessing and protection. Then he hammered and chipped and smoothed and polished the building blocks he made from the stones he took out of the mountain.

Although he worked hard and his days were long, he never minded until the day he delivered some blocks of stone to repair a wall at the home of a rich man.

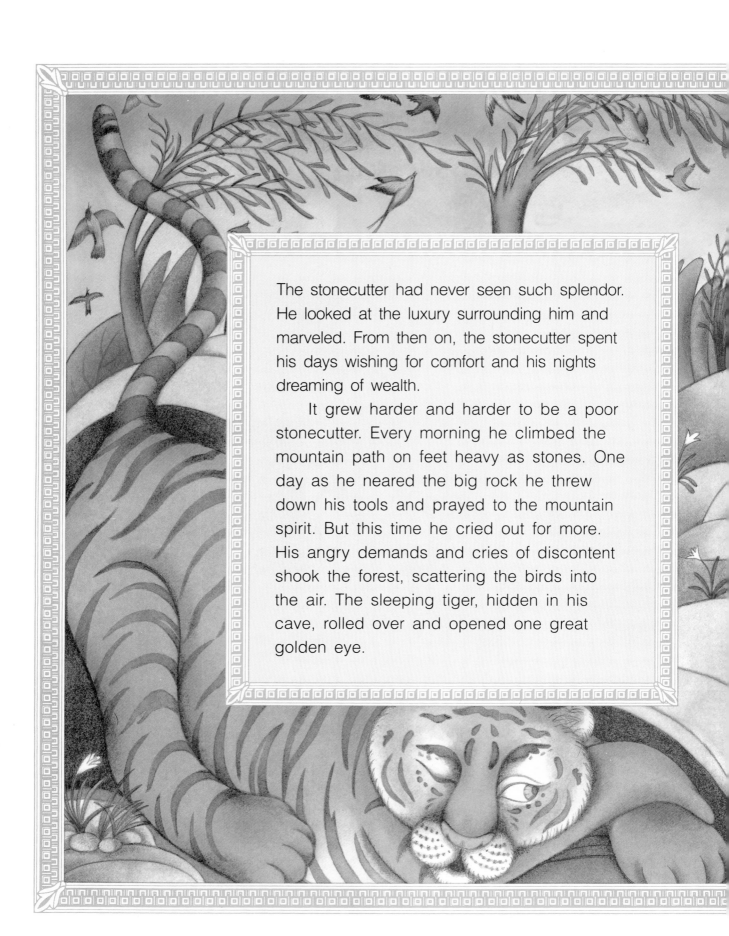

The stonecutter had never seen such splendor. He looked at the luxury surrounding him and marveled. From then on, the stonecutter spent his days wishing for comfort and his nights dreaming of wealth.

It grew harder and harder to be a poor stonecutter. Every morning he climbed the mountain path on feet heavy as stones. One day as he neared the big rock he threw down his tools and prayed to the mountain spirit. But this time he cried out for more. His angry demands and cries of discontent shook the forest, scattering the birds into the air. The sleeping tiger, hidden in his cave, rolled over and opened one great golden eye.

Deep within the mountain the spirit heard the stonecutter's cries and decided to grant his prayers.

The spirit stilled the trees and calmed the birds and soothed the tiger back to sleep. The stonecutter's heart was filled with hope so that when he raised his hammer and began to work, he believed his prayers would soon be answered.

The next day, as he walked to the city to deliver some blocks of stone, the stonecutter saw a merchant leading camels heaped high with silks and spices for the market. He stood by the side of the road and watched.

"A stonecutter is nothing compared to a rich merchant," he said, sighing, and squeezed his eyes shut against the dust.

"If only I were a rich merchant," he cried, as he covered his ears to keep out the shouts of the camel drivers. "Then I could be truly happy."

Far away inside the mountain, the spirit heard his wish and made it true.

When the stonecutter opened his eyes, his blocks of stone had disappeared and in their place stood all the wealth of a merchant. He bowed his richly turbaned head and murmured his gratitude.

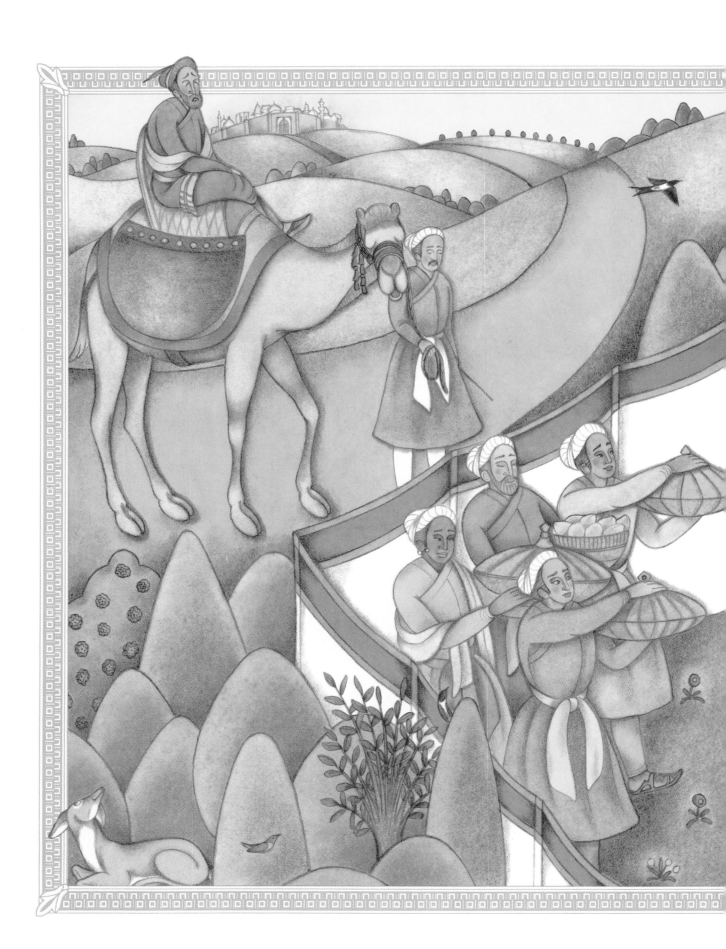

508

Surrounded by his new wealth, he began his journey to the city to sell his goods.

But even a wealthy merchant grows tired and thirsty traveling a long, hot road in the middle of the day.

"I will stop there for rest and refreshment," the stonecutter said to his camel drivers, pointing at a distant bright-flowered hill.

But as his caravan drew closer the stonecutter could see that it was not a flower-covered hill at all, but a king and his courtiers, clad in petal-bright silks, having a picnic on the hillside.

From his camel-high seat the stonecutter could see just over the cloth screen meant to shield the royal court from the curious eyes of passersby. When he caught sight of the king sitting on a carpet spread end-to-end with a feast of delicacies, the stonecutter frowned and shook his head. His own wealth seemed small compared to the king's.

"A merchant is nothing compared to a king," he said. "If only I were a king, then I could be truly happy."

The words were barely spoken when—wonder of wonders—the stonecutter became a king!

A servant offered him a tray of sherbets. The sweet pink ices cooled his dry throat. Perfumed courtiers hovered like butterflies, filling the air with the scent of roses and sandalwood. The stonecutter kicked off his slippers and settled into his cushions, nibbling first from one tray of delights and then another.

Though his every desire was fulfilled, the afternoon sun burned down on the hillside and the stonecutter began to feel hot. His beard glistened with sweat and his skin blistered and itched.

Shielding his eyes with his hand, the stonecutter tried to look heavenward. High above, the sun blazed powerful and brilliant, too great for even a king to gaze upon.

"I was wrong," moaned the stonecutter, wiping his brow with a silk scarf. "A king is nothing compared to the sun. If only I were the sun, then I could be truly happy."

His wish spoken, the stonecutter at once became the scorching sun, whirling red-hot across the heavens, and dazzling the world with his fiery strength.

"Now there is nothing more glorious than I am," he declared, seeing each flower's face turn to him and every tree reach up, up to embrace him.

"Even a powerful king cannot stop me from burning his skin," declared the stonecutter, as his thousand wheeling arms searched the earth for a king.

Just then a small cloud drifted across the sky and passed between the sun and the earth. The stonecutter cried out, for his face was hidden from the earth.

He was utterly powerless.

"I was wrong," he groaned. "The sun is nothing compared to a cloud. If only I were a cloud, then I could be truly happy."

And so saying, the stonecutter was transformed into a pale gossamer cloud, with the sun scowling at his back, the earth spread below, and the sky all around. He had nothing better in the world to do but float along effortlessly, puffed up with the pride and power of his new position.

But not for long.

As quickly as the cloud had covered the sun, a wind arrived and swept the cloud away.

"Oh-h-h," sobbed the stonecutter, as the wind's icy breath tore him apart. "A cloud is nothing compared to the wind. If only I were the wind, then I could be truly happy."

At once the stonecutter became the wind, tossing the clouds across the sky as he rushed to earth.

"Whee-e-e-e!" He blew over the ocean making waves.

"Whir-r-r-r!" He rolled across the fields, bending flowers and grasses.

"Who-o-o-sh!" He rustled through the trees, snapping branches.

Everywhere the stonecutter went he made a great commotion until he met a mountain. Although he blustered and raged and blew he could not move it. Not even a little.

"The wind is nothing compared to a mountain," huffed the stonecutter. "If only I were a mountain, then I could be truly happy."

"Now," boasted the stonecutter as once again his wish was granted, "a wind cannot move me."

"A cloud cannot cover me."

"The sun cannot burn me."

"A king cannot equal my majesty."

"And surely a merchant is nothing compared to a mountain."

But as he spoke, a man climbed up the side of the mountain. He carried a hammer, and when he began to pound, pound, pound, the stonecutter cried out: "I am the mountain and there is nothing on earth or in the heavens as powerful as I am."

The man continued to hammer and chip and smooth and polish, making building blocks from the stones he took out of the mountain.

"Oh-h-h, no-o-o," wailed the stonecutter. "I was wrong."

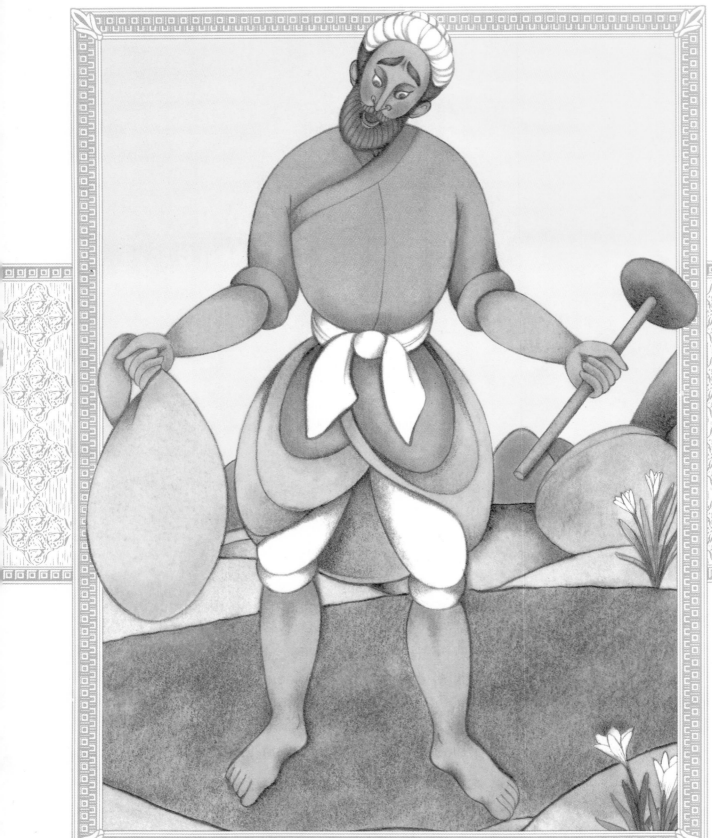

"Stone by stone, even a mountain is nothing compared to a stonecutter. If only I were a stonecutter, then I would be truly happy."

His wish spoken, he found himself standing on the side of the mountain. He was a stonecutter once again.

As he climbed his well-worn path, trees waved and birds soared and sang. The tiger slumbered in his cave.

The stonecutter offered a prayer of thanks to the mountain spirit. A feeling of contentment settled over him.

"At last I am happy to be a stonecutter—truly happy."

Then he began to hammer and chip and smooth and polish, making building blocks from the stones he took out of the mountain.

Meet Pam Newton

Pam Newton says, "I knew from kindergarten that I wanted to be an artist. I liked to draw horses." As a child, Newton also liked to read. Her favorite stories were fairy tales by the Brothers Grimm and Hans Christian Andersen. She still spends all her extra time reading.

Today, as Newton reads, she looks for folk tales and myths that she can retell and illustrate. Newton chooses folk tales very

carefully. She knows the story is good, she says, "if it makes pictures in your head."

The Stonecutter began not with a picture in her head but with one outside a window. When she and her family lived in Turkey, she awakened one morning to see a camel caravan passing by. Years later, Newton read the tale about the stonecutter and realized she had found a place for the long-remembered caravan.

The Story Song

Where do stories come from? Tell me if you know.
Where do stories come from, and where do stories go?
Stories come from deep inside, then they travel far and wide—
That's where stories come from, that's where stories go.

Where do stories come from? Tell me if you can.
Where do stories come from? History of man, and woman.
Stories come from me to you, travel on to who knows who—
That's where stories come from, that's where stories go.

If you like my stories, tell them to a friend.
Keep the chain a-growing, stories never end.
From a golden story box, turn the key, unlock the locks—
That's where stories come from, that's where stories go.

That's where stories come from . . . that's where stories go!

Marcia Lane

INFORMATION ILLUSTRATED

YOUR GUIDE TO A WORLD OF INFORMATION— WITH EXAMPLES RELATED TO THE THEMES YOU ARE EXPLORING!

CONTENTS

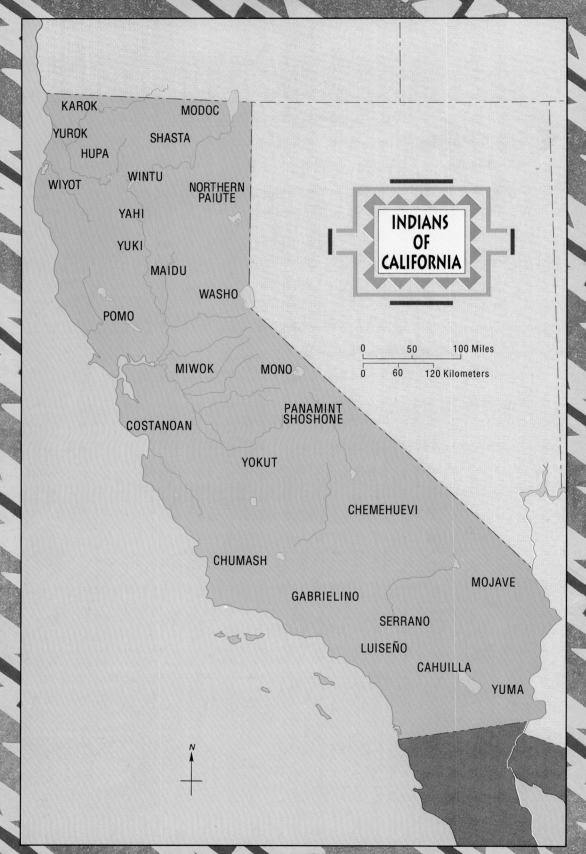

KAROK
MODOC
YUROK
SHASTA
HUPA
WINTU
WIYOT
NORTHERN
PAIUTE
YAHI
YUKI
MAIDU
WASHO
POMO
MIWOK
MONO
COSTANOAN
PANAMINT
SHOSHONE
YOKUT
CHEMEHUEVI
CHUMASH
MOJAVE
GABRIELINO
SERRANO
LUISEÑO
CAHUILLA
YUMA

**INDIANS
OF
CALIFORNIA**

0   50   100 Miles
0   60   120 Kilometers

N

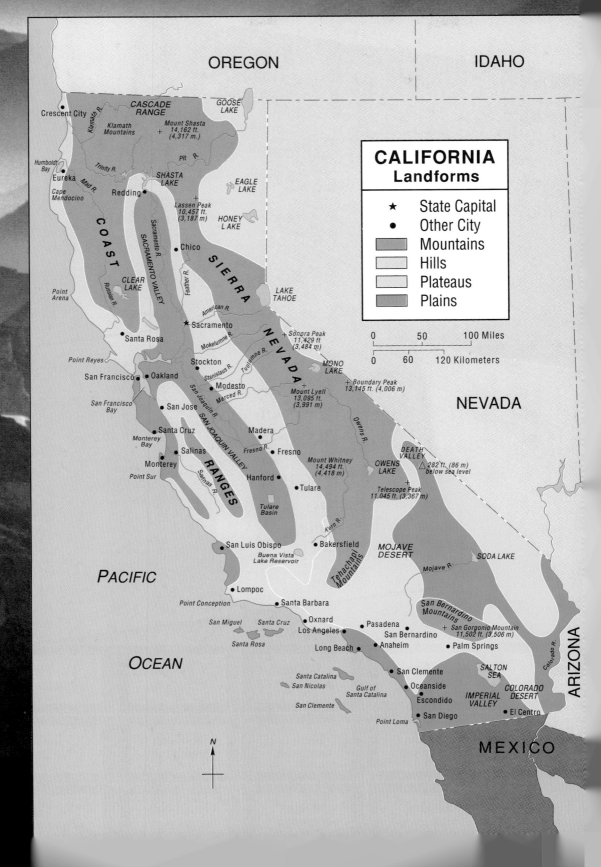

CALIFORNIA
Landforms

★ State Capital
● Other City

Mountains
Hills
Plateaus
Plains

| 0 | 50 | 100 Miles |

| 0 | 60 | 120 Kilometers |

OREGON

IDAHO

NEVADA

ARIZONA

MEXICO

PACIFIC

OCEAN

CASCADE RANGE

GOOSE LAKE

Crescent City

Klamath R.

Klamath Mountains

Mount Shasta 14,162 ft. (4,317 m.)

Pit R.

EAGLE LAKE

Trinity R.

Humboldt Bay

Eureka

Cape Mendocino

Mad R.

SHASTA LAKE

Redding

Lassen Peak 10,457 ft. (3,187 m)

HONEY LAKE

COAST

SACRAMENTO R.

SACRAMENTO VALLEY

Chico

SIERRA

Point Arena

CLEAR LAKE

Russian R.

Feather R.

Point Reyes

Santa Rosa

American R.

★ Sacramento

Sonora Peak 11,429 ft (3,484 m)

LAKE TAHOE

NEVADA

Mokelumne R.

Stockton

Tuolumne R.

MONO LAKE

San Francisco

Oakland

Stanislaus R.

Modesto

Mount Lyell 13,095 ft. (3,991 m)

Boundary Peak 13,145 ft. (4,006 m)

San Francisco Bay

San Joaquin R.

San Jose

Merced R.

SAN JOAQUIN VALLEY

Santa Cruz

Madera

Owens R.

DEATH VALLEY

Monterey Bay

Fresno R.

Fresno

Salinas

RANGES

Mount Whitney 14,494 ft. (4,418 m)

OWENS LAKE

△ 282 ft. (86 m) below sea level

Monterey

Point Sur

Salinas R.

Hanford

Telescope Peak 11,045 ft. (3,367 m)

Tulare

Tulare Basin

Kern R.

San Luis Obispo

Bakersfield

MOJAVE DESERT

SODA LAKE

Buena Vista Lake Reservoir

Tehachapi Mountains

Mojave R.

Lompoc

Point Conception

Santa Barbara

San Bernardino Mountains

San Miguel

Santa Cruz

Oxnard

Pasadena

San Gorgonio Mountain 11,502 ft. (3,506 m)

Colorado R.

Santa Rosa

Los Angeles

San Bernardino

Long Beach

Anaheim

Palm Springs

SALTON SEA

Santa Catalina

San Nicolas

Gulf of Santa Catalina

San Clemente

Oceanside

COLORADO DESERT

IMPERIAL VALLEY

San Clemente

Escondido

El Centro

Point Loma

San Diego

N

CARD CATALOG

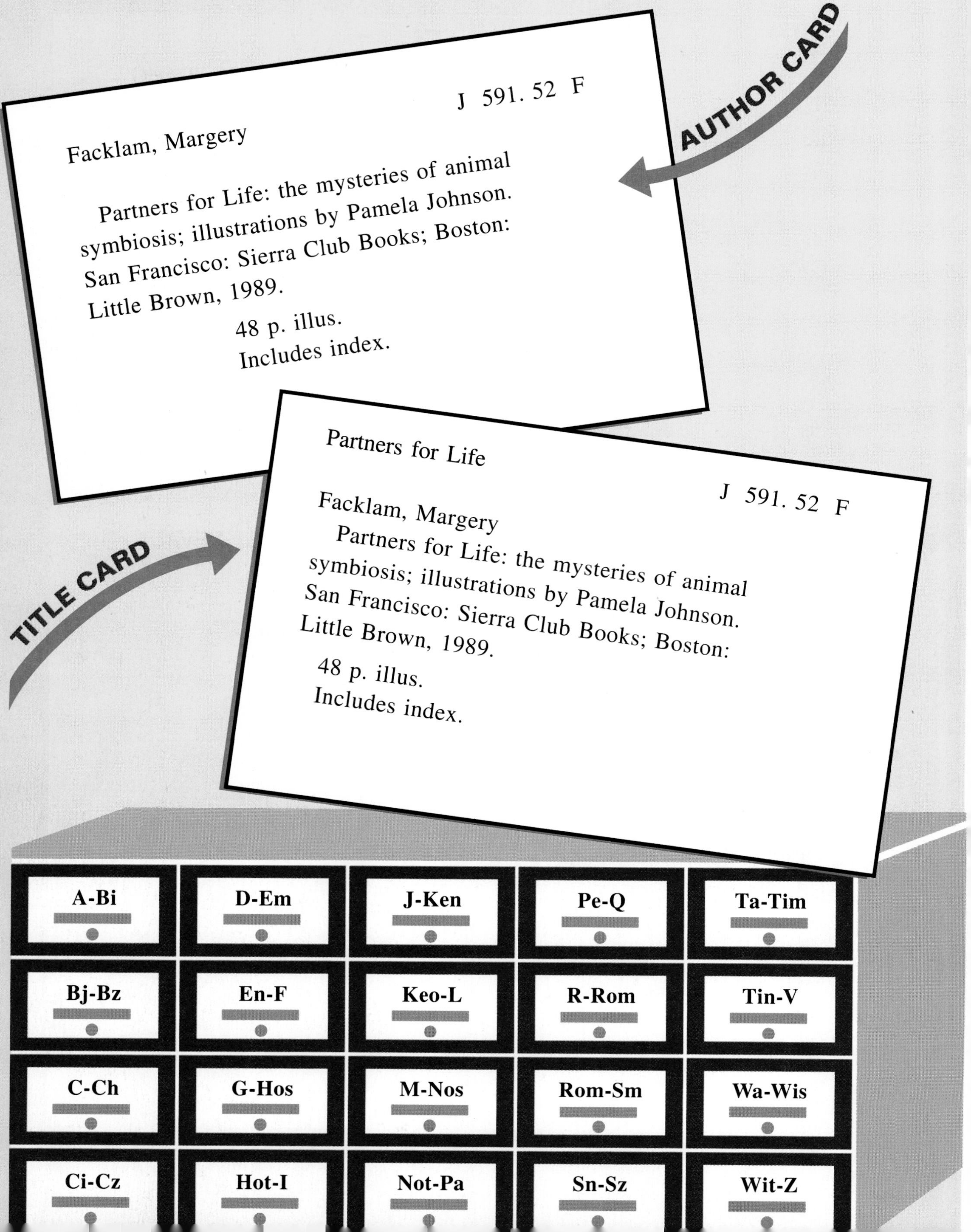

AUTHOR CARD

J 591. 52 F

Facklam, Margery

Partners for Life: the mysteries of animal
symbiosis; illustrations by Pamela Johnson.
San Francisco: Sierra Club Books; Boston:
Little Brown, 1989.

48 p. illus.
Includes index.

TITLE CARD

Partners for Life

J 591. 52 F

Facklam, Margery
Partners for Life: the mysteries of animal
symbiosis; illustrations by Pamela Johnson.
San Francisco: Sierra Club Books; Boston:
Little Brown, 1989.

48 p. illus.
Includes index.

A-Bi	D-Em	J-Ken	Pe-Q	Ta-Tim
Bj-Bz	En-F	Keo-L	R-Rom	Tin-V
C-Ch	G-Hos	M-Nos	Rom-Sm	Wa-Wis
Ci-Cz	Hot-I	Not-Pa	Sn-Sz	Wit-Z

CARD CATALOG

SYMBIOSIS

J 591. 52 F

Facklam, Margery
   Partners for Life: the mysteries of animal symbiosis; illustrations by Pamela Johnson. San Francisco: Sierra Club Books; Boston: Little Brown, 1989.

   48 p. illus.
   Includes index.

1. Symbiosis 2. Animal Behavior 3. Animal Ecology
1. Johnson, Pamela, illus. ll. Title

SUBJECT CARD

COMPUTERIZED FORM
OF THE CARD CATALOG

BOOK FORM OF THE
CARD CATALOG

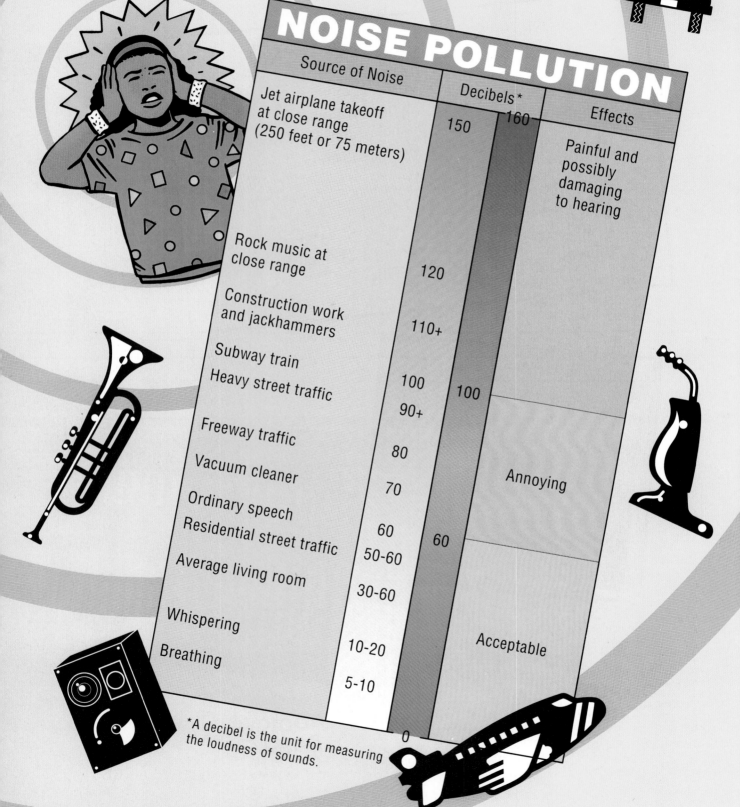

NOISE POLLUTION

Source of Noise	Decibels*	Effects
Jet airplane takeoff at close range (250 feet or 75 meters)	150 160	Painful and possibly damaging to hearing
Rock music at close range	120	
Construction work and jackhammers	110+	
Subway train	100	
Heavy street traffic	100	
	90+	
Freeway traffic	80	Annoying
Vacuum cleaner	70	
Ordinary speech	60	
Residential street traffic	50-60	60
Average living room	30-60	
Whispering		Acceptable
Breathing	10-20	
	5-10	
	0	

*A decibel is the unit for measuring the loudness of sounds.

LARGE ZOOS
IN THE UNITED STATES

Name	YEARLY BUDGET (Millions of Dollars)	YEARLY ATTENDANCE (Millions of People)	NUMBER OF ACRES	NUMBER OF SPECIES
Bronx Zoo (New York)	24.6	2.2	265	657
Lincoln Park Zoo (Chicago)	8.8	4.5	35	382
National Zoo (Washington, D.C.)	13.0	3.0	163	509
St. Louis Zoo	11.3	2.8	83	720
San Diego Zoo	40.0	3.5	100	800

A SAFE LANDFILL

Landfills are not the solution to the problem of too much waste. However, it is possible to build a safe landfill in places where there is a thick layer of clay above the water table. Pipes with holes on the top side are laid on top of the clay. The pipes lead to a reservoir that has a clay bottom and clay sides. The clay prevents the water from leaking out. Waste is deposited on top of the pipes. Rain water seeps through the waste into the pipes, and is carried to the reservoir. The water in the reservoir is treated for purification. The treated water may go back into the ground to become part of the groundwater, or it may go into a lake.

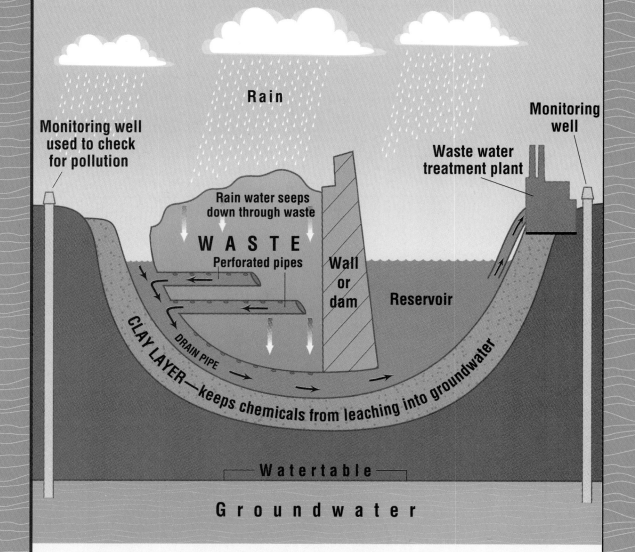

Rain water filters through waste into pipes leading to a reservoir. The water is treated and allowed to go into a lake or back into the ground.

A FOOD CHAIN

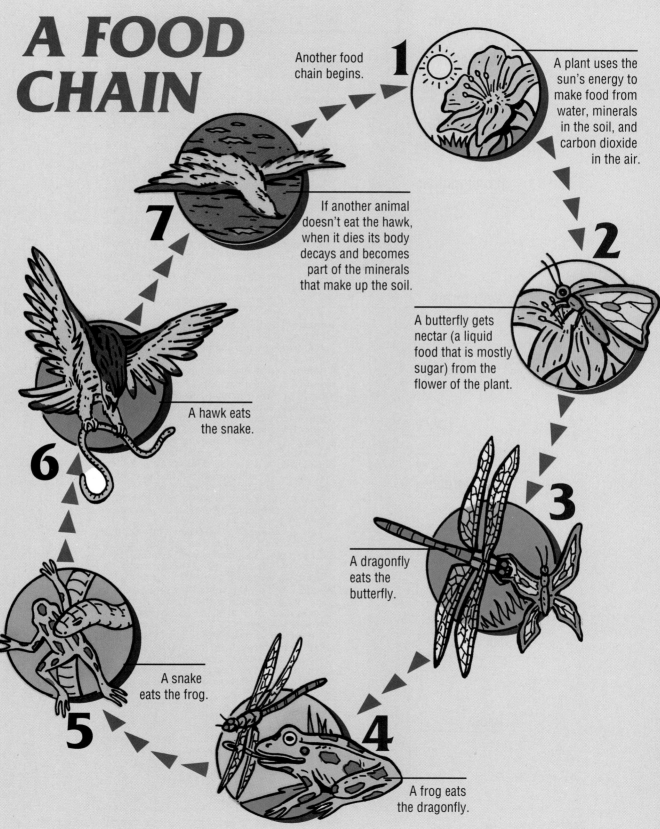

Another food chain begins.

1 A plant uses the sun's energy to make food from water, minerals in the soil, and carbon dioxide in the air.

7 If another animal doesn't eat the hawk, when it dies its body decays and becomes part of the minerals that make up the soil.

2 A butterfly gets nectar (a liquid food that is mostly sugar) from the flower of the plant.

A hawk eats the snake.

6

3 A dragonfly eats the butterfly.

A snake eats the frog.

5

4 A frog eats the dragonfly.

Dictionary

Guide words

Main entry

willing Wanting or ready to do something. Are you *willing* to help us? To be hypnotized, you have to be a *willing* subject.
will·ing (wil'ing) *adjective.*

Definition

willow A tree or bush that has long, thin branches that bend easily and narrow leaves. Willows usually grow in wet areas.
wil·low (wil'ō) *noun, plural* **willows.**

Pronunciation

wilt To become limp; droop. The flowers *wilted* soon after they were cut.
wilt (wilt) *verb,* **wilted, wilting.**

win **1.** To do better than any other in a race or contest; gain a victory. The home team *won* the hockey game. We flipped a coin, and I *won.* **2.** To get as a prize. The winner of the baking contest will *win* a set of bread pans. **3.** To get by effort; gain. The explorer is *winning* new fame as an author. *Verb.*
—A victory or success. The team had six *wins* and five losses this season. *Noun.*
win (win) *verb,* **won, winning;** *noun, plural* **wins.**

Verb forms

wince To draw back slightly from something painful, dangerous, or unpleasant. The child *winced* when the doctor gave the injection.
wince (wins) *verb,* **winced, wincing.**

winch A machine for lifting or pulling things. A winch is made up of a large spool or pulley with a rope or chain around it. Ships' anchors are hoisted on a winch.
winch (winch) *noun, plural* **winches.**

Homographs

wind¹ **1.** Air that is moving over the earth. The *wind* blew my hat off. The strong *winds* made the trees bend and sway. **2.** The power to breathe; breath. The hard blow knocked the *wind* out of me. *Noun.*
—To cause someone to be out of breath. Climbing the long flight of stairs *winded* us. *Verb.*
• **to get wind of.** To receive information or hints about. If my cousin *gets wind of* the party, the surprise will be ruined.
wind (wind) *noun, plural* **winds;** *verb,* **winded, winding.**

Part of Speech

wind² **1.** To wrap something around on itself or on something else. Please *wind* this loose yarn into a ball. The vine *wound* around the pole. **2.** To move or cause to move in one direction and then another. The road *winds* through the mountains. I *wound* through the traffic on my bicycle. **3.** To give a machine power by tightening its spring. Don't forget to *wind* your alarm clock. *Verb.*

Idiom

• **to wind up.** **1.** To end; finish; conclude. Let's *wind up* the work today. The meeting *wound up* at six o'clock. **2.** To make movements with the arms and body

DICTIONARY

before pitching a ball. The batter watched carefully while the pitcher *wound up.*
wind (wīnd) *verb,* **wound, winding.**

wind instrument   A musical instrument that is played by blowing into it. Trumpets and flutes are wind instruments.
wind instrument (wind).

windmill   A machine that uses the power of the wind to turn vanes or sails at the top of a tower. Windmills are used to pump water, grind grain, or generate electricity.
wind·mill (wind′mil′) *noun, plural* **windmills.**

windmill

window   An opening in a wall or roof that lets in air and light. Panes of glass fill the openings of most windows.
win·dow (win′dō) *noun, plural* **windows.**

Word History

The word **window** comes from two Scandinavian words meaning "wind" and "eye." A window was thought of as an opening, or "eye," in a wall to let the wind through.

windowpane   A single pane of glass in a window.
win·dow·pane (win′dō pān′) *noun, plural* **windowpanes.**

windpipe   The tube in the body that carries air from the throat to the lungs.
wind·pipe (wind′pīp′) *noun, plural* **windpipes.**

DIRECTIONS

Planting Seeds

1

Fill the containers almost full of potting soil. Press the soil down slightly as you put it in.

SUPPLIES:
- containers with holes in them (peat pots)
- potting soil
- seeds
- stakes or popsicle sticks
- a watering can or plant sprayer

2

Put one (or two) seeds in each container. (Some seeds don't sprout. If both do, you can transplant one later.)

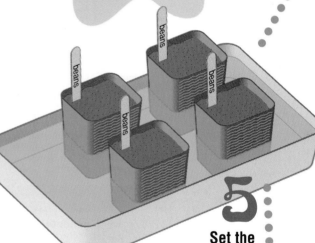

5

Set the containers in a pan of shallow, warm water. Leave them there until the water seeps up and moistens the soil.

3

Cover the seeds with more soil—just a thin layer. Pat the soil down.

4

Write the name of the plant on a marker—a stake or a popsicle stick. Put the marker in the soil near the edge of the container.

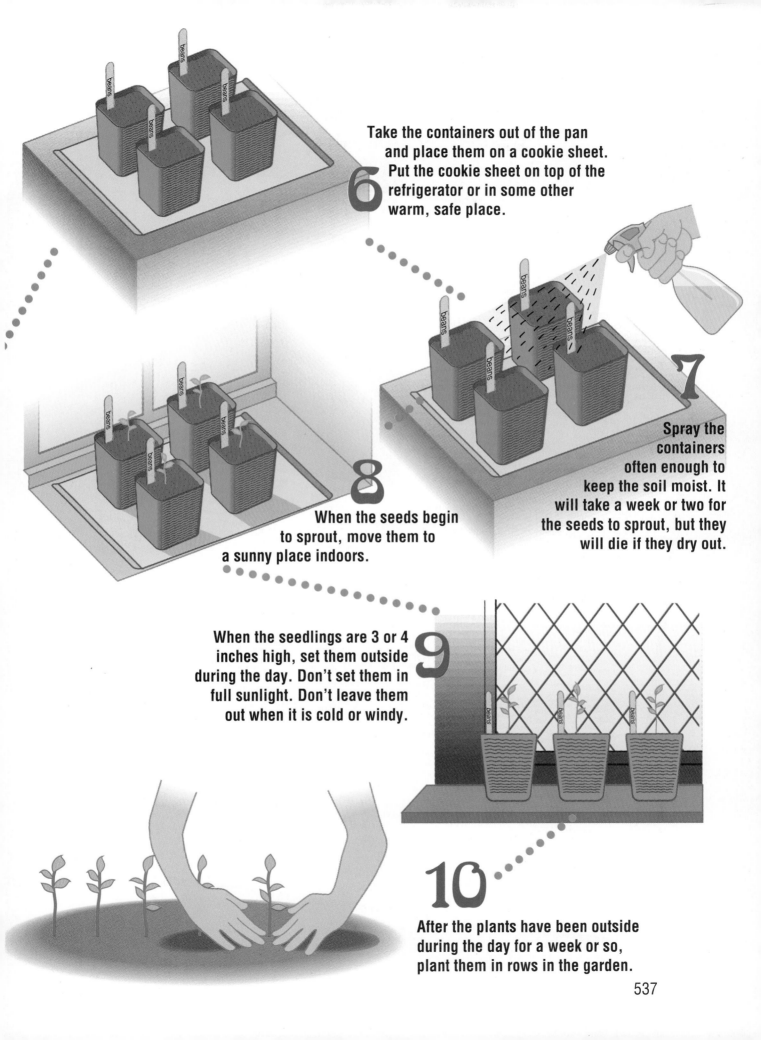

6 Take the containers out of the pan and place them on a cookie sheet. Put the cookie sheet on top of the refrigerator or in some other warm, safe place.

7 Spray the containers often enough to keep the soil moist. It will take a week or two for the seeds to sprout, but they will die if they dry out.

8 When the seeds begin to sprout, move them to a sunny place indoors.

9 When the seedlings are 3 or 4 inches high, set them outside during the day. Don't set them in full sunlight. Don't leave them out when it is cold or windy.

10 After the plants have been outside during the day for a week or so, plant them in rows in the garden.

558 Hiawatha

Hiawatha (hī′ə woth′ə), a 16th-century North American Indian chieftain credited with founding the Iroquois Confederacy of tribes in what is now New York State. Since every new chief of the Tortoise Clan of the Mohawk Indians inherited the name Hiawatha, the Iroquois hero is believed to have been a Mohawk. A disciple of the great Indian prophet Deganawidah, Hiawatha wanted to unite all North American tribes in universal peace. In about 1570 he and Deganawidah persuaded four nearby tribes to join the Mohawks in the Iroquois Confederacy, which dominated most Indians of the northeastern United States early in the 18th century. By that time, Iroquois legends described Hiawatha as a magical figure who had brought civilization to his people by teaching them agriculture, medicine, political cooperation, and the arts.

In the 19th century, scholars mistakenly attached Hiawatha's name to a group of legends about the mythical Chippewa hero Manabozho. Henry Wadsworth Longfellow based his famous *The Song of Hiawatha* on the Chippewa tales.

•Frederick J. Dockstader

A hibernating ground squirrel is insensitive to touch.

hibernation (hī′bər nā′shən), also called winter sleep, a state of reduced activity that occurs in many animals during the winter. In cold weather most animals need relatively large amounts of food to carry on their normal body activities. In winter, however, food often becomes scarce, and many animals could not survive unless they hibernated. In the state of hibernation normal body activities are so greatly reduced that very little food is required. As a result, hibernating animals may survive for months on fat stored in the body.

Hibernation occurs in many mammals, including woodchucks, ground squirrels, hamsters, hedgehogs, and certain bats. It also occurs in most reptiles and amphibians, some insects, and a few fishes and birds. Although the condition varies slightly from one animal to the next, all hibernating animals undergo certain similar changes. The rate of metabolism is always greatly decreased, and the body temperature falls until it approaches the temperature of the animal's surroundings. Both the rate of breathing and the heartbeat slow down considerably. The animal is not sensitive to touch or sound, and it remains in a coma-like state of unconsciousness. Usually a rise in temperature arouses a hibernating animal. With the arrival of warm weather in spring, the body processes begin to speed up. Soon the animal awakens and becomes active again, searching for food that is once more available.

Mammals. Toward winter, many mammals seek out sheltered burrows or tree hollows in which to hibernate. Shortly after they fall asleep, their rate of metabolism and their body temperature fall. Breathing slows down to about the rate of one breath every five minutes, and the heart beats only four or five times a minute.

The length of time a mammal hibernates depends on the severity and length of the winter season. For example, some arctic animals hibernate for as long as eight months. Since hibernating animals live on stored body fat, mammals that hibernate for a long time may lose as much as one-third of their original weight.

Contrary to popular belief, bears do not hibernate. Although they enter a deep sleep and live on stored fat, their body temperature does not fall more than a few degrees, and their rate of metabolism decreases very little. They remain sensitive to touch, and they can be awakened by prodding. Certain other mammals, including opossums, skunks, and raccoons, enter a deep sleep similar to that of bears. However, they do not really hibernate.

Reptiles and Amphibians. Unlike mammals, reptiles and amphibians are cold-blooded. They do not generate their own body heat, and they depend on their surroundings to provide the warmth needed to carry on their body activities. As winter approaches, many lizards and snakes enter burrows and crevices in the ground. Freshwater turtles spend the winter at the bottom of a lake or pond. Frogs, toads, and other amphibians hibernate by burying themselves in mud.

In hibernating reptiles and amphibians, the body temperature drops to only one or two degrees above that of the surroundings and sometimes almost to freezing. Almost no air is taken in, and no food is eaten.

Fishes, Insects, and Birds. Hibernation is rare in fishes. However, some freshwater species, such as the carp, move into deep water for the winter, and some freshwater eels bury themselves in mud. Certain kinds of insects, such as yellow jackets and some butterflies, also hibernate in winter. Hibernating insects usually crawl under bark or stones or into the ground.

Only a few kinds of birds are known to hibernate. Such birds include the poorwill, a small bird native to the western United States and Mexico, and some species of swifts and hummingbirds.

•Lorus and Margery Milne

Hibernia (hī bèr′ni ə), the Latin name given to Ireland by the ancient Romans. It is derived from Ierne, the ancient Greek name. Today, Hibernia is occasionally used as a poetic name for Ireland. See also IRELAND.

•Norman J. G. Pounds

ENCYCLOPEDIA

which was the strike force of Haganah, the underground Jewish army. During World War II he fought for the British in Lebanon and Syria. In the Israeli war for independence in 1948, he was deputy commander of the Palmach, and he commanded the brigade that kept the supply lines to Jerusalem open. Rabin remained in the army as a career soldier, eventually becoming chief of staff in 1964. He retired from the army in 1968 and served as ambassador to the United States from 1968 to 1973. He was minister of labor in early 1974.

Charles Radding

Raccolta (rə kōl′tə), in the Roman Catholic church, a collection of material describing the various ways of gaining indulgences, or reductions of the time a soul must pass in Purgatory. These include prayers, good works, and pilgrimages. The Raccolta was first published in 1807.

*Rev. Thomas H. McBrien, O.P.

raccoon (ra kün′), also called coon, a stout-bodied mammal with a pointed face and long bushy tail. Raccoon live in many regions throughout the continental United States, Mexico, and Central America. They are especially abundant in parts of southern Canada, and some raccoon are found as far south as the equator.

The raccoon's fur was used as money by early settlers in North America, and raccoon hats were often worn by explorers. Raccoon were also trapped and hunted for their tasty flesh. In some parts of the United States and Canada they are still hunted for their flesh and for their fur, which is used to make coats, collars, hats, pocketbooks, and other apparel. Raccoon from northern climates are widely used for these purposes because their coat is denser than that of raccoon living in southern areas.

Raccoon are often kept as pets, particularly in rural areas. However, it is not recommended that raccoon be taken into the home as pets. While the young are playful and mischievous, raccoon tend to become surly as they grow older.

Size and Appearance. When fully grown, large raccoon are about 2½ feet (75 cm) long, including their 9-inch-long (23-cm-long) tail. They range in weight from 10 pounds (4.5 kg) to more than 30 pounds (13.5 kg).

A raccoon's coat is usually one or more shades of gray, but it may range from yellow to black. Red, brown, and even pure-white coons are occasionally born. Across the eyes of the coon's face is a black band, which extends sideways like a mask. Another black band extends up from the tip of the nose and flares out into the gray fur that covers the head. The short rounded ears are light at the tips and edges, and the feet are also light in color. The tail is banded, usually with five bands of light gray.

Behavior. Most raccoon live in hollow trees. They may also live in holes in the ground, rocky ledges, beaver dams, or even abandoned houses. Usually they remain in the nest during the day and leave only at night to search for food. Raccoon are completely omnivorous. They eat crayfish, fish, worms, and rabbits, as well as plant products, such as nuts and corn and other grains.

Contrary to popular belief, raccoon do not wash their food before eating. A raccoon may dip its food in water, but it never washes anything. The belief

Raccoons live in many regions of North America and Central America. They are skillful climbers, and they frequently escape from their predators by rapidly ascending a tree.

that it washes its food has arisen because the raccoon has a keen sense of touch and investigates objects by feeling them. Because it can feel moist objects better than dry ones, it frequently dips objects in any available water, whether it is clean or dirty. The feeling motions made by the coon are often mistaken for washing, but the animal also makes the same feeling motions with dry objects.

Like many other animals, raccoon slow down their activities during the cold winter months. They do not hibernate, but they do enter a deep sleep from which they are difficult to rouse. They are nourished through this period by deposits of fat, which they store in the body in the fall.

Reproduction. The mating season usually occurs during February and March, and the young, called cubs, are born about 61 days later. A litter generally consists of four cubs, but there may be as few as one or as many as eight. The newborn young, which are about 4 inches (10 cm) long and weigh about 6 ounces (170 gm) remain with the mother until they are about 6 months old. Raccoon mature at about the age of 8 months, but they continue to grow for 18 months. The first litter is born to females in the second year of life. Raccoon may live as long as 20 years, but the average life-span is 9 or 10 years.

Coon Hunting. On fall and early winter nights, coon hunters and their dogs invade the areas where coons are known to live. The dogs are usually a kind of hound that has been bred for hunting, but sometimes they are crosses between hounds and other breeds.

In a typical coon hunt, a party of hunters walks through the woods until a dog crosses a raccoon's track. The dog follows the trail to the tree that the animal has climbed and barks steadily until the hunters arrive to shoot the coon. Some dogs are trained to run ahead of a hunter's slow-moving automobile. When the dog crosses a coon's trail, the hunters park the car and follow the dog through the woods until it trees the coon. After a hunt, raccoon are often eaten.

The raccoon, *Procyon lotor*, is classified in the order Carnivora, family Procyonidae.

Leon F. Whitney

If you enjoyed **Folktales of the United States**, you may want to read some of the other books included in WORLD-WIDE PUBLISHERS' series FOLKTALES OF THE WORLD. Use the handy order form below to receive copies.

— — — — — — — — — — — — — DETACH HERE — — — — — — — — — — — — —

ORDER FORM

Folktales of China	#1002	$4.95	**Folktales of England**	#1007	$4.95
Folktales of Africa	#1003	$4.95	**Folktales of Australia**	#1008	$4.95
Folktales of Mexico	#1004	$4.95	**Folktales of Canada**	#1009	$4.95
Folktales of South America	#1005	$4.95	**Folktales of Greece**	#1010	$4.95
Folktales of France	#1006	$4.95	**Folktales of the Pacific**	#1011	$4.95

Please Print

NAME _Douglas Montero_

ADDRESS _732 West Alameda_

CITY _Goshen_   STATE _Ala._   ZIP _00000_

PHONE (_000_) _555-7231_

ITEM #	QTY.	NAME OF BOOK	ITEM PRICE	TOTAL	POSTAGE ($.50 per item)	TOTAL ITEM CHARGES
1006	2	Folktales of France	$4.95	$9.90	$1.00	$10.90
1007	1	Folktales of England	4.95	4.95	.50	5.45
1008	1	Folktales of Australia	4.95	4.95	.50	5.45
1010	1	Folktales of Greece	4.95	4.95	.50	5.45

PAYMENT METHOD (check one)

☑ CHECK

❏ MONEY ORDER

(SORRY – NO CREDIT CARDS)

Price & Postage TOTAL	$27.25
Special handling ($.50 per item)	
Tax: 5% for residents of Iowa	
TOTAL	$27.25

SEND TO: WORLD-WIDE PUBLISHERS
 Folktales of the World
 2200 North Mississippi
 Chanticlere, Iowa 00000

ALLOW 3-4 WEEKS FOR DELIVERY

LAKESIDE LIBRARY
APPLICATION FOR LIBRARY CARD

PLEASE PRINT

NAME ___Lung Wei___

ADDRESS ___439 Coolidge___

number and street   apt. # if applicable

HOME PHONE ___555-7019___

MAILING ADDRESS _____
(only if different from above address)   number and street

___Privet Point,   Michigan   00000___

city   state   zip

PARENT/GUARDIAN NAME ___Ying Wei___

SCHOOL ___Garrison Elementary___

(if attending)

EMPLOYER NAME _____

EMPLOYER ADDRESS _____

number and street

_____

city   state   zip

WORK PHONE _____ EXT. _____

I AGREE TO FOLLOW ALL LIBRARY RULES AND BE RESPONSIBLE FOR ALL MATERIALS THAT ARE CHARGED TO THIS CARD.

X ___Lung Wei___

signature of patron

X ___Ying Wei___

signature of parent/guardian if patron is under 18

The library requests your VOLUNTARY assistance in providing information in order to select materials, plan services and programs, and apply for possible grants. This information is confidential. **PLEASE CIRCLE THE APPROPRIATE LETTERS:**

BORN BETWEEN:
A. BEFORE 1900   D. 1921-1930   G. 1951-1960   (J.) 1981-2000
B. 1901-1910   E. 1931-1940   H. 1961-1970
C. 1911-1920   F. 1941-1950   I. 1971-1980

CIRCLE YOUR PRIMARY READING LANGUAGE:
A. Arabic   E. German   I. Maltese   M. Tagalog
(B.) Chinese   F. Italian   J. Portuguese N. Tongan
(C.) English   G. Japanese   K. Russian   O. Vietnamese
D. French   H. Korean   L. Spanish   P. Other _____

THANK YOU FOR YOUR COOPERATION

STAFF USE ONLY

DATE: _____

INIT/LIB: _____

BAR CODE #: _____

OTHER ID: _____

MAIL CODE:
1   2   3

AGE: _____

READ. LANG: _____

_____

DATE ENTERED:

_____

INITIALS: _____

GRAPHS

WORLD PRODUCTION OF CRUDE OIL IN 1989

Country	Production
OPEC Countries	
Canada	
China	
Mexico	
United Kingdom	
United States	
USSR	
All other countries	

 = 1 million barrels per day   = 2 million barrels per day

PICTOGRAPH

GRAPHS

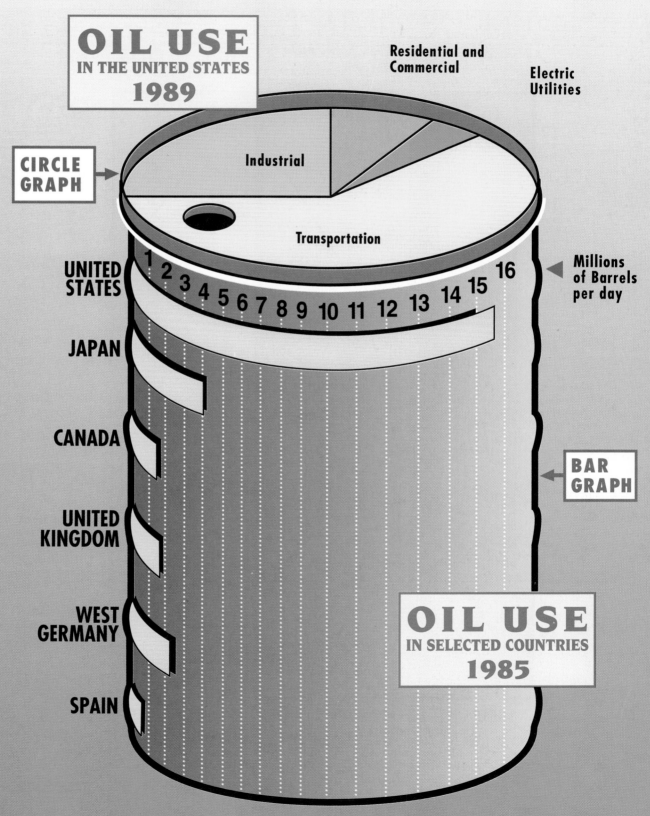

OIL USE IN THE UNITED STATES 1989

CIRCLE GRAPH

Industrial

Residential and Commercial

Electric Utilities

Transportation

UNITED STATES

1 2 3 4 5 6 7 8 9 10 11 12 13 14 15 16

Millions of Barrels per day

JAPAN

CANADA

UNITED KINGDOM

BAR GRAPH

WEST GERMANY

SPAIN

OIL USE IN SELECTED COUNTRIES 1985

GRAPHS

USE OF OIL IN THE UNITED STATES: 1960-1985

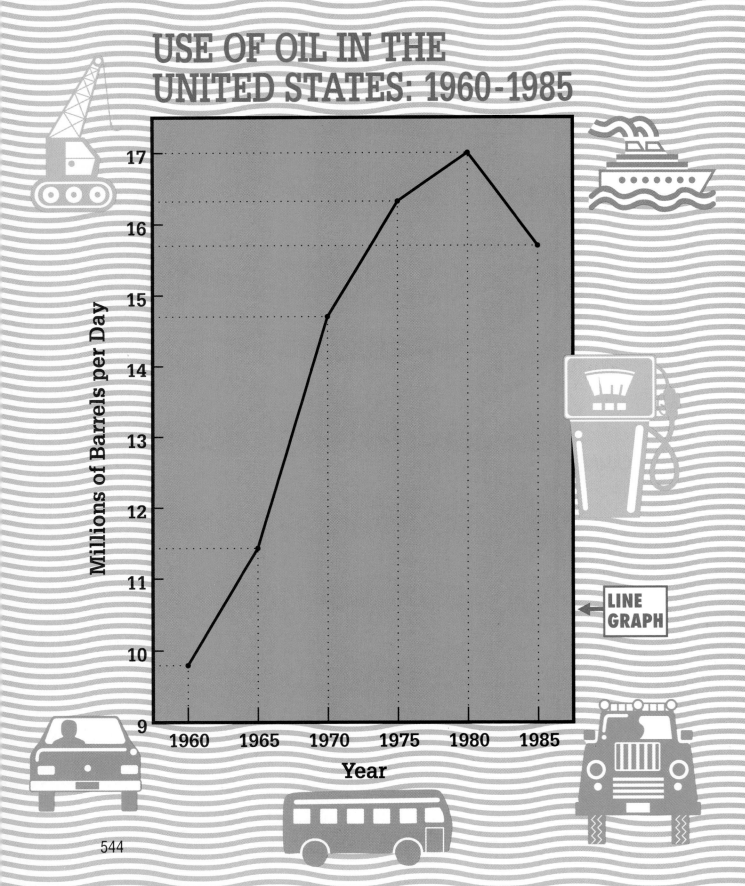

LINE GRAPH

INDEX

115

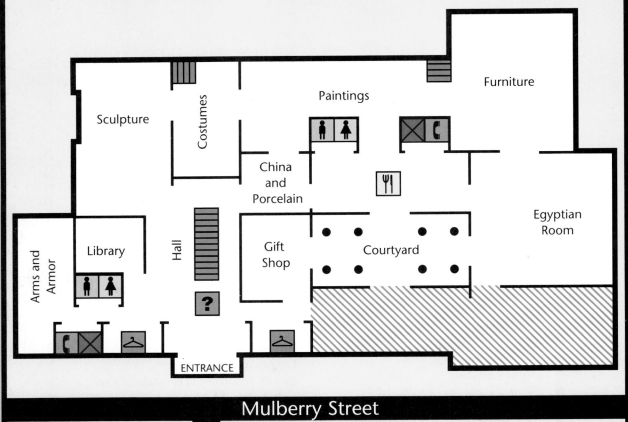

CITY MUSEUM
FLOOR PLAN – GROUND FLOOR

Sculpture · Costumes · Paintings · Furniture · China and Porcelain · Library · Hall · Arms and Armor · Gift Shop · Courtyard · Egyptian Room · ENTRANCE

Mulberry Street

Fourth Avenue

KEY

Symbol	Meaning	Symbol	Meaning	Symbol	Meaning
⊠	Elevator	?	Information	♨	Restaurant
▤	Stairs	🧥	Coat Check	☎	Telephone
👨	Men	👩	Women	▨	Special Exhibits

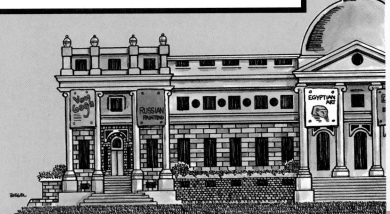

Maps

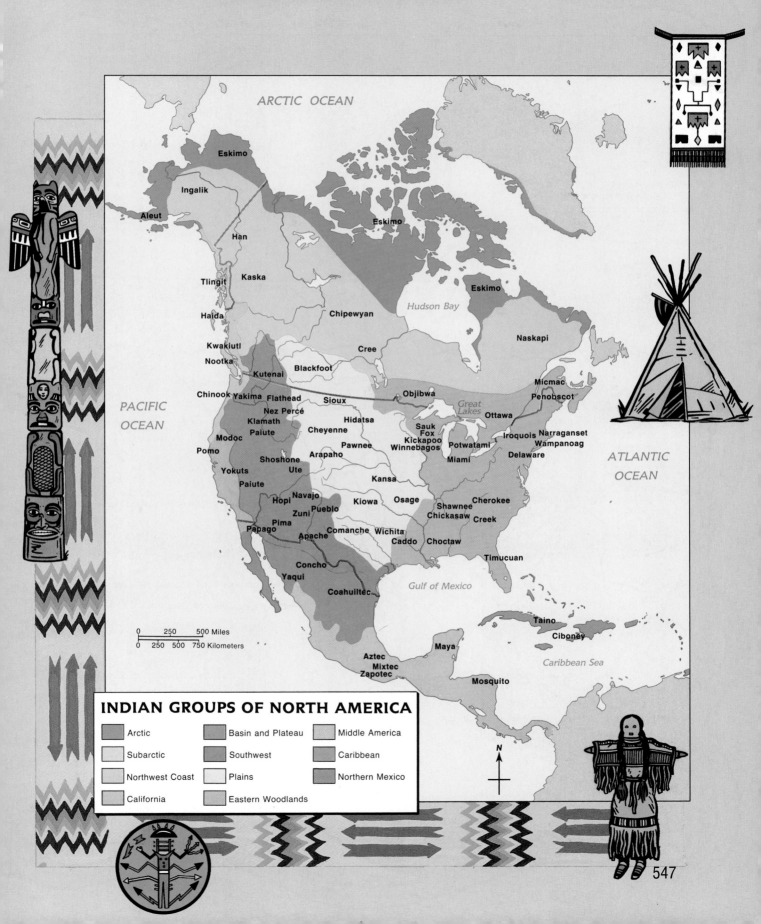

ARCTIC OCEAN

Eskimo

Ingalik

Aleut

Han

Tlingit — Kaska

Haida

Kwakiutl
Nootka

Kutenai — Blackfoot

Chinook Yakima Flathead

Nez Percé
Klamath
Paiute

Modoc

Pomo

Shoshone
Yokuts — Ute

Paiute

Hopi — Navajo
Zuni — Pueblo

Pima
Papago — Apache

Concho

Yaqui

Coahuiltec

Eskimo

Chipewyan

Cree

Sioux

Hidatsa

Cheyenne

Pawnee

Arapaho

Kansa

Kiowa

Comanche — Wichita

Caddo

Hudson Bay

Eskimo

Naskapi

Objibwa

Great
Lakes — Ottawa

Sauk
Fox
Kickapoo
Winnebagos — Potwatami
Miami

Osage

Shawnee
Chickasaw

Choctaw

Micmac
Penobscot

Iroquois Narraganset
Wampanoag
Delaware

Cherokee

Creek

Timucuan

PACIFIC
OCEAN

ATLANTIC
OCEAN

Gulf of Mexico

Taino

Ciboney

Aztec
Mixtec
Zapotec

Maya

Mosquito

Caribbean Sea

0   250   500 Miles
0 250 500 750 Kilometers

INDIAN GROUPS OF NORTH AMERICA

- Arctic
- Subarctic
- Northwest Coast
- California
- Basin and Plateau
- Southwest
- Plains
- Eastern Woodlands
- Middle America
- Caribbean
- Northern Mexico

N

547

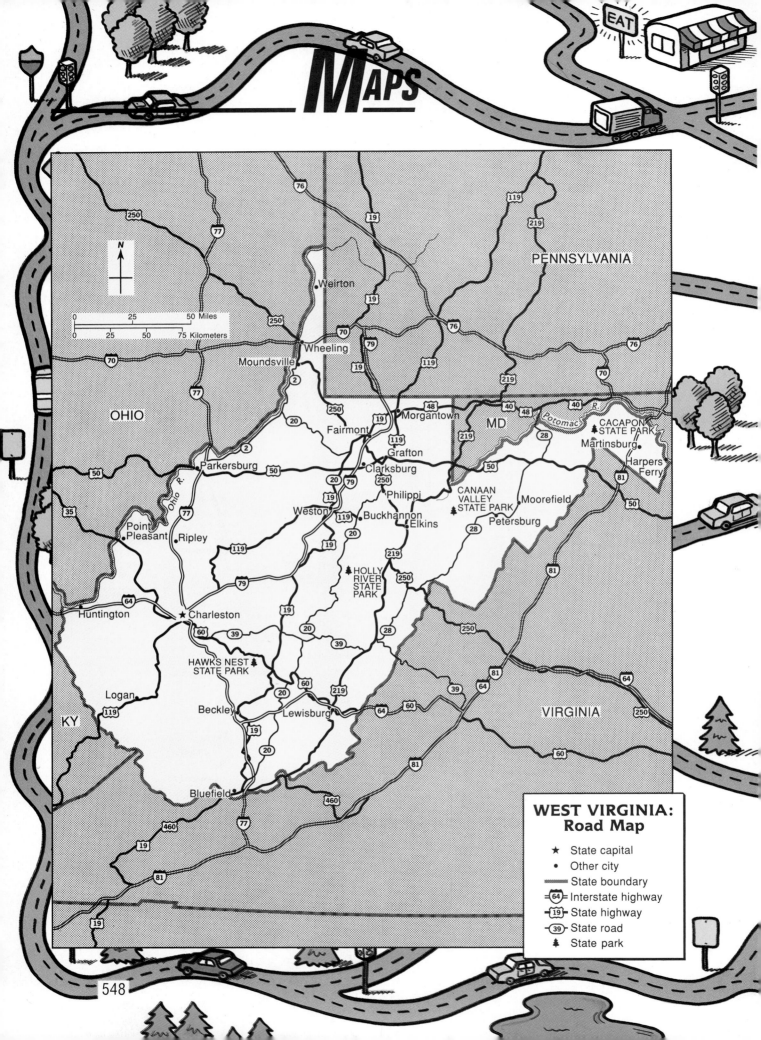

MAPS

PENNSYLVANIA

Weirton

Wheeling
Moundsville

OHIO

Morgantown
Fairmont
MD
Grafton
Parkersburg
Clarksburg
CACAPON
STATE PARK
Martinsburg
Harpers
Ferry
Philippi
CANAAN
VALLEY
STATE PARK
Moorefield
Weston
Buckhannon
Point
Pleasant
Ripley
Elkins
Petersburg

HOLLY
RIVER
STATE
PARK

Huntington
Charleston

HAWKS NEST
STATE PARK

Logan

KY
Beckley
Lewisburg

VIRGINIA

Bluefield

548

WEST VIRGINIA:
Road Map

★   State capital
•   Other city
    State boundary
64 Interstate highway
19 State highway
39 State road
    State park

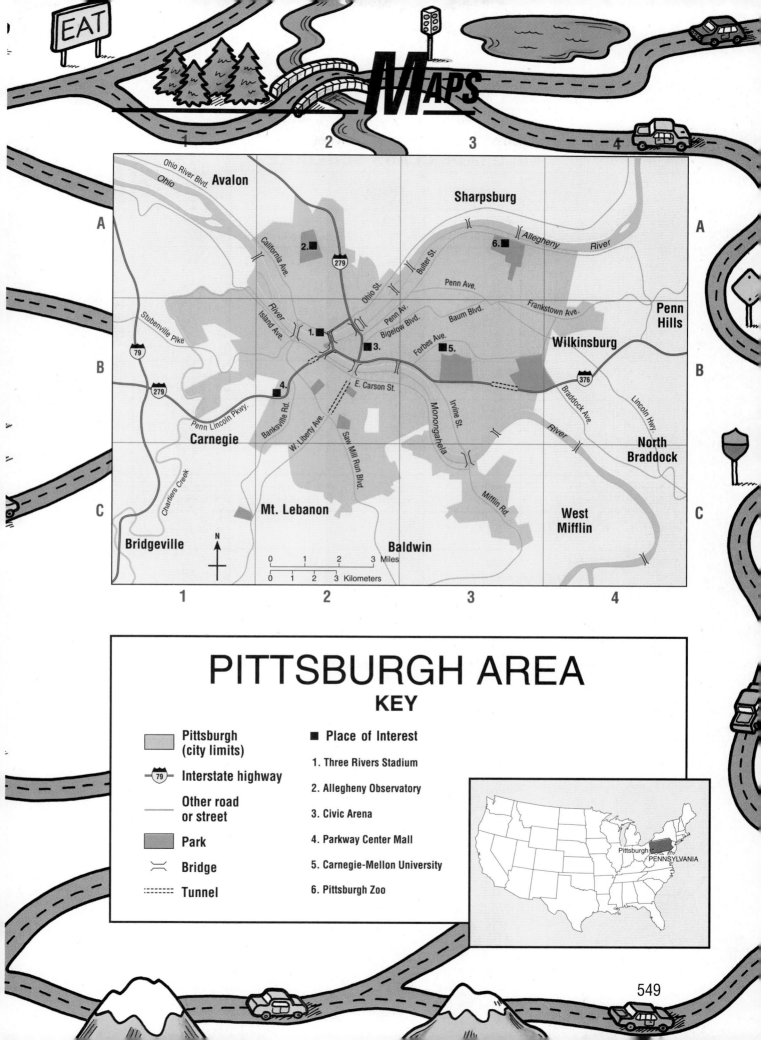

PITTSBURGH AREA
KEY

Pittsburgh (city limits)

🛣 79 Interstate highway

Other road or street

Park

⋈ Bridge

┄┄ Tunnel

■ Place of Interest

1. Three Rivers Stadium

2. Allegheny Observatory

3. Civic Arena

4. Parkway Center Mall

5. Carnegie-Mellon University

6. Pittsburgh Zoo

Pittsburgh
PENNSYLVANIA

549

SCHEDULES

4th GRADE CLASS SCHEDULE

TIME \ DAY	MONDAY	TUESDAY	WEDNESDAY	THURSDAY	FRIDAY
8:00-8:10	Flag Salute, Announcements	Flag Salute, Announcements	Flag Salute, Announcements	Flag Salute, Announcements	Flag Salute, Announcements
8:10-9:50	Language Arts	Language Arts	Language Arts	Language Arts	Language Arts
9:50-10:10	P.E.	P.E.	P.E.	P.E.	P.E.
10:10-11:10	Art	Music	Art	Music	Art
11:10-11:50	Lunch & Recess	Lunch & Recess	Lunch & Recess	Lunch & Recess	Lunch & Recess
11:50-12:15	SSR	SSR	SSR	SSR	SSR
12:15-1:00	Math	Math	Math	Math	Math
1:00-1:30	Health	Health	Health	Health	Health
1:30-1:45	Recess	Recess	Recess	Recess	Recess
1:45-2:20	Science	Science	Science	Science	Science
2:20-2:45	Social Studies	Social Studies	Social Studies	Social Studies	Social Studies
2:45	D I S M I S S A L				

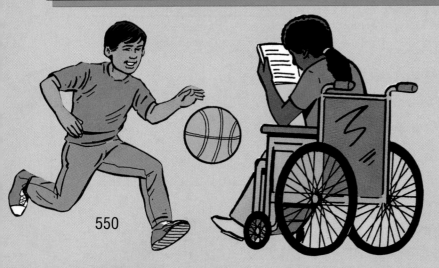

SCHEDULES

CALTRAIN

Sundays/Holidays*

SAN FRANCISCO TO SAN JOSE

			TRAIN NO. — AM		TRAIN NO. — PM						
MILES /	ZONE /	STATION	92	40	44	48	94	98	76	78	80
0.0		Lv San Francisco @									
		4th & Townsend Sts.	8:00	10:00	Noon	2:00	4:00	6:00	7:15	8:00	10:00
1.9	SF	Lv 22nd Street	8:05	10:05	12:05	2:05	4:05	6:05	7:20	8:05	10:05
4.1		Lv Paul Avenue	8:09	—	—	—	4:09	6:09	—	—	—
5.2		Lv Bayshore	8:12	10:10	12:10	2:10	4:12	6:12	7:25	8:10	10:10
9.3		Lv So. San Francisco	8:17	10:15	12:15	2:15	4:17	6:17	7:30	8:15	10:15
11.6	1	Lv San Bruno	8:21	10:19	12:19	2:19	4:21	6:21	7:34	8:19	10:19
13.7		Lv Millbrae	8:25	10:23	12:23	2:23	4:25	6:25	7:38	8:23	10:23
15.2		Lv Broadway	8:28	10:26	12:26	2:26	4:28	6:28	7:41	8:26	10:26
16.3		Lv Burlingame	8:31	10:28	12:28	2:28	4:30	6:30	7:44	8:28	10:28
17.9	2	Lv San Mateo	8:34	10:31	12:31	2:31	4:33	6:33	7:47	8:31	10:31
18.9		Lv Hayward Park	8:36	10:34	12:34	2:34	4:36	6:36	7:50	8:34	10:34
20.0		Lv Bay Meadows ●	—	—	—	—	—	—	—	—	—
20.3		Lv Hillsdale	8:39	10:37	12:37	2:37	4:39	6:39	7:53	8:37	10:37
21.9		Lv Belmont	8:42	10:40	12:40	2:40	4:42	6:42	7:56	8:40	10:40
23.2	3	Lv San Carlos	8:45	10:43	12:43	2:43	4:45	6:45	7:59	8:43	10:43
25.4		Lv Redwood City	8:49	10:47	12:47	2:47	4:49	6:49	8:03	8:47	10:47
27.8		Lv Atherton	8:53	10:51	12:51	2:51	4:53	6:53	8:07	8:51	10:51
28.9		Lv Menlo Park	8:56	10:53	12:53	2:53	4:55	6:55	8:10	8:53	10:53
30.1		Lv Palo Alto	8:59	10:56	12:56	2:56	4:58	6:58	8:13	8:56	10:56
31.8	4	Lv Stanford Stadium ●	—	—	—	—	—	—	—	—	—
34.8		Lv California Avenue	9:02	10:59	12:59	2:59	5:01	7:01	8:16	8:59	10:59
36.1		Lv Mountain View	9:08	11:05	1:05	3:05	5:07	7:07	8:22	9:05	11:05
38.8		Lv Sunnyvale	9:12	11:09	1:09	3:09	5:11	7:11	8:26	9:09	11:09
40.8	5	Lv Lawrence	9:16	11:12	1:12	3:12	5:15	7:15	8:30	9:12	11:12
44.3		Lv Santa Clara	9:20	11:17	1:17	3:17	5:19	7:19	8:35	9:17	11:17
46.9		Ar San Jose	9:28	11:25	1:25	3:25	5:28	7:28	8:43	9:25	11:25
		Ar Santa Cruz	10:30	12:30	2:30	4:30	6:40	8:30		10:30	

   Indicates bus connection to Santa Cruz.

*   New Year's Day, Memorial Day, Independence Day, Labor Day, Thanksgiving Day and Christmas Day. (CalTrain may operate reduced service on holiday eves and day after Thanksgiving). Call the CalTrain Hotline for details.

●   Special train service during racing, football, Giants baseball seasons only.

Emergency 1

EMERGENCY NUMBERS

Blairtown

Fire	**555-2323**
Police (Alternate number 555-2616)	**555-2452**
Sheriff (Night 555-2412)	**555-2501**
Ambulance	**555-2104**

Grenfell

Fire	**911**
Police	**911**
Sheriff	**555-6180 or 555-3822**
Ambulance	**911**

San Ruiz

Fire	**555-2123**
Police	**555-3031**
Sheriff (Night 555-2412)	**555-2501 or 555-2940**
Ambulance	**555-2104**

Other Emergency Numbers

Police Control Center	**1 + 800-555-6633**
Highway Patrol	**1 + 555-2562**
FBI	**1 + 555-555-8181**
If no answer call	**1 + 555-555-6100**

For Other Helpful Numbers see page 14

On the

KREEL – MURRAY   GRENFELL   30

Kreel Floyd 519 S Burr	555-1665
Kreen Mae 418 W 1	555-2644
Kruger Al 215 N Spencer	555-2936
Kruger Burt Rt 1	555-3428
Kruger John 202 Lebow	555-3952

L

L & S Hardware 101 Webster	555-3400
Lamb Otto 560 Benton	555-2857
LARSON GRAIN CO Hwy 44	555-4000
Lee K T 110 N Burr	555-2242
Leery Jacob 811 E 10	555-2901
Lemon Alice 806 Lebow	555-2865
Lester Betty L 112 W 1	555-5254

Lucas Ben 220 S Adams	555-9778
Lumis Roger Rt 1	555-2705
Lunez Martin 502 N Spencer	555-2345
Lyman C E 519 Lebow	555-3143
Lymann Carl 820 Webster	555-6167
Lyon Margaret 113 S Spencer	555-7881
Lyons Ed 220 Benton	555-5274
Lyons Frances 531 E 2	555-5201
Lyons Juanita 1555 N Adams	555-2667
Lyons Max 117 Benton	555-3788

M

Macer Tim 333 W 7	555-6778
...b 609 S Denison	555-4287

WHITE PAGES

---

18   FARM – FLEET

Farm Equipment

Bane Bros Farms Inc
620 Lebow Blairtown 555-5500

FARMER AND RANCH INC

Combines	Tractors	Irrigation Equipment

Hwy 44 San Ruiz **555-6666**

Gard Farm Supply Rte 1 555-4646

FARM EQUIPMENT

Tractors new and used
Forage tools
Combines and other harvest machines

Parts • Service • Finance

JUSTIN FARM SUPPLY
555 6700

FEDERAL OFFICES - See Government-United States

Feed Dealers

Argo Agri Services
Blairtown 555-7990
BLAIRTOWN FEED AND SEED
W Hwy 37 555-7855

CENTERTOWN COOP
Feed and Fertilizer Supply
Equipment to Lease
201 W 23 .... **555-4488**

Midway Suppliers
E Hwy 37 555-8345
Sutton Feed & Fertilizer Supply
3400 W Jackson San Ruiz 555-6652
WESTERN SUPPLY
1616 N Burr San Ruiz 555-3435

WILLIAMS EQUITY EXCHANGE
Liquid & Dry
Fertilizer
209 E 17 Grenfell **555-2562**

YELLOW PAGES

Gl os

This glossary can help you to pronounce and find out the meanings of words in this book that you may not know.

The words are listed in alphabetical order. Guide words at the top of each page tell you the first and last words on the page.

Each word is divided into syllables. The way to pronounce each word is given next. You will be able to understand the pronunciation respelling by using the key to the right. A shorter key appears at the bottom right corner of every other page.

When a word has more than one syllable, a dark accent mark (´) shows which syllable is stressed. In some words, a light accent mark (´) shows which syllable has a less heavy stress.

Glossary entries are based on entries in *The Macmillan/McGraw-Hill School Dictionary 1*.

a	at, bad	d	dear, soda, bad
ā	ape, pain, day, break	f	five, defend, leaf, off, cough, elephant
ä	father, car, heart		
âr	care, pair, bear, their, where	g	game, ago, fog, egg
e	end, pet, said, heaven, friend	h	hat, ahead
ē	equal, me, feet, team, piece, key	hw	white, whether, which
i	it, big, English, hymn	j	joke, enjoy, gem, page, edge
ī	ice, fine, lie, my	k	kite, bakery, seek, tack, cat
îr	ear, deer, here, pierce	l	lid, sailor, feel, ball, allow
o	odd, hot, watch	m	man, family, dream
ō	old, oat, toe, low	n	not, final, pan, knife
ô	coffee, all, taught, law, fought	ng	long, singer, pink
ôr	order, fork, horse, story, pour	p	pail, repair, soap, happy
oi	oil, toy	r	ride, parent, wear, more, marry
ou	out, now	s	sit, aside, pets, cent, pass
u	up, mud, love, double	sh	shoe, washer, fish, mission, nation
ū	use, mule, cue, feud, few	t	tag, pretend, fat, button, dressed
ü	rule, true, food	th	thin, panther, both
ù	put, wood, should	<u>th</u>	this, mother, smooth
ûr	burn, hurry, term, bird, word, courage	v	very, favor, wave
		w	wet, weather, reward
ə	about, taken, pencil, lemon, circus	y	yes, onion
b	bat, above, job	z	zoo, lazy, jazz, rose, dogs, houses
ch	chin, such, match	zh	vision, treasure, seizure

A

Abuelita A Spanish word for "Grandmother."
  A•bue•li•ta (ä´bwā lē´tä) *noun.*

abuse **1.** A practice or custom that is unfair or does harm. **2.** Harsh or insulting language.
  a•buse (ə būs´) *noun.*

accomplishment Something successfully completed; an achievement. Landing on the moon and the first spacewalk were both great *accomplishments.*
  ac•com•plish•ment
  (ə kom´plish mənt) *noun.*

altitude The height that something is above the ground or above sea level. The plane flew at an *altitude* of 1 mile (1.6 kilometers).
  al•ti•tude (al´ti tüd´) *noun.*

Word History

The word **altitude** comes from the Latin word *altus,* meaning "high" or "deep." When an airplane gains altitude, it flies higher.

---

amphibian **1.** Any of a group of cold-blooded animals with backbones. Amphibians have moist skin without scales. They usually live in or near water. Frogs and toads are amphibians. **2.** An airplane that can take off from and land on both land and water.
  am•phib•i•an (am fib´ē ən) *noun.*

amphibian

Antarctic The continent around the South Pole. The Antarctic is almost completely covered with ice all year long.
　　Ant•arc•tic (ant ärk´tik *or* ant är´tik) *noun.*

Appalachia A region of the United States that includes the Appalachian Mountains. Appalachia extends from southern New York to central Alabama.
　　Ap•pa•la•chi•a (ap´ə lā´chē ə *or* ap´ə lach´ē ə) *noun.*

Arctic The islands and ocean around the North Pole. Most of the Arctic is very cold and snowy, except in the summer.
　　Arc•tic (ärk´tik *or* är´tik) *noun.*

azure Having a clear sky-blue color.
　　az•ure (azh´ər) *adjective.*

B

Baja California A long, narrow strip of land in northwestern Mexico, separating the Gulf of California from the Pacific.
　　Ba•ja Cal•i•for•nia (bä´ hə kal´ə fôr´nyə) *noun.*

barren Not able to produce anything. No plants could grow in the sandy, *barren* soil.
　　bar•ren (bar´ən) *adjective.*

bidding An order or command. I closed my book at the teacher's *bidding.*
　　bid•ding (bid´ing) *noun.*

bizarre Very odd or strange.
　　bi•zarre (bi zär´) *adjective.*

Antarctic

at; āpe; fär; câre; end; mē; it; īce; pîerce; hot; ōld; sông; fôrk; oil; out; up; ūse; rüle; pu̇ll; tûrn; chin; sing; shop; thin; **th**is; **hw** in **wh**ite; **zh** in treasure. The symbol ə stands for the unstressed vowel sound in about, taken, pencil, lemon, and circus.

bluster To blow in a noisy or violent way. The wind *blustered* through the trees.
    blus•ter (blus′tər) *verb*, **blustered, blustering.**

bulldogging Wrestling a steer to the ground by taking hold of its horns and twisting its neck.
    bull•dog•ging (bul′dôg′ing) *noun*.

Caleb (kā′ləb)

caravan A group of people who travel together. In Africa and Asia, merchants and their camels travel in caravans across the desert. A *caravan* of trucks rolled slowly down the highway.
    car•a•van (kar′ə van′) *noun*.

carnivore An animal that eats the flesh of other animals. Lions and dogs are carnivores.
    car•ni•vore (kär′nə vôr′) *noun*.

carnivore

casting The selection of actors or performers. The *casting* for the play has been completed.
    cast•ing (kas′ting) *noun*.

churn A container in which cream or milk is shaken or beaten to make butter.
    churn (chûrn) *noun*.

churn

cinder A piece of coal, wood, or other material that has burned up or that is still burning but no longer flaming.
    cin•der (sin′dər) *noun*.

conjure Magic and magical charms. Many folk tales tell about people practicing conjure. *Noun.* —Having to do with magic. *Adjective.*
    con•jure (kon′jər *or* kun′jər) *noun; adjective.*

Consuela (kōn swā′lä)

contaminate To make dirty; pollute. Garbage thrown in the river will *contaminate* the water.
    con•tam•i•nate (kən tam′ə nāt′) *verb*, **contaminated, contaminating.**

courtier An attendant of a king or queen. The faithful *courtiers* went everywhere with the queen.
cour•ti•er (kôr′tē ər) *noun.*

crokasack *Also,* **crokersack.** A burlap bag. He put his clothes in a large *crokasack.*
crok•a•sack (krōk′ə sak′) *noun.*

D

damsel A young girl.
dam•sel (dam′zəl) *noun.*

debris 1. Waste material. **2.** The scattered remains of something that has been broken or destroyed. Broken tree limbs and other *debris* from the storm littered my front yard.
de•bris (də brē′ *or* dā′ brē) *noun.*

courtier

Word History

The word **debris** comes from the French word *debriser,* meaning "to break into pieces." Debris is often made up of bits of broken material.

at; āpe; fär; câre; **e**nd; mē; **i**t; īce; pîerce; hot; ōld; sông; fôrk; **oi**l; **ou**t; **u**p; ūse; rüle; pu̇ll; tûrn; **ch**in; si**ng**; **sh**op; **th**in; <u>th</u>is; **hw** in **wh**ite; **zh** in trea**s**ure. The symbol ə stands for the unstressed vowel sound in **a**bout, tak**e**n, penc**i**l, lem**o**n, and circ**u**s.

destination A place to which a person is going or a thing is being sent. I told the train conductor that my *destination* was New York City.
des•ti•na•tion (des´tə nā´shən) *noun.*

draft 1. A current of air. I could feel a cold *draft* from the open window. 2. A version of something written. The second *draft* of my report about ants reads better than the first.
draft (draft) *noun.*

Ekoomiak, Normee (ē kü´mi ak, nôr´mē)

enclosure An area that is fenced in or surrounded on all sides.
en•clo•sure (en klō´zhər) *noun.*

essential Very important or necessary. It is *essential* that we leave now or we'll miss the last train.
es•sen•tial (i sen´shəl) *adjective.*

Ezel (ēz´əl)

fauna The animals that live in a particular region, time, or environment. The *fauna* of the African plains includes lions and hyenas.
fau•na (fô´nə) *noun, plural* **faunas** *or* **faunae** (fô´nē).

fauna

560

fictitious Not real or true; made up. He wrote a science-fiction story about a *fictitious* hero who lives in the future.
fic•ti•tious (fik tish´əs) *adjective.*

flamboyant Showy or without restraint. The acrobat did a *flamboyant* backflip.
flam•boy•ant (flam boi´ənt) *adjective.*

flan A sweet dessert made from eggs, milk, sugar, and flavorings. Flan is baked in an oven.
flan (flan *or* flän) *noun.*

flora The plants that live in a particular region, time, or environment. Tall trees covered with moss are part of the *flora* in the rainforest.
flo•ra (flôr´ə) *noun, plural* **floras** *or* **florae** (flôr´ē).

fluke¹

flora

fluke¹ Either of the two fins of a whale's tail.
fluke (flük) *noun.*

fluke² An unexpected turn of luck; chance happening. By a *fluke,* we saw our friends in the large crowd at the parade.
fluke (flük) *noun.*

formation 1. The way in which the members or units of a group are arranged. The band marched into a square *formation.* 2. Something that takes a shape. The rock *formations* looked like huge animals.
for•ma•tion (fôr mā´shən) *noun.*

at; āpe; fär; câre; end; mē; it; īce; pîerce; hot; ōld; sông; fôrk; oil; out; up; ūse; rüle; pùll; tûrn; chin; sing; shop; thin; <u>th</u>is; hw in white; zh in treasure. The symbol ə stands for the unstressed vowel sound in about, taken, pencil, lemon, and circus.

fossil fuel A fuel that was formed from the remains of prehistoric plants and animals. Coal and petroleum products, such as oil and gasoline, are fossil fuels.
　　fos•sil fu•el (fos′əl fū′əl) *noun.*

Fuentes (fwen′tes)

generation

G

gait **1.** A rate of movement. The years seemed to go by at a slow *gait*. **2.** A way of walking or running. The horse's *gait* changed from a trot to a gallop. ▲ Another word that sounds like this is **gate.**
　　gait (gāt) *noun.*

generation **1.** One step in the line of descent from a common ancestor. A grandparent, parent, and child make up three *generations*. **2.** A group of persons born around the same time. My parents call me and my friends the younger *generation*.
　　gen•er•a•tion (jen′ə rā′shən) *noun.*

gossamer Light, filmy, or delicate in appearance. Look at the butterfly's *gossamer* wings.
　　gos•sa•mer (gos′ə mər) *adjective.*

562

gratitude A feeling of thanks for a favor one has received or for something that makes one happy. Our neighbors were full of *gratitude* for the help that we gave them.
grat•i•tude (grat´i tüd´ *or* grat´i tūd´) *noun.*

Greene, Silas (grēn, sī´ləs)

greenhouse effect The trapping of heat from the sun within the earth's atmosphere. This can result from an increase in the amount of carbon dioxide and other gases created by the burning of fossil fuels on earth. These gases prevent the heat from escaping into space, just as the glass windows keep heat inside a greenhouse.
green•house ef•fect (grēn´hous´ i fekt´) *noun.*

groove A long, narrow cut or dent. The wheels of the car made *grooves* in the muddy road.
groove (grüv) *noun.*

harmony A pleasing combination or mixture of parts. The rainbow was a *harmony* of colors.
har•mo•ny (här´mə nē) *noun.*

hazardous Likely to cause harm or injury; dangerous. Walking on an icy sidewalk is *hazardous* because you can slip and fall.
haz•ard•ous (haz´ər dəs) *adjective.*

hazardous

at; āpe; fär; câre; **e**nd; mē; it; īce; pîerce; hot; ōld; sông; fôrk; oil; out; up; ūse; rüle; pu̇ll; tûrn; chin; sing; shop; thin; **th**is; hw in **wh**ite; zh in treasure. The symbol ə stands for the unstressed vowel sound in **a**bout, tak**e**n, penc**i**l, lem**o**n, and circ**u**s.

heritage Something that is handed down from earlier relatives who lived a long time ago or from the past; tradition. Children of African *heritage* learned about the food and dress of their ancestors in Africa.
her•i•tage (her´i tij) *noun.*

heroine The main female character in a play, story, or poem. The name of the *heroine* in the story is Tanya.
her•o•ine (her´ō in) *noun.*

hibernation The act of spending the winter in a deep sleep. Many animals, such as bears, squirrels, snakes, a few fish and birds, and some insects, go into hibernation in the winter.
hi•ber•na•tion (hī´ber nā´shən) *noun.*

Word History

The word **hibernation** comes from the Latin word *hibernare,* meaning "to pass the winter." An animal that hibernates passes the winter by sleeping.

---

host¹ 1. The living plant or animal in or upon which another animal or plant lives and gets nourishment. **2.** A person who entertains guests, often at home. The guests thanked the *host* for a fun-filled party.
host (hōst) *noun.*

**host² ** A large number. On a clear night I can see a *host* of stars.
host (hōst) *noun.*

hover 1. To remain in the air above something. The helicopter *hovered* over the landing pad. **2.** To stay close by. The reporters *hovered* around the mayor while waiting to ask their questions.
hov•er (huv´ər *or* hov´ər) *verb,* **hovered, hovering.**

humiliation A feeling of shame or extreme embarrassment.
hu•mil•i•a•tion (hū mil´ē ā´shən) *noun.*

hibernation

Inuit

I

ignite To set on fire. A spark *ignited* the dry leaves.
    ig•nite (ig nīt´) *verb,* **ignited, igniting.**

immortal Living, lasting, or remembered forever.
    im•mor•tal (i môr´təl) *adjective.*

incinerate To burn to ashes.
    in•cin•er•ate (in sin´ə rāt´) *verb,* **incinerated, incinerating.**

ingot A mass of metal that is often shaped like a bar or block.
    in•got (ing´gət) *noun.*

intimidate To influence or frighten by threats or violence. The snarling dog *intimidated* everyone who walked by.
    in•tim•i•date (in tim´i dāt´) *verb,* **intimidated, intimidating.**

Inuit Eskimo people of North America living in Greenland, Canada, and mainland Alaska.
    I•nu•it (in´ü it *or* in´ū it) *plural noun, singular* **Inuk** *or* **Inuit.**

investigate To look into carefully in order to find facts and get information. The police are responsible for *investigating* crimes.
    in•ves•ti•gate (in ves´ti gāt´) *verb,* **investigated, investigating.**

J

jowl Heavy, loose flesh hanging from or under the lower jaw.
    jowl (joul) *noun.*

---

at; āpe; fär; câre; **e**nd; mē; **i**t; īce; pîerce; h**o**t; ōld; sông; fôrk; **oi**l; **ou**t; **u**p; ūse; rüle; p**u̇**ll; tûrn; **ch**in; si**ng**; **sh**op; **th**in; **th**is; **hw** in **wh**ite; **zh** in trea**s**ure. The symbol ə stands for the unstressed vowel sound in **a**bout, tak**e**n, penc**i**l, lem**o**n, and circ**u**s.

jubilee An occasion of joyful celebration and rejoicing. Our city has a strawberry *jubilee* every summer.
    ju•bi•lee (jü´ bə lē´ *or* jü´bə lē´) *noun.*

Kaffir (kaf´ər)

kayak A type of canoe first used in arctic regions. It is made by stretching animal skins over a frame of wood. It has an opening in the center where the person who paddles can sit.
    kay•ak (kī´ak) *noun.*

linger To stay on as if not wanting to leave; move slowly. The children *lingered* at the circus so they could see the elephants again.
    lin•ger (ling´gər) *verb,* **lingered, lingering.**

lithe Easily bent. The *lithe* dancer easily did a backbend.
    lithe (līth) *adjective.*

lithe

mammoth

lope To run with long, easy, and bounding steps. The dog *loped* through the park.
    lope (lōp) *verb,* **loped, loping.**

lurk **1.** To lie hidden. My kitten *lurked* in the bushes, waiting to pounce on a bug. **2.** To move about in a secretive manner.
    lurk (lûrk) *verb,* **lurked, lurking.**

Maidu Belonging to a Native American tribe that lived in the Sacramento Valley area of California.
    Mai•du (mī´dü) *adjective.*

Maldonado, Felicidad (mäl´dō nä´dō, fe lē´sē däd´)

mammoth Of immense size; huge; gigantic. *Adjective.* —A kind of elephant that lived long ago. Mammoths had long, curving tusks and shaggy brown hair. They were larger than elephants living now. The last mammoths on earth died about 10,000 years ago. *Noun.*
    mam•moth (mam´əth) *adjective; noun.*

Mercado (mer kä´dō)

migration The act of moving from one place to another. During their *migration* north, geese stop at a pond near our house.
    mi•gra•tion (mī grā´shən) *noun.*

mill¹ To move around in a confused way. The crowd *milled* around the football field after the game. *Verb.* —A building where machines grind grain into flour or meal. *Noun.*
    mill (mil) *verb,* **milled, milling;** *noun.*

---

at; āpe; fär; câre; end; mē; it; īce; pîerce; hot; ōld; sông; fôrk; oil; out; up; ūse; rüle; pull; tûrn; chin; sing; shop; thin; **th**is; **hw** in **wh**ite; **zh** in treasure. The symbol ə stands for the unstressed vowel sound in about, taken, pencil, lemon, and circus.

567

mill² A unit of monetary value equal to one-tenth of a cent.
   mill (mil) *noun.*

Mis Poinsettia (miz poin set´ē ə *or* miz poin set´ə)

modest **1.** Not thinking too highly of oneself. A modest person does not brag or show off. **2.** Within reason. We spent a *modest* amount of money on the trip.
   mod•est (mod´ist) *adjective.*

mollusc Another spelling of **mollusk.** Any of a group of animals without backbones that usually have a soft body protected by a hard shell. Mollusks often live in or near water. Clams, snails, and oysters are mollusks.
   mol•lusc (mol´əsk) *noun.*

Word History

The word **mollusk** (also spelled **mollusc**) comes from the Latin word *molluscus,* meaning "soft." Mollusks have soft bodies.

mollusk

Mount Everest A mountain in the Himalayas; the highest mountain peak in the world (29,028 feet, or 8,848 meters).
   Mount Ev•er•est (mount ev´ər əst *or* mount ev´rəst) *noun.*

Mount Everest

N

native **1.** Originally living or growing in a region or country. Raccoons are *native* to North America. **2.** Born in a particular country or place. She is a *native* Californian.
   na•tive (nā´tiv) *adjective.*

New Orleans A city in southeastern Louisiana, a port on the Mississippi River.
   New Or•le•ans (nü ôr´lē ənz, nü ôr´ lənz, *or* nü ôr lēnz´) *noun.*

O

Okpik An Inuit word meaning "snowy owl."
Ok•pik (ok´pik) *noun.*

opponent A person who is against another in a fight, contest, or discussion. The soccer team beat all the *opponents* and won the championship.
op•po•nent (ə pō´nənt) *noun.*

organism A living thing. Animals, plants, amebas, and bacteria are all organisms.
or•gan•ism (ôr´gə niz´əm) *noun.*

organism

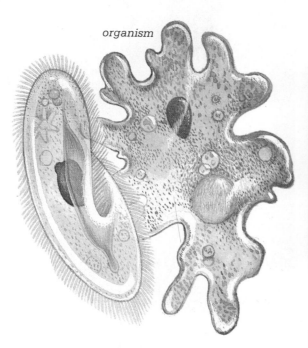

origin How something begins or where it comes from. The island's *origin* was from a volcano that erupted in the ocean thousands of years ago.
or•i•gin (ôr´i jin *or* or´i jin) *noun.*

ozone layer A layer of the gas ozone that is between ten and thirty miles above the earth. The ozone layer soaks up harmful ultraviolet rays and keeps them from reaching the earth's surface.
o•zone lay•er (ō´zōn lā´ər) *noun.*

P

Paquito (pä kē´tō)

pavilion A building that is used for a show or exhibit, or for play. A pavilion often has open sides. The dance was held at a *pavilion* in the park.
pa•vil•ion (pə vil´yən) *noun.*

pavilion

Paye, Won-Ldy (pā, wun´dā)

at; āpe; fär; câre; end; mē; it; īce; pîerce; hot; ōld; sông; fôrk; oil; out; up; ūse; rüle; pu̇ll; tûrn; chin; sing; shop; thin; **th**is; hw in **wh**ite; zh in treasure. The symbol ə stands for the unstressed vowel sound in about, taken, pencil, lemon, and circus.

peninsula

peninsula A piece of land that sticks out into water from a larger body of land. The southern part of Florida is a peninsula.
    pen•in•su•la (pə nin′sə lə *or* pə nin′syə lə) *noun.*

Word History

The word **peninsula** comes from two Latin words, *paene*, meaning "almost," and *insula*, meaning "island." A peninsula is a strip of land surrounded by water on three sides, so it is almost an island.

---

petition A formal request that is made to a person in authority. All the people on our street signed a *petition* asking the city to put a stop sign on the corner.
    pe•ti•tion (pə tish′ən) *noun.*

Pittsburgh A city in southwestern Pennsylvania, the leading center of iron and steel production in the United States.
    Pitts•burgh (pits′bûrg) *noun.*

plait To braid.
    plait (plāt *or* plat) *verb,* **plaited, plaiting.**

Plymouth, Massachusetts A town in southeastern Massachusetts, on the Atlantic Ocean, settled in 1620 by the Pilgrims.
    Plym•outh, Mas•sa•chu•setts (plim′əth mas′ə chü′sits) *noun.*

poncho A cloak made of one piece of cloth or other material. It has a hole in the middle for the head.
    pon•cho (pon′chō) *noun.*

poncho

predator

predator An animal that lives by hunting other animals for food. Lions, wolves, sharks, and owls are predators.
    pred•a•tor (pred′ə tər) *noun.*

prejudice Hatred or unfair treatment of a particular group, such as members of a race or religion.
    prej•u•dice (prej′ə dis) *noun.*

preservation The process of keeping and protecting wildlife. Our city zoo encourages the *preservation* of several endangered birds and animals.
    pres•er•va•tion (prez′ər vā′shən) *noun.*

primate A group of mammals that includes humans, apes, and monkeys. All primates have large brains, eyes that look forward, and fingers and thumbs that can grasp things.
    pri•mate (prī′māt) *noun.*

provoke 1. To cause (something) to happen on purpose. One of the men *provoked* a fight with the other. 2. To make angry. We didn't know why Steve was upset; we hadn't done anything to *provoke* him.
    pro•voke (prə vōk′) *verb,* **provoked, provoking.**

pungent Sharp or strong to the taste or smell. Ammonia has an unpleasant, *pungent* odor.
    pun•gent (pun′jənt) *adjective.*

R

racial Having to do with relations between races of human beings. Racial prejudice is prejudice against people because of their race.
    ra•cial (rā′shəl) *adjective.*

at; āpe; fär; câre; end; mē; it; īce; pîerce; hot; ōld; sông; fôrk; oil; out; up; ūse; rüle; pu̇ll; tûrn; chin; sing; shop; thin; this; hw in white; zh in treasure. The symbol ə stands for the unstressed vowel sound in about, taken, pencil, lemon, and circus.

rainforest

rainforest A thick forest that receives a large amount of rain during the year.
  rain•for•est (rān´fôr´ist) *noun.*

ravine A deep, narrow valley.
  ra•vine (rə vēn´) *noun.*

reluctant Unwilling. I am *reluctant* to pet the cat because it scratched me yesterday.
  re•luc•tant (ri luk´tənt) *adjective.*

S

sage¹ A very wise person, usually also old and very respected. People of the village consulted the *sage* for advice.
  sage (sāj) *noun.*

sage² A small plant whose leaves are used to flavor food.
  sage (sāj) *noun.*

Sedna (sed´nə *or* sed´nä)

segregation The practice of setting one racial group apart from another. Since our government passed laws against *segregation*, children of all races attend public schools together.
  seg•re•ga•tion (seg´ri gā´shən) *noun.*

shang ya (shäng yä)

shoat A young hog, usually less than one year old.
  shoat (shōt) *noun.*

Shonah (shō´nä *or* shō´nə)

Sierra Nevada Mountains A mountain range in eastern California.
  Si•er•ra Ne•vad•a Moun•tains (sē er´ə nə vad´ə moun´tənz *or* sē er´ə nə vä´də moun´tənz) *noun.*

silhouette A dark outline seen against a lighter background. At dusk, you can see the *silhouettes* of the mountains against the sky.
  sil•hou•ette (sil´ü et´) *noun.*

slag Waste material left after metal is separated from the rock it is found in.
  slag (slag) *noun.*

span To extend over or across. The fallen log *spanned* the mountain creek.
span (span) *verb,* **spanned, spanning.**

Word History
The word **span** comes from the Dutch word *spannen,* which means "to stretch."

squall

squall A strong gust of wind that arises very suddenly. Squalls often bring rain, snow, or sleet.
squall (skwôl) *noun.*

stable¹ A building where cattle or horses are kept and fed. A stable often has stalls for the animals that are kept there.
sta•ble (stā´bəl) *noun.*

stable² Not easily moved, shaken, or changed. After the earthquake, only *stable* buildings were left standing.
sta•ble (stā´bəl) *adjective.*

streamlined Designed or shaped so as to give the least possible resistance to air or water. The *streamlined* boat moved quickly through the water.
stream•lined (strēm´līnd´) *adjective.*

tapir An animal that looks like a large pig but is related to horses and rhinoceroses. Tapirs live in Central and South America and Asia.
ta•pir (tā´pər) *noun.*

taunt An insulting or scornful remark. The basketball team heard the *taunts* from the angry crowd.
taunt (tônt) *noun.*

technology 1. Methods, machines, and devices that are used to do a specific task in a science or profession. **2.** The use of science for practical purposes.
tech•nol•o•gy (tek nol´ə jē) *noun.*

Tío Jorge Spanish for "Uncle George."
Tí•o Jor•ge (tē´ō hôr´hā) *noun.*

transform To change in shape or appearance. The fuzzy yellow caterpillar was *transformed* into a beautiful butterfly.
trans•form (trans fôrm´) *verb,* **transformed, transforming.**

tribal Having to do with a group of people who have the same ancestors and social customs. We studied African *tribal* customs.
trib•al (trī´bəl) *adjective.*

---

at; **āpe**; **fär**; **câre**; **end**; **mē**; **it**; **īce**; **pîerce**; **hot**; **ōld**; **sông**; **fôrk**; **oil**; **out**; **up**; **ūse**; **rüle**; **pùll**; **tûrn**; **ch**in; **si**ng; **sh**op; **th**in; **th**is; **hw** in **wh**ite; **zh** in treasure. The symbol **ə** stands for the unstressed vowel sound in **a**bout, tak**e**n, penc**i**l, lem**o**n, and circ**u**s.

573

U

undaunted Not discouraged or frightened; fearless. *Undaunted* by the cold and the darkness, the hero in the fairy tale continued to hike through the snow.
 un•daunt•ed (un dôn´tid) *adjective.*

urban In, having to do with, or like a city or city life. New York City is a large *urban* area.
 ur•ban (ûr´bən) *adjective.*

urban

V

vigil The act or period of remaining awake to guard or observe something. My dog held a *vigil* by the door all afternoon, waiting for me to return.
 vig•il (vij´əl) *noun.*

vigilante group A group of people who, without the law's permission, take it upon themselves to punish criminals.
 vig•i•lan•te group (vij´ə lan´tē grüp) *noun.*

Y

Yeh-Shen (yā´shən)

Yellowstone National Park A national park in northwestern Wyoming and neighboring sections of Montana and Idaho.
 Yel•low•stone Na•tion•al Park (yel´ō stōn´ nash´ə nəl pärk) *noun.*

Yosemite National Park A national park in east-central California.
 Yo•sem•i•te Na•tion•al Park (yō sem´i tē nash´ə nəl pärk) *noun.*

Z

Zimbabwe A country in south-central Africa.
 Zim•bab•we (zim bäb´wē *or* zim bäb´wā) *noun.*